Old-Time Conversations

Old-Time Conversations

Finding Health, Happiness and Community Through Traditional Music

CRAIG R. EVANS

Foreword by Clare Milliner

McFarland & Company, Inc., Publishers
Jefferson, North Carolina

LIBRARY OF CONGRESS CATALOGUING-IN-PUBLICATION DATA

Names: Evans, Craig R., 1952– author. | Milliner, Clare, writer of foreword.
Title: Old-time conversations : finding health, happiness and community through traditional music / Craig R. Evans ; foreword by Clare Milliner.
Description: Jefferson, North Carolina : McFarland & Company, Inc., Publishers, 2024. | Includes bibliographical references and index.
Identifiers: LCCN 2024015202 | ISBN 9781476694726 (paperback : acid free paper) ∞
ISBN 9781476652092 (ebook)
Subjects: LCSH: Old-time music—History and criticism. | String band music—United States—History and criticism. | Folk musicians—United States—Interviews. | Banjoists—United States—Interviews. | Banjo makers—United States—Interviews. | Musicologists—United States—Interviews. | Evans, Craig R., 1952– | BISAC: MUSIC / Genres & Styles / Folk & Traditional | LCGFT: Interviews.
Classification: LCC ML3551 .E78 2024 | DDC 781.62/13—dc23/eng/20240419
LC record available at https://lccn.loc.gov/2024015202

BRITISH LIBRARY CATALOGUING DATA ARE AVAILABLE

ISBN (print) 978-1-4766-9472-6
ISBN (ebook) 978-1-4766-5209-2

© 2024 Craig R. Evans. All rights reserved

No part of this book may be reproduced or transmitted in any form or by any means, electronic or mechanical, including photocopying or recording, or by any information storage and retrieval system, without permission in writing from the publisher.

Front cover images: (Instrument Builders, left to right) Bart Reiter, Patrick "Doc" Huff, Zachary Hoyt, Pete Ross, Bill Rickard; (Performers and Teachers) Rayna Gellert, John McCutcheon, David Holt, Paul Brown, James "Sparky" Rucker; (Historians and Authors) Dwight Diller, Josh Turknett, Dom Flemons, Tim Brooks, Bill Malone; (Performer, bottom left) Clare Milliner.
Back cover image: The Clifftop water tower (all photographs courtesy of the author)

Printed in the United States of America

McFarland & Company, Inc., Publishers
Box 611, Jefferson, North Carolina 28640
www.mcfarlandpub.com

To my mom.
The role she played in our small farming community,
providing music when and where it was needed, was enormous.
And she did it with such grace.
I'm just sorry it took me close to 40 years
to recognize just how important her role was.
Thanks, Mom.
Now I get to carry on the legacy.

And also to all the old-time performers, luthiers and historians
for carrying the torch of traditional music into the future.

Acknowledgments

Famous composer and conductor Gustav Mahler once said, "Tradition is not to preserve the ashes, but to pass along the flame."

Thank you to the flamekeepers of today's traditional music, and to those that have inspired our species for millenia past.

To my mentors and friends who provided me with inspiration and encouragement to write this book, I say thank you.

Tom Burkett, Bryan Iwamoto, Tim Voigts, Howard Rains, Tricia Spencer, Sam and Stella Roberts, Donald Zepp, Tim Brooks, James "Sparky" Rucker, Bart Reiter, James Leary, Daniel Sheehy, Jeff Place and my dear friend Stephen Wade, your knowledge and support were foundational. It happened because you were a part of it.

Thank you to my Smithsonian Folkways colleagues: Daniel Sheehy, Jeff Place, Atesh Sonneborn and new director and curator Maureen Loughran. Your ongoing friendships and support for my traditional music community films made this book possible.

And finally, thank you to my artistic friend and life partner, DeAnne L. Parks, without whose encouragement this grand adventure would not have happened.

Table of Contents

Acknowledgments vi
Foreword: Is This Heaven? by Clare Milliner 1
Preface 5
Introduction 9

Part I. My Story 13
   1. The Early Years   14
   2. The Artist's Choice   26
   3. College, Career and Crash   30
   4. Life Interruptus: My Hero's Journey   43

Part II. Talking Old-Time Community 65
   <u>*Instrument Builders*</u>   69
     5. Bart Reiter   70
     6. Patrick "Doc" Huff   77
     7. Pete Ross   84
     8. Zachary Hoyt   90
     9. Bill Rickard   98
     10. William Seeders Mosheim   103

   <u>*Performers and Teachers*</u>   109
     11. Rayna Gellert   110
     12. David Holt   119
     13. James "Sparky" Rucker   129
     14. Clare Milliner   140
     15. Mac Benford   147
     16. Sheila Kay Adams   154
     17. Paul Brown   163
     18. John McCutcheon   172

Table of Contents

Historians and Authors 181
    19. Dwight Diller 182
    20. Bill Malone 188
    21. Dom Flemons 198
    22. Tim Brooks 209

Part III. In the Company of Music 227
    23. Clifftop 228
    24. Why Play Old-Time Music? 250
    25. How Music Works Magic:
    A Conversation with Josh Turknett 259

Epilogue: An Invitation to Join the Fun 273
Bibliography 275
Index 277

Foreword:
Is This Heaven?

Clare Milliner

I was 28 and broke, the single mother of an impossibly cute little tyrant who was infinitely smarter than I. I was at odds with my family. And I had no self-esteem. I was lonely.

But I understood music. When I was four, my mother had propped me up on three telephone books to reach the piano keys and taught me to play notes from a book with beautiful silhouette drawings. Violin started at age seven, with drives to Wilmington every week to take lessons along with my cousin.

In my family, music was a discipline … a language my mother was determined that my brothers and I would learn. It offered me an escape from my senior year of high school; I spent my time at college studying piano. But the specter of performing, alone and naked in front of an audience, was more than my fragile psyche could bear.

I come from a long line of introverts; social gatherings were anathema. But I had heard some scratchy tapes of old men playing old-time music at Lenape Park that my brother had recorded. And one magical summer, his friend sat in our kitchen night after night, drinking my brother's homemade dandelion wine and playing "Over the Waterfall" on the banjo. What magic was this? I wrote down the notes on manuscript paper so I could remember how it went.

After I got married, it seemed music had no place in my life. Besides, who was there to play with? I knew nothing of the constellations of old-time gatherings happening all around me—so many young souls searching for rhythm and harmony and ecstasy—playing wildly untethered, free from the constraints of musical convention that I was familiar with.

And here I was, at 28. I got a job as a table-waiter, for which I was uniquely unqualified. I neither knew how to ingratiate myself nor how to remember what people had ordered. I don't remember how the subject of music came up, but my friend, the bartender, miraculously said, "Why don't you get my husband to show you some fiddle tunes? He's just sitting at home, watching the kids."

A few days later, I drove up along the edge of a field of corn stubble to the top of a hill where a lone house stood. Chris Ferrier sat on the porch, playing a fiddle. He played "Buck Mountain" and "June Apple" and I tried to follow along.

What do you call the feeling when you teach someone something and they get it? Or when someone shows you how to do something really cool and you realize you're able to do it, too? Teaching makes you care about your student, and being taught makes you feel loved. It's give and take; it creates intimacy.

From the beginning, I felt I could understand how the tunes were supposed to go, what the old tune-wright was getting at when he first played it. The form of the tunes was just like the old Bach minuets and dances, AABB, and the combinations of notes and turns of phrase were familiar. But these tunes were like snippets of classical music, leaving more unsaid than said, evoking a mysterious, undefinable, irresistible emotion.

The keys had different personalities. D was bright and fast and full of scalar runs, while C was jazzy and lazy and swingy. C was an enigma to me; I grew up on Bach. G was fat and welcoming. Its notes covered the entire fiddle. But I loved A; there were modal tunes and cross tunes that sounded primal.

I wanted to remember the tunes *exactly*. I started bringing along manuscript paper and pencil to write down the notes, the spells and incantations, so I could play them when I got home.

Chris decided to start "Tunes" again; a bunch of us would gather each week and play. The guys knew the tunes from way before. They always talked about how they'd started playing "when the Highwoods String Band came through" as if it were a seismic, mythical event in the distant past, before everyone had married up and had children and gotten jobs that took them away from the intoxication of playing tunes all night.

Before I knew it, I was part of a group. I realized that these people didn't care what I had done or hadn't done in the past. They liked me just because I could play. All I had to do now was learn the spell and play it well.

Who hasn't searched for that perfect place, that safe haven, where everyone is glad to see you, and there's an element of the supernatural? Where there's the possibility of achieving zero gravity, floating on that sea-bed of rhythm and harmony, playing effortlessly. This group became my family, my church. I didn't want to miss a single session.

One day Chris said, "We're going to play for a dance." My old fear of performance swelled up. But Chris said, "Get right up to the microphone." And there I was—playing in a group for an audience of dancers; it sweeps you along and keeps you from dwelling on your mistakes. I felt as if Woody Woodring's guitar-playing was taking care of me, helping me play, because hearing the right chords made it so easy.

Pete LaBerge started a series of square dances in an old school gym. When our little band played, we were propelled along by the enthusiasm of the dancers, and of Pete himself, as he turned and gazed grinning down upon us from his great height, bobbing to the beat.

Meanwhile, I amused myself by transcribing all the tunes that floated my way. I filled books of manuscript. I catalogued them in a notebook so I could find them. I made lists upon lists: D tunes, dance tunes, cow and pig tunes, good tunes to play in a session.

Word was that a local music festival at Lake Genero was great. I went to check it out. As I arrived, someone said, "There's Walt Koken." I had no idea who Walt Koken was. "You know—the Highwoods String Band." What? That mythic force from the distant past?

It was later, in a whiskey-soaked session, that Walt and I exchanged tunes. He played something I'd never heard. I played something that he apparently didn't know, and it was off to the races. He moved to Pennsylvania and we started having tunes at our house, every Saturday, religiously, starting around 9 p.m. and going 'til 2 a.m. The whiskey and wine flowed. The rug gobbled up bottles of champagne. Cannabis perfumed the air. It was Party Central and our musical family grew.

Walt found my manuscript books and became passionate about preserving them. We traced each tune to its earliest recording, or the recording that introduced it to the current old-time repertoire. We spent hours meticulously correcting the transcriptions and finally it was born: the Milliner-Koken Collection of American Fiddle Tunes.

Much like a meditation, I felt it important to play through the entire collection ... all 1,404 tunes. The only place we could accomplish this, where time was on pause for an entire week, was the Appalachian String Band Festival in Clifftop, West Virginia. So, in 2011, we sat with our faithful bandmates, 10 hours a day, for eight straight days ... but we only got through half the Book. We did the second half the next year. People came and went, filling in behind us in wing formation, later exclaiming, "I was there for the Ds and Es!" or some such thing. A couple from Iowa brought sandwiches and milk and taped the whole thing.

We formed a band, like you do. Pete Peterson played a Supertone banjo and Walt played an Orpheum banjo, so along with Kellie Allen (guitar) and later Hilary Dirlam (bass), we became the Orpheus Supertones. The next thing we knew, we were playing in England and California. We found that this virtual old-time community existed not only in the States but the rest of the world. *What was it that draws people to this music?*

There's a high when it goes right. In a small session of five or six musicians, where everyone can hear each other, and you strive to play the right notes and chords, you lift up and are lifted up by your fellow musicians. The many become one ... individual fallacies fall away. It's such a euphoria that you keep trying to reach that point, that transcendent moment, session after session. *Is this heaven?*

Music exists in time and space. It's fundamental *to be physically present* in the vibrations from other people's instruments to achieve that consonance. Playing it with other people in real time is how it happens. For instance, when Walt records, it's live. There's no studio separation of the players, or parts patched in later. What's played together *in that moment* is what we get. We are living beings, not AI.

Now that we're older, some of our closest music friends have passed. We sit, play our music and remember how it was in the old days. But for you, reading this book, these *are* the old days, or the young days, whatever—you *always* have the opportunity for that real, *in-the-moment joy* in front of you. Why not bring somebody else into it and turn them on, just like someone did for you? *It's worth it.*

Craig knows about this. He revels in the utopia of the old-time community. In his interviews, he wants *you* to evoke that vision of heaven. Yes, he's got rose-colored glasses on, but don't you have to be able to imagine heaven in order to get there? Thanks, Craig, for pointing out the way to heaven and helping us know when we're here.

Clare Milliner is an attorney, musician, and writer. She lives on the farm she grew up on in Chester County, Pennsylvania, with her beloved husband, Walt Koken, and her cat, Tiglath-Pileser.

Preface

"Without music, life would be a mistake"—Friedrich Nietzsche

"Music produces a kind of pleasure which human
nature cannot do without."—Confucius

"Music gives a soul to the universe, wings to the mind,
flight to the imagination and life to everything."—Plato

Embracing Music and Community

As passions and careers go, my life's journey has come full circle. From my earliest memories, music has had a profound impact on me. Growing up in a small Iowa farm town, I witnessed the transformative power of music through my mother, a humble church organist. Whether it was the joyous celebration of weddings, the solemn reverence of funerals, or the commemoration of anniversaries, her music brought solace and healing to our rural community. She was often compensated with meager offerings like a five-dollar bill, or a dozen eggs. But her true reward lay in the happiness she received from sharing her music with others. She was indeed an artist.

As a kid, I wanted to follow in her footsteps and make music my life's calling. Yet, well-intentioned advice from my dad steered me down a different path. With a desire to help animals, I pursued degrees in biology and physiology, setting my sights on becoming a veterinarian. Despite my academic achievements, an unforeseen obstacle derailed my admission to vet school. A single interviewer, citing what he saw as *an inclination toward promotion*, twice denied me entry. Looking back, I realize that it was a pivotal moment, a sign that the direction of my life would follow a different, unknown path.

After that door closed, I started a different journey, one that led me down the path of business success. Armed with an MBA, I thrived in promoting the products and services of others. On the surface, I appeared fulfilled, but a lingering sense of incompleteness gnawed at my soul. The worldly achievements and recognition I gained failed to compare to the sacrifices I had made along the way. At the age of 50, I found myself depleted and yearning for a fresh start.

It was then, after a quarter-century of dormancy, that I dusted off my banjo and guitar, tucked away under my bed. Determined to reclaim my passion for music, I serendipitously immersed myself in a world of joy and community. The revival of my mental, emotional, physical, and spiritual well-being was nothing short of miraculous. Surrounded by a group of smiling, vibrant and engaging friends, I rediscovered the sense of belonging and connection I had experienced as a child. It was as if the community I had longed for had never ceased to exist, patiently awaiting my return. It was within this nexus of music and community that I found myself asking the question "What kind of magic is going on here?" Little did I know that what I was experiencing was just the tip of the iceberg.

Driven by an unexplainable sense of purpose and blessed with my wife's unwavering support, I used my 60th birthday to justify a personal search for meaning. I set out on a journey across North America, documenting the artisans who craft open-back banjos. Next, I captured the stories of performers and teachers of traditional music, filling 12 DVDs with their interviews. My now–12-year, 60,000-mile quest expanded to include historians, authors, festival players, and other instrument builders, ensuring that the diverse tapestry of the North American traditional music community was represented. To my delight, Smithsonian Folkways recognized the historical value of these documentaries and offered to preserve and share my film collection for posterity.

The bulk of this book features the personal stories of a score and more of these precious human beings. Everyone has a unique role in the traditional music community and these folks demonstrate the best of the best of both music and community. It was hard to winnow these down. You can find and listen to the first series of these films at Smithsonian Folkways Recordings.

Through this odyssey, I discovered that the lives, stories and community roles of these remarkable individuals formed the most captivating and enriching chapter of my own life. The people I encountered not only possessed immense talent but also radiated an inner joy that emanated from doing what they loved and sharing it with others. They embodied the true essence of music and community—an alchemy that fills the heart and nurtures the soul. And they smiled, a lot.

As a child, I had witnessed my mother's music bring healing to those in need. As an adult, I experienced firsthand the transformative power of music and community in healing my own wounds. Since then, scientific research has emerged, shedding light on the myriad benefits of music and community engagement. Playing or even listening to music has been found to ignite our brains, illuminating pathways of neural plasticity (aka learning) and keeping us youthful regardless of age.

In writing this book, I am elated to assume the role of a promoter once again. However, this time, my aim is to champion the cause of music itself—an inspiring and uplifting force that has the potential to bring joy and fulfillment to all who embrace it. With each page, I hope you also begin to appreciate the profound impact of music and community, offering a beacon of hope in a world that yearns for healing.

May this book be a source of inspiration, guiding you toward a deeper understanding of the magic that unfolds when music intertwines with community. May it resonate with your heart, offering solace, joy, and a renewed sense of purpose. May the stories of these traditional music community members invite you to become a part of the group, knowing that with open hearts, and open minds, sharing the gift of music with the world can indeed make it a better place. And may you, too, find yourself smiling.

Introduction

After an exhausting 11-hour drive the night before, I woke up to sunbeams in a brightly-lit room. The walls were beautiful pine logs. Pleasant pictures of a young girl at various ages posing in jerseys with different sports paraphernalia were scattered about. I remembered that my host had offered me his daughter's bedroom for my two-night stay at the banjo workshop I was attending outside of Lansing, Michigan. There was a freshness in the air, a newness that was a nice change from my dim, depressing apartment back in Minneapolis.

I thought to myself, here's where the path to my new life begins—free of mental and emotional stress—at a five-string, clawhammer banjo camp in the middle of nowhere. I had a hollow feeling, but anything other than tension and stress seemed a welcome relief.

I'd chosen my banjo teacher, Dwight Diller, billed as the keeper of West Virginia banjo traditions, based on his newly-released CD, *Just Banjo '99*. I didn't know much about him other than I really liked his music. I'd later learn it was called Southern Appalachian traditional music, commonly referred to as old-time. There was an energy about it that lifted my heart. I'd heard rumors that Dwight, also a Mennonite minister, could be a bit curmudgeonly. Due to personal dilemmas in my life, I had been beat up so badly by lawyers by that time, I figured even that would be a tolerable change.

I pulled on some clothes and walked downstairs to the open fireplace. The room was empty, but I heard voices from outside. Through the front door window, I saw a grizzled old man standing on the porch. There were some folks around him chattering excitedly, ready for the day to begin. I opened the door. The old guy—my new teacher, Dwight Diller—was standing off to the side, gazing off into the pines. I walked out on the porch toward him.

As I approached, his friends noticed me, but Dwight stood still, fixated on the woods. I smiled at the other folks, including one who turned out to be my host, but I continued toward Dwight. I stopped a few feet away. A few long moments passed. I was waiting for him to notice me, at least my presence. That didn't work. So, to his back, I offered…

"Dwight, I wanted to tell you, I listened to a bunch of CDs before I decided to come to your camp. The way you played 'Arkansas Traveler' and 'Turkey in—'"

Me (left) and Dwight Diller. Back in the day, in 2000. I had no idea how important Dwight's influence would be to me and others in our music community.

"How old are you?" Dwight barked into the wood, not bothering to turn in my direction.

"What?"

Without moving, Dwight repeated, "How old are you?!"

"Uh, 50. Why?"

Pause. "Good. You're starting to sense your own mortality."

Since I didn't really have a follow-up to that, I think I backstepped at bit. Dwight continued staring off into the woods, so I turned back to my previously-smiling hosts. Their eyes darting back and forth between Dwight's back and me told me perhaps they also found his comments a bit unnerving. Dwight remained stoic, looking elsewhere. And me? I probably looked lost.... I know I felt naked.

After a few more uncomfortable moments, my host asked, "Do you like my daughter's room?" Very nice, I said, and turned to collect my thoughts someplace else. Like every unexpected life experience I'd been hit with up to that point, that little episode with Dwight was a shock.

Since then, I've learned the shock, like my own mortality, is meant simply to get one's attention. Once anything superficial has been removed, and you're genuinely tuned in, the truth is revealed to the beginner's eyes, mind and heart. Dwight wasn't doing or saying anything he hadn't experienced himself. He also wasn't being coy. Like his music, he was speaking his truth, his way, unfiltered, from the heart.

I wasn't aware of it yet, but I'd just started on my successful road to recovery … to rediscover the happiness and meaning I'd first experienced growing up as the son of a church-organist mom in small-town Iowa. I was deeply longing to recover my mental and physical health. I missed connecting with people, and I had no idea where to find them. I intuitively knew that I *had* to get my head out of my troubles—I had to get *out of my own head*! No matter how much I stewed about the situation I was in, my brain was not going to figure me out of this one. I needed something new, something beyond me.

A few hours later, in a rough-hewn outdoor shed in remote Michigan, my introduction to the music and community that would rebuild (and become) my life would begin. The biggest and best blessing of my life happened *when time stopped*. Because I then *let joy begin*. The entrance to this awakening—traditional music has been there since humans first walked upright on this rock. I'd also found myself in a community of 11 other pilgrims looking for the same connections and meaning. Along with them, I guess you could say Dwight Diller introduced us to that old-time religion (pun intended).

If you're now feeling lost, looking for connection and fulfillment, I'm leaving my story here for you. Read on, dear pilgrim, and consider taking this journey. You, too, can share musical redemption with friends and a smile.

Part I

My Story

Early Traditional barn raising, 1908 (History and Art Collection / Alamy Stock Photo).

1

The Early Years

I grew up in Early, a tiny northwest Iowa town. Founded in 1882, Early celebrated its centennial, which is a pretty big deal for a small town that survived that long. Singer-songwriter Greg Brown was invited to perform his song by the same name, made famous by Robin and Linda Williams on Garrison Keillor's *Prairie Home Companion* radio program. In it, he waxes poetic about the early morning sunrise, the history of the generous Midwestern prairie, and how it provided for many early immigrant families. It also acknowledges the complications of weather—and that farming is a risky proposition. First time I heard the song, I, too, fell in love with the romantic sentiments. A backstory to the tune is that Greg was hired by the Iowa Arts Council, along with other young, emerging Iowa songwriters, painters and photographers, to let their creative juices flow as they traveled across the state for a few days. They were paid a $250 stipend for the inspiration.

The night before Greg was to travel his last leg of his journey across the state, he stayed in Sac City, the county seat 10 miles from Early. As he tells the story, his mind wandered to Early as an adjective, as in *early in the morning*. And henceforth came a song. Beautiful, right? Not sure anyone told him the story that I'd heard about the town's dawn. The story I learned growing up, there was a Judge D. Carr Early that won the property where Early was originally built, two miles due south of its present location, in a poker game. The story goes that a very large oak tree was there. So large, in fact, when the road was built, it was directly in the line of construction. But due to its enormous size, and the fact that locals had used the "big tree corner" as a landmark for at least as long as anyone could remember, they decided to let it stand and simply curved the road around it. The tree and the winding road are long since gone. And the people that told me these stories were mostly family and neighbors, also gone. When I approached the Early library for some confirmation of the lucky judge card game, I came away empty-handed. Nothing on record. Let's just call it family folklore for now. I can see how it made for a good story when folks from small towns got together and told tales about back home to entertain themselves.

All was well with Early for a time. Next came the railroad. As with the roads, the railroad construction engineers wanted to build it on a straight line from point A to point B. The goal was to connect as many commerce centers along the way as possible. There weren't many large cities in Iowa at that time, but there were some

1. The Early Years

The ancient Early, Iowa, water tower that I actually climbed as a kid.

towns that showed promise. Early, Iowa, certainly thought of itself as one. Unfortunately, it failed the commerce requirements (too small) and thus was ignored as the Chicago and Northwestern track was laid two miles north of the big tree corner. Not being people to gamble on missing out, the good folks of Early decided their town would be better served by moving closer to the ways and means they believed would eventually connect the world. So the town pulled up roots and relocated two miles north to its current location—and left Judge Early's namesake intact. A couple of buildings were left behind; they're all gone now, but the early Early cemetery remains. As a kid, I used to love reading the dates on the headstones.

My great-grandfather from Wales was one of those early, homesteading immigrants. As farm help was sorely needed in those days, large families were commonplace. Besides, one or two might die off along the way. Therefore William Drury had three wives and 12 kids: Maude, Millard, Blanche, Clara (my grandma), Merrill, Grover, Bill, Sarah, Howard, Homer, Joyce, and Dean—just one more would make 13. Will's first wife, Sarah (my great-great grandmother), died of a ruptured appendix shortly after Clara's birth. His second wife, Mae Dell, died in childbirth with twins Howard and Homer. His third wife, Laura Gathman, outlived him. Times were challenging back then.

My grandmothers, Clara Evans (left) and Stella Weaver, in the 1970s. It's amazing how much we can learn listening to "the old people."

My grandma Clara Evans was an incredibly positive, loving influence, with a mellow, throaty laugh. Her family life was typical for a Plains' farm family. She shared an upstairs bedroom, and bed, with several siblings whom she'd care for during the day. The room had a table, a chair, and a kerosene lamp that she would read by in the evenings. The chair, which came from Scotland, was from her mother, Sarah Wilson. I've still got that lamp and chair. Grandma also delighted in talking about a small piano that sat in the front parlor where, in those days, one would officially meet outside folks. She learned how to play hymns on that piano. When Grandpa Elmer came a-courtin' at the age of 15, and Grandma was 13, she played piano for him. Pretty sure Grandpa was smitten. Married a few years later, they were together close to 60 years when he passed. Before Grandma joined him, she gave me a box of more than 50 pencil-written letters from Elmer that followed that early recital. *Young love on the prairie was a beautiful thing.* Love that family legacy.

By the time I came along, the land Great-Grandpa Will homesteaded was being farmed, but the house had been abandoned. All that I remember seeing of the place was a corncrib with many of the 12 kids' names carved into the boards. The corncrib blew down in a storm a few years later. I also remember seeing a very early picture—a late 18th-century cabinet card of the beautiful shade trees that lined the long entrance to the house. Hard not to feel sentimental while dwelling on such things. Thanks to Grandma, there was some music in my family in those early years. She would play a more important role in my musical journey later on.

My mom, Beth, was born in another small town, Hawarden, Iowa. Her father, William Sherman Weaver, died of a heart attack at work (an accountant at a lumber company) about the time she was readying to leave the nest for college. Within the next few years, she lost her younger brother Barton when he was captured at the Battle of the Bulge in World War II. He spent three very cold, wintry days and nights in a rail car along with other Allied prisoners being shipped to a POW camp. By the time Bart arrived, he'd contracted pneumonia, and he died shortly after. Bart was my mom's only sibling. She had doted on him, but now that he was gone, she became the caretaker of my Grandma Weaver. There was very deep love in that family. They picked up and went forward without self-pity. She showed me that *from great challenges can come great strength.* Not sure where her love of community came from, but throughout her life, she was always focused on families in need. And in a small farming community, that's a fair number of folks.

Mom had learned how to play the piano early on. She told me stories of Grandpa Weaver singing ballads on his guitar in the evenings. Apparently, he had a beautiful baritone voice. She couldn't remember the names of any of the songs, but it's clear the family enjoyed musical time together. She attended Iowa State Teachers College to become a grade-school teacher and met her future sister-in-law Shirley while teaching in Cherokee, Iowa. Shirley introduced my mom to my dad and that was that. He the handsome service man, and she the willowy, long-haired brunette with bright blue eyes and a warm, genuine smile. Once married, Mom and Dad moved to Early, Dad's home. Grandma Weaver had her own room in our house and visited often—as in, I pretty much grew up with her. Grandma Weaver's ever-present influence of kindness and attention to the small, beautiful things that surround us shaped my world. She once told me, "Now remember to put your shoes together when you go to bed at night. That way, they won't get lonely for each other."

I knew my dad as a brilliant guy. Growing up in Early, he attended Kemper Military Academy and then Coe College in Cedar Rapids. He served in the Coast

Guard during World War II and found work with Grandpa right after the war. The Rural Electrification Association (REA) was a government initiative formed around that time to help connect farmers to the growing electrical grid taking root in cities and small towns in the Midwest. Ever the entrepreneur, Grandpa bought a bunch of Army surplus machinery shipped back from Korea, painted all the pieces a bright yellow, and stenciled Evans Construction Company on the sides. For the next couple of decades, Dad and Grandpa installed electrical power to farmers in northwestern Iowa and southwestern Minnesota.

Connecting rural people to electricity was a part of the upgrade. Powering pumps, machinery and lights immediately improved productivity, but as appliances and communications media appeared like radio, phones and TV, Dad's work proved much more significant in connecting these previously isolated folks to the local community than anyone would have known.

Mom was like most women of the '50s, assigned to care for the family and, in her spare time, provide for others. The role came easy for her. At that time, Early was about 600 people with four churches, three Protestant and one Catholic. All the church musicians knew each other. If someone like an organist got sick, someone else from another church might fill in. The congregation's needs came first, the denomination's second. Since everyone playing piano or organ pretty much knew everyone else's music, filling in was a small road-bump sort of thing. Regarding doctrines, you could all be different, that was okay; however, if trouble threatened, community came first.

Even in good times, that sharing of resources spilled over to community events. Anytime there was a church social, or celebration of some sort, someone from another congregation might be invited in to play or sing as part of the entertainment. I went to all the churches as a kid, especially the summer Bible school programs offering lots of music opportunities. I thought that's what everyone's church was about. I did know, when we sang together, we smiled a lot. We were all kin. That's the message we kids took home.

Mom would play for weddings, funerals and anniversaries, accompany high school students at the music contests, and more. Folks would pay her with whatever they could or whatever they had. In a cabinet in the corner of the kitchen, my mom kept an old, weathered envelope with penciled entries scribbled on the outside.

Sometimes she got paid with a dozen eggs or sweetcorn. Although she called it her "egg money," it never was about the money—it was about *providing what was needed for the gathering*. Her music wasn't always the central focus, but because of what music does—and how it affects human beings—she served a significant role.

Mom instinctively knew how music could comfort those suffering. She knew what to play at funerals and would add last-minute requests to her set list with a smile. She wanted to perform the numbers most meaningful to the deceased and their family. Music is a healing and soothing balm at such times. *It heals not just individuals, but families.* Current research shows how good it is for mental health.

1. The Early Years

Mom's egg money envelope showing where she performed and how much money she earned.

My mom, Beth, an organist in the Early United Methodist church for 55 years, in 1972.

Same goes for happy events like weddings, birthdays, and anniversaries. We now know that music helps with the release of happy hormones known as endorphins. Spontaneous joy might lead to dancing, laugher, and, then, even more joy.

That can help us physically. If someone starts dancing, the body benefits through movement. Everything works better.

Not to be left out, the elderly people in Early would come, sit, watch and listen to the music, witness the community celebrate, *and receive the same benefits*. If you were in small-town Iowa, you were considered part of the greater community. If you were lonely, you were always welcome at a public event. Somehow this was understood. I remember lots of smiling folks, all served up scoops of healthy benefits through the music. *Music + community are good medicine.*

Communities are constructs to describe a group of people who share common interests or goals. In the case of a small farm town, it's to provide a safe, viable space for people to live, work, worship, raise families and, if all goes well, celebrate and enjoy life. They can take many forms. Early, Iowa, is a geographic community. They can also be around interests like music, hobbies, politics and much more. Today there are virtual communities pretty much everywhere online. What's amazing is what communities can do for us as a group:

- *The sharing of knowledge:* Communities allow people to exchange and advance their knowledge/expertise with one another, which in turn leads to faster learning and innovation. Knowledge-sharing can take many forms, including spoken word, written word, tool building, pottery and textile construction (traditions), and music.
- *Division of labor:* In a community, people can specialize in different tasks and professions, allowing for a more-efficient use of resources and greater productivity. In the traditional music community, some make the instruments that others play, perform on, and teach. The historians like authors and filmmakers save the developments for both current and future generations.
- *Protection and security:* Strength in numbers. By banding together, communities of individuals can protect themselves from external threats such as predators or hostile groups. Communities also provide a safety net for member individuals who fall on hard times or face personal challenges.
- *Social support:* Communities offer emotional support, companionship, and a sense of belonging, which can have positive effects on mental and physical health. Being part of a community can also help individuals cope with stress and adversity.
- *Resource sharing:* In communities, individuals can share resources such as food, water, and shelter. This helps to ensure that everyone has access to the basic necessities of life, including happiness, even in times of scarcity.

By simply witnessing her actions, Mom roped me into the small-town community mindset early on. I was a pudgy little kid, much more interested in my coin collection, riding bikes with my friends, reading or spending time down at the creek catching frogs and turtles than thinking of others. When I'd come home from school, or on Saturdays before I'd get started playing outside, she'd load me up with freshly baked pastries and old magazines that she'd saved and send me out on my bike with deliveries for the "old folks."

Early had lots of older shut-ins, many retired farmers or veterans with limited resources, and only a few could drive. Once again, the community would provide for them. One old couple that I clearly remember was the Zimmermans, who were in their 80s or 90s.

One Saturday morning when I was six or so, my mom interfered with my routine of self-indulgence. She handed me a grocery bag to deliver to the Zimmermans before I went out to play with friends. Grumpy because, well, I was a kid, I flew down the alley on my high-handlebar, banana-seat Schwinn with a load of warm, tasty cinnamon rolls and a stack of *Newsweek* magazines, hoping to make it to my friend's house before cartoons started. I had no idea how witnessing my mom's simple act of *kindness shown to others* would positively affect me later on in life. But it started that day.

The Zimmermans were like every other older family she'd serve. Let's start with how welcome they made me feel. Immediately invited in, I was received as a family member, served at least a glass of water at the kitchen table as the other elder in the house made his or her way to a chair next to me so they could hear. Both were already smiling, but one would then start a conversation. "What are you doing in school, Craig?" was a good starter. "Did you read this magazine you brought?" was next. "What did you learn from it?" might have been a follow-up. I wasn't old enough to know I should be asking them about their lives and their experiences—that wouldn't come until I grew up. But boy, did they show me what real, attentive listening looks, sounds, and *feels* like. They were focusing on me. Both were "present," completely into the conversational moment. *Time stops. Joy starts!* Not just for them; I was a part of it. Makes me smile again, just thinking about it.

I remember that it felt warm … delightful. I didn't realize they were honoring me in that moment, but they were. They were giving me their complete, undivided attention. Now, I realize that even in my naivete, the simple fact that I took the time to talk and listen to them was honoring them. They showed me how real listening is simple, but it requires focus … time free of distractions. And how good it feels for everyone sharing in that moment. That skill is mostly lost today due to competitive noise and limited time. *What a blessing those old people gave me. Listening matters.* Thank you, small-town Iowa.

Small Iowa towns also produce lots of what I call "Midwestern extroverts," which means, in social situations, you pretty much smile all the time. Some eye contact is allowed, but no staring, though. This technique also serves as encouragement to a conversation, if spoken to first. Other than that, we're okay with just our own company. Elsewhere, you'd be called an introvert.

By the time I was in high school, I knew my mom was really busy. She was always scheduling in some social event that required her music. I didn't really realize how important her role as musician was to the community was until 30 years later. You see, my mom served a very important community role. Vibrant small towns usually have a doctor to care for the sick and injured, teachers to prepare young minds for life, firefighters and law enforcement to keep us safe, grocery store owners to provide all with their daily manna and, of course, pastors of various denominations to offer that spiritually. Equally as contributing are other community-serving members with more diverse labels like Good Samaritan, Helpful Volunteer, even Town Bully as an example of who not to be. I would label my mom Early and Sac County's music and entertainment director. Dad would joke *no one could get married or buried without first checking her schedule.* He was spot-on with that comment. But she loved it! I never saw her complain about this role. I'm not sure she really knew how important what she selflessly did was to the community. She was simply doing what came naturally to her, using her gift of music to *help* others. That's the way community works.

Music can express joy and celebration as easily as it comforts sorrow and grief. In a community setting, it's cathartic, settling, comforting and uniting. Where the local doctor was in charge of healing our bodies through medicine, *music was equally as good for us physically, mentally, emotionally, and spiritually.* But I wasn't thinking big thoughts like that back then. I was intrigued with her *popularity.* Folks hiring her to play knew the importance of what she provided. And she was invited to everything, everywhere. I liked the social aspect that the music seemed to facilitate. Also, the good humor that seemed to be present when she played, even the funerals. I had no idea that music was a language that humans instinctively respond to, whether they know it or not. I did know *music was somehow associated with fun.*

Me and music? I started on piano around age five or six but didn't really like it. However, I did find something that would rock my musical world. One day, I was exploring my Grandma Evans' attic. I could find all sorts of interesting stuff up there. I'd just returned from the grocery store for her, so she indulged me having a look. This time, I found a ukulele with a canoe and a romantic couple rowing down a small stream stenciled on it. For reasons unknown, my heart jumped. I grabbed it and ran downstairs.

"Grandma, can I have this?"

"What is it, child?"

"It looks like a small guitar."

"Oh, that was your Uncle Bill's. He bought it at college. I'm sure he wouldn't mine you playing it."

And play, I did. I bought a Mel Bay's instructional chord book from a small music store in Storm Lake and took off.

My mother was the church organist to a small Methodist congregation. To prepare for church, she'd practice hymns all week on a beautiful old Baldwin organ in our living room that Dad bought her as a gift. He loved her music and also saw the important role she played in the little farm town. I grew up hearing all the great melodies: "The Old Rugged Cross," "Leaning on the Everlasting Arms," "To All Things Now Living," "It Is Well with My Soul." Early on, Mom recognized I had an interest in music, and when I was about five she gave us both a single subscription to the Columbia Record Club as a Christmas present. My music world exploded overnight.

Every month brought us something new and exciting. As soon as the 33⅓ LP record arrived, it was saddled up on the RCA record player. From the electric energy present in the "French Cancan," to the rousing refrain of Franz von Suppé's "Charge of the Light Brigade," to the delayed anticipation and climax of the Gershwin's "Rhapsody in Blue," all were played until they were worn out. I couldn't get enough of the rush I felt listening to these dynamic treasures. Literally, time would stop for me … and, the best word I could find was that *joy*, which Webster defined as *a feeling of great pleasure and happiness*, filled my chest. At times, I found myself smiling, holding my breath as I listened. In a single sitting of sometimes up to three hours, I could be laughing or crying out loud, based on how those amazing musical strains affected me. No thoughts, just non-stop goose bumps. I'd lose all track of time. Time stopped. Joy followed! That's what I was feeling at age five. Later in life I would learn what I was experiencing was *delight*, when the excitement within fills you with such blissful feelings, you feel like you could burst. I also later learned to describe music as *awe*-inspiring. Eventually, after listening, my emotions would subside enough to let my brain ask, "What the heck is that? And why does it make me feel that way?" It's a simple question, but I could find no internal answer. I had to read more, investigate. Music and its effect on us humans is so vast. That mystery drew me in … for life. Who knew those moments would eventually direct me to the most rewarding, fulfilling musical experience one could have in life—traditional music—but I digress.

At this point between age five and 10, I was pretty much a music junkie. Although I liked some music more than others, I couldn't really tell the difference between good and bad. Some gave me more feelings, but I thought it all significant. One observation: aside from the hymns Mom played, most of what I was experiencing were instrumentals. And what lyrics I paid attention to in church were mostly about hope, love and salvation. What was not to like?

Mom loved the traveling performer Fred Waring. I remember seeing him on a grainy TV surrounded by a bunch of odd-looking folks with their faces painted black (it was his "Pennsylvanians" chorus in Blackface). Their appearances were peculiar and unexplained at the time, but the music was deep, emotional, electric. When I was older, Mom drove the two of us to a high school gymnasium somewhere in Sioux City, Iowa, where Fred and his Pennsylvanians were giving a concert. Now, this was *live*, not a recording. I loved our Columbia Records, but what I witnessed from the first concert number on was *one full step above the previous experience*!

Instantly, *time stopped and joy started*! Before that event, I had *never* experienced what I did that night. The blending of voices. The four-string banjo, the upbeat dance tempos. All performers working in sync with each other, a giant *community* of music. I found myself holding my breath for no reason other than to try and contain what I was feeling inside. I can picture that stage and the chorus as it happened even today. As fate would have it, I would reconnect with Fred and the blissful experience again through a historian, 60 years later, but all I knew back then was that something inside of me was alive and present when this music happened. I was hooked.

Dad loved music but couldn't play anything beyond the radio. But he fully supported Mom's music habit. So when I showed an interest in the Columbia Records and was trying to sing and play along with Peter, Paul and Mary on my ukulele, like the great dad he was, he tuned in. He told me a singing group I might enjoy was coming to the Schaller Auditorium at Buena Vista College in Storm Lake, Iowa. They were called the New Christy Minstrels. Since Mom was normally the music contact in the family, this was something new. But I was game. I had no time to prepare for what I was about to experience that night. Dad and I simply showed up. The highs I'd experienced from discovering Uncle Bill's ukulele, to the Columbia Record Club, to Fred Waring were about to be topped.

OMG! We were center stage, seated somewhere in the first 10 rows. Then, out of nowhere, 12 smiling, handsome young people lined up across a stage. The first number was like a bucking bronco exploding out of the gate! The singers were all riding it in sync. I was barely holding on. I clearly remember balanced, tight, magnificent harmonies. They were dancing and moving in sequence with the beat. They weren't individuals, they were one unit. *The community of them was acting as a single organism.* It was a force of nature!

The set list was all traditional music, much of it early minstrel-era, like the original Christy Minstrels from the 1870s. Songs like "Follow the Drinkin' Gourd" made my hair stand on end. When I studied the lyrics years later, I would finally understand why. It's song about a repressed group of suffering, enslaved Africans helping each other escape through a community of those supporting them in finding freedom. Gives me goosebumps even now as I type this page. Back then, as now, I instinctively cry because I *delight* in such works. It takes my breath away! I still hold my breath again and again while listening. The swells of emotion are omnipresent now as then. To this day, I've never felt closer to God than I was at that concert. Pretty sure I experienced the Divine in that moment. *Time stopped. Joy started.* Smiling now.

The impact those young musicians had on me that night has been lifelong. How can something, anything be that powerful?! This *is* just music, right? What is the emotional, physical, even spiritual connection that keeps rattling my overwhelmed little earth suit? I had no idea then, but 60 years later, I'm getting closer to an explanation. For now, though, back to the story.

Popular music was in the midst of a tectonic shift in the early to mid 1960s. The Folk Scare (traditional music scene) was about to end. And rock 'n' roll was going to be the future wave. Falling asleep at night, I'd listen to my brother Jack's AM radio placed on the floor, between our twin beds. The doo wop of the late '50s was fun, but I was inexplicably drawn to the folk singers and acoustic music.

As a teen, listening to rock 'n' roll lyrics my parents pretty much didn't know about, but would not have allowed, became sort of a special interest. "Louie Louie" was interesting—what did he say, what did that mean? But it was not quite as compelling as a Peter, Paul and Mary story about mythical magic dragons or cars, toys or lost loves. No doubt about it, story songs were cool. I started buying albums and teaching myself the songs.

From high school through college, I taught myself guitar and banjo just to play the melodies and retell the stories that filled my head and heart. Since girls liked to hear ballads, I learned enough to raise their interest in me. But the lyrics I was singing—mostly written by old English characters using arcane language—were probably beyond my scope of understanding. I don't remember a time when I sat down and actively thought, "I wonder what a rake or a bard really is?" As a teenager, if a girl smiled when whoever the good guy was got the gal in the story I was singing, I was happy. End of thought.

My childhood introduced me to the concept of community and how it can unite, feed, and support us. And how its members, in attending to the suffering and lonely, keep the tradition strong. I also learned about how joy, happiness, delight, and awe can come out of nowhere—and how active listening and music facilitates time that seems to stop in certain moments. It's a by-product of music when facilitated by and within a community.

All this is made possible in the language of music. Too bad it took me another 50 years to connect the dots. But if I hadn't, this book wouldn't be here, in your hands, offering you an invitation to join this community and feel the rush. But again, I'm getting ahead of myself. Like Odysseus, I had to start my own personal odyssey. It was time for me to make some decisions and grow up.

2

The Artist's Choice

First Time, Old-Time: "What's that noise?!"

I was seven going on eight years old. It was a summery mid-afternoon in 1960, and Dad and I were somewhere in downtown Deadwood, South Dakota. We'd been sightseeing at Mt. Rushmore most of the morning. I was impressed but found myself daydreaming while looking at static, stoic stone statues. I was much more interested in the beaded leather coin pouches and arrowheads I'd discovered in a souvenir shop. Pretty sure I was probably whining, so to my family's delight, my good-natured dad volunteered to entertain me. We left my mother and brother behind and headed to town. I remember thinking, "Score! Me n' Dad get to go exploring."

Walking the streets of Deadwood, I heard a shocking sound best described as two cats fighting … or one being strangled. It was coming from the covered boardwalk in front of a souvenir store across the street. When I asked Dad if we could investigate, he nodded. Dad always encouraged an adventure, and off we went.

My eye was more on the souvenir store than my ear was on the raucous sound, but as we got closer, I saw a crumpled old character resting on a folding chair, leaning forward. His bony knees touched at an odd angle, and his worn boots pointed toward each other, toes almost touching. His face was covered by a gigantic gray hat. As I got closer, I could see this old man was playing a fiddle. I couldn't really see the instrument as the upper part of his body was covered by his dusty fedora. I did occasionally see a bony hand and the ends of his bow as it emerged, traveling back and forth across the strings. But the sound grabbed me, and it was exciting, electric. I can't explain why. It seemed to lift my heart upward, right in my chest. I know I was holding my breath, but I felt like dancing. Was this joy? Somehow that music was lighting up every neuron in my brain. Time stopped…. I was floating.

We stopped a few feet in front of him. The old fella finished his tune about the same time I noticed an open violin case at his feet. It held a few coins and a bill or two. I turned to Dad and asked if I could give him some money. Dad produced a quarter, handed it to me, and I tossed it toward the case. The silver coin hit a few others and made a jingling sound. I was looking down at the case as that happened. Suddenly the old man's hat turned upward, toward me. To my shock, I found myself peering dead-on into his ancient face. I accentuate the "ancient" part.

His high, bony cheeks framed a gaunt, small, open mouth. He had a stubble of beard on his chin. His blue eyes were wide, staring in my general direction. The bright blue was accented by an odd *white* (not black) pupil. Clearly, he had cataracts. He was blind.

"Thank you!" he garbled through very few teeth. His face immediately broke into a wide, craggy, hillbilly-toothless grin. His crumpled hat promptly dropped back down, and he began scratching out another cat-skinning melody. Meanwhile, I'd recoiled backward into my dad's leg. The old fiddler's appearance scared me half to death. But the shock passed quickly as the music once again filled my ears and heart with excitement. I went from fear to joy

My dad, Bob Evans, in 1975.

in seconds. I think the old fellow's enthusiastic smile caught up with me. I know the music did. But what's most interesting is that, here I am, 64 years later—and I can relive this scenario as if it just happened. I didn't know it, but that day, that blind old man and his love of playing and sharing the music, which I later found out was traditional music, would become a major part of my life. It only took me another 50 years to figure out what I had experienced that day changed my life … for good.

John Lennon Was Right

Dad was very much a product of his culture and era. Like Mom, he too followed the socially-assigned roles of his generation, the '50s and '60s. As the stoic head of the family, Dad was "the provider." Mom took care of the kids. I really don't make that statement with remorse or to diminish either of them—that was the way it was. Frankly, I had a childhood that would make Norman Rockwell jealous. It *was* that good. That being said, Dad was attuned to my curiosities and interests, but he didn't often indulge in a conversation about them. There was an event, though, when that all changed. First, a little more background.

It's important to introduce a conversation about life paths, careers, dreams and goals. I started out life thinking I could be anything I wanted. Dad would say "the world's your oyster." I was a Midwesterner so didn't really understand what that meant (what's an oyster?). Dad would talk about careers. He'd had many and enjoyed them all. Being around and working on farms, I learned I really liked animals. Maybe I could be a veterinarian. I also really liked history and current events. Maybe I could be a journalist. And I *really* liked what Mom did ... *playing music*. Maybe I could be a musician.

I was having fun with my four-string uke. Listening to my record albums, I'd taught myself songs from the New Christy Minstrels as well as Peter, Paul and Mary, the Serendipity Singers and more. Songs were filling my heart with the same joy I felt when listening to the old fiddler from Deadwood. I also was witnessing more of Mom's involvement in the community of Early, Iowa. There wasn't a wedding or a funeral or a social event that didn't involve her and her best friend, Smitty Nellis, who played piano. The two of them were the entertainment for almost any gathering, dances included.

I now understand that Beth and Smitty were providing *the social elixir and the glue* that helped make our community strong. That's what music does. It bonds us together, helps us celebrate, and can fill us each individually with the joy the old fiddler exposed me to. Mom was really popular! As a young man looking for something to do as a job, I could see myself providing music like that.

About this time, my parents invested in the World Book Encyclopedia. That was a game changer. First thing I looked up was an oyster. I remember thinking I should find something more desirable to shoot for; then I lost myself in these amazing books. I spent most evenings reading, studying the world, history, science and more as it was presented. Grainy black-and-white photos came to life. It was astonishingly satisfying. They opened my eyes and made me want to learn more. I was especially intrigued with past cultures—the Mayans, Incas, Romans, and Greeks. Being a collector of early American coins, I began focusing on how people paid for things back then. It was fascinating.

About age 10, I started noticing even more coins on my trips to the grocery store. One day as I walked in, I saw a hand-scribbled note tacked to the neighborhood "notice" board. It was from an old fellow in Sac City, 10 miles away. He had a coin collection he wanted to sell. It contained some foreign coins and about 20 old silver dollars. I had some lawn-mowing and bean-walking cash in my bank (old BAND-AID canister) so I was in a position to buy.

When I asked my dad if he would drive me there, he agreed, although he did raise a skeptic eyebrow when I told him I was going to pay $2 in bills for each $1 silver coin. He asked me if I thought that made sense. I don't remember if he was smirking or serious, but it was a good question. I knew that the silver in that dollar was probably worth more than its face value—it was clearly worth more than paper. Jack Kennedy was president (1961-1963). And for longer than I care to remember, Walter Cronkite would remind us of Nikita Khrushchev and his nukes. If bad times did happen, I figured the silver dollar would be more appealing if we needed to buy food. No kidding. That *was* a thought.

By that time, I'd assembled a pretty fair coin collection. Dad was a director at the Early Savings Bank. On Saturdays, I'd stop in, wait for an opening and then walk up to one of the three tellers' booths and ask if I could look over all the silver dollars they had stacked off to the side. Back then silver certificates were still legal tender—and if someone wanted to, they could ask the bank to exchange the paper for actual silver, so banks had them on hand. The teller would take me back to a table and let me look through the 20 or so she had at her station and also let me do the same with the stacks from the other two booths. I'd bring my own silver dollars and exchange duplicates for those with other dates or in better condition. And if I found some I really wanted, I'd turn in a silver certificate for it. But I genuinely believed that every silver dollar, whether it was a collectable date or not, had more value than the paper. Besides, it represented history, and I liked building up my stash. Okay, back to Dad.

Once I told him about the status of my coin collection, he was intrigued. He commented that I had done well saving. He also commented on how I was investing in the future; that silver might become more of a commodity. He agreed to drive me to meet the old fellow in Sac City.

The day came. We were both excited, me for buying more silver dollars—and going on an adventure with Dad—and Dad with a plan of his own. He thought it was time to ask a rather important question that I hadn't seen coming. We were driving down the road when he started in.

"Son, what do you want to be when you grow up?"

I told him, "I want to be a musician. I want to play music like Mom."

Dad was silent. After a few thoughtful moments he said, "That's great, son, but what's your *day job*?" I was stunned. Given how much Dad supported Mom's music, and his pride in her selflessly serving the community, his question surprised me. I guessed a day job meant providing an income—more than a few five-dollar bills and a dozen eggs. I thought about Mom's job. Apparently, music must be what you do for fun? Not serious enough for "day" work? Hmmm. Money matters a lot, I guess.

In 1969, John Lennon wrote a prophetic statement: *"Every child is an artist until he's told he's not an artist."*

As an artist, Lennon clearly knew music could be a day job. It's also what filled him up, as much as money. Of all the times in my life that Dad provided me valuable information, this was the one time he missed. He *was* thinking of my best interests, I know that. But the values he was using in convincing me to avoid following a passion, possibly a career in music, were based on *his* life values. It's okay, and I forgave him long ago.

I decided to become a veterinarian.

3

College, Career and Crash

My choices for college were limited to the Midwest. I'd be close to home, and most were affordable. Dad offered to pay if I went to Buena Vista College in Storm Lake, the place we'd watched the New Christy Minstrels. "You can stay here and commute. Sleep in your own bed every night. Mom can make you breakfast and even type up your term papers." That probably sounded pretty good to him, but I had more in mind—so I started looking at other small colleges in Iowa. Grinnell is where my cousin Joey met her husband, Raleigh. "That's too much of a hippie school, son. You need to go somewhere you can learn, not just be around those that are unruly." Dang, I was naïve back then. Iowa State and the University of Iowa were too big for my comfort level. I didn't want to be lost in a crowd. Dad and brother Jack went to Coe, so of course I didn't want to. I settled on Drake University in Des Moines. Right size student body (under 5,000), right location (central Iowa), not too progressive, not too conservative, in the state's capitol (big town) and three hours away from home. Turns out, it was a good fit for me.

I majored in biology early on, thinking I'd be going to Iowa State next to study veterinary medicine. I had a plan. Then life came knocking.

College is a wonderful experience for a small-town kid. I'd really enjoyed reading the encyclopedia, but this, *this* was learning and exploring in real time. I signed up for some history and journalism classes to see what they were about.

After a couple of semesters, discovering that I could handle the workload, I was looking for more to do. I thought I'd find a part-time job somewhere. I had a short-lived starter stint delivering Charles Chips Potato Chips. Next, I landed a really good job as a singing waiter at the new downtown Holiday Inn with the rotating circular restaurant on top. I had to sing, dance, and play an instrument as an audition, along with a couple hundred other kids from Des Moines, Ames, and neighboring towns. What a fun group!

The restaurant hired a dance instructor, taught us some show tunes for a couple of all-cast sets. They also polished up whatever we could do on our own or in small groups and taught us how to formally wait tables. Then they put us to work, if one could call it that. I called it fun! That had to be one of the best jobs *ever*! Being from different cities and campuses, we kids came together as a community to perform the music. The barriers to entry were low. In fact, we were seeking each other to see what we could do together. For the first time in my college life, I had a community experience similar to my days in Early; they felt like old friends. Didn't realize how much I'd actually missed it. College felt more solitary.

The Holiday Inn Singers proved one of my college highlights. We played, sang, partied, and made money. Time stopped when our "work" started. Did I say money? On a good night, I'd clear $250 in cash. This is 1972. Our hourly pay was small, but we'd perform our own music for our tables, and we had been given permission to sing to other diners, if it looked like they were open. And they tipped most generously, by Iowa standards. I learned the basics of busking—and making money playing music.

Mentors

Where would we be without the people that act as signposts for us? Trouble is, most of us didn't pay attention at the time they were trying to show us the way. I was fortunate in that I kinda did, or, more likely, they kept coming around until one day, I got the message.

It seems every time wisdom is served up to me, it's by somebody I love. It started with my dad. He was happy, pleasant, optimistic, and kind. His mother, my grandmother Evans, was also very kind and taught me how to watch out for others. My tiny little grandmother Weaver—all four feet, four inches of her—was the same way. Like putting my shoes together at night (so they wouldn't be lonesome), all were lessons about love and kindness. Regarding her height, my brother would joke "poor thing, she's always the last one to know when it rains."

I had these angels visiting me all through college, too. I graduated early with a bachelor's degree. And I was awarded a teaching assistantship to finish my master's degree in physiology while waiting to get into veterinary school. In the meantime, I had a nice office in the brand new biology building, along with a bunch of interesting laboratories to teach. Several were groups of nurses.

One bright fall morning, as I was about to lecture a class of nurses on the circulatory system, Dr. Rodney Rogers, head of the biology department, knocked on my door and said, "I have a job for you!" Seems that a research company from Chicago was coming to Des Moines to determine if the local rendering plant did indeed smell—a complaint often made by the people who lived closest to the plant. The research company was hired to determine at what concentration of odor molecules people actually recognize "that smells!" They needed 200 people to sample, um, odors. They would get paid something like $2.50 an hour. A smiling Dr. Rogers said, "This is right up your alley!" I wondered, what does that mean … or, how did he know?

I worked all through college. At that time, I was a producer and a floor assistant at KRNT, a local TV station in Des Moines. It was the latest of my many jobs, including bill collector for the phone company, Charles' Chips delivery person, and singing waiter at the Holiday Inn's rotating restaurant. TV was still mainstream media back then. I thought about the best way to reach and recruit a bunch of local people, and bingo! Dr. Rogers was right. I was in the best position possible to reach pretty much all of Des Moines ... *on the 6 p.m. news.*

I called up the news department at my television station and asked, "How would you like to film a segment on people getting paid to smell ... simply using their nose?" The reporter said they would be right out. That was too easy. I decided to call the other two networks. A half hour later, I had three TV stations coming out *that day* at 10 a.m., 2 p.m. and 4 p.m. All went as planned. That day I decided I loved journalism.

I prepped to watch the 6 o'clock news that night. I put three televisions in my living room, invited over a bunch of friends, and filled the fridge with beer. The hour approached. My station came on with news report first, *lead story*! "How would you like to get paid for using your nose?" The reporter went on, showed a short interview with me describing what I was looking for and a few cut-away shots of people's noses. At the very last, he listed the phone number people were to call to reach me—*first thing in the morning*—to take their name. Oh, no! The telephone number was wrong! I grabbed the phone and quickly called the station to give the proper number.

Moments later the second television channel gave a similar story, slightly different angle but same visuals of noses. Whew, they listed the correct number. The third station followed suit but before that happened, about halfway through their newscast, my television station came back on and reported that *we gave the wrong number*! Some poor little lady from Clive, Iowa, was finally able to get through to the television station. She reported, "Every time I picked up the phone to call you, there was someone new calling me to sign up!" Hmm. I liked the sound of that. My station then listed what they thought to be the real number.

Unfortunately, the second time my station posted the number, it too was wrong. I got back on the phone, and at the end of the newscast, a sheepish anchor came on and said, "I'm sorry we've given the wrong number a second time," and then laughed. This time, they did give the correct number. My smelling story had won the day. I wasn't yet in advertising, but this was like a dream come true.

The next morning, as I was walking down the hall to my office, I could hear the phone ringing. Once seated at my desk, I'd wait for the ring, pick it up, take down a name and a phone number, and then hang up. I'd count to three and, before it rang, I'd pick the phone up again, and there would be another person on the line. Same experience as the little old lady from Clive. By the end of the day, I lined up enough people to do the sampling. Two of the stations came back for a follow-up report later in the week, which I was happy to oblige. It was fun!

Fast forward to my second attempt to enter veterinary school at Iowa State University. I had applied twice; the second time I was put on hold, which meant there were 30 applicants, from which they would select 15. My grades were great, my test scores were stellar, but what I needed was a good interview in front of the five veterinarians on the admission board. The first year I went I didn't really know what I was doing. I'd really felt pressure, and I floundered. I was rejected, and it broke my heart. I genuinely thought I was supposed to be a veterinarian—so I tried a second time.

This time I knew what I was facing. I went in with a very conservative suit, tie, shined shoes, short haircut and I was prepared to thoroughly answer all questions to the best of my ability. I walked in and sat down in front of the same group of five. The older man that led the committee looked at me and said, "Welcome back. This is your second time..." and then paused. He said, "I know you!" A smile spread across his face as he said, "You're that smeller guy from Des Moines. How did that program turn out?" at which point he leaned back in his chair to genuinely listen. I took the opportunity to fully explain the entire engagement, how I responded, and how it was successfully completed. Four out of the five members listening to me asked follow-up questions and laughed about the experience. The fifth one sat straight up throughout my nine minutes, with minimal eye contact. Clearly, he was not enjoying the story. It only takes one to blackball admission.

Later, I was told by the head of the interview committee that I had the highest-scored interview that year. Not sure how they figured that, but apparently, I'd done the right thing ... for four out of the five. I found this out because, when I received my second rejection letter from Iowa State University's veterinary school, I once again went around and spoke to every person on the board to find out how I could better my chances of admission the following year. Four out of the five voted for me and said they would again. The one that didn't, Dr. R. folded his arms, leaned back in his chair and told me, "I don't think you'd make a good veterinarian. You're too promotional." Promotional?

My heart sank a second time. I didn't know being promotional—whatever that meant—was necessarily a bad thing, especially when all I did was explain myself and the process I'd followed to be successful with the task.

Many years later, it turns out Dr. R. did me a favor. Yes, I would've been a good veterinarian, but I never would have experienced the other things in my life that have given it significance and meaning. Thanks, Dr. R.; you still were a jerk. Meanwhile, it was clear from the first four doctors that they found me competent or at least interesting.

That's when I decided to join the rat race. Up to now, I'd majored in biology and physiology, with music as an unofficial elective, outside of college. In addition to the Holiday Inn Singers, I was a regular with my cousin Raleigh's jug band out of Ames. We played the finest dive bars in central Iowa. Many with chicken wire in front of the stage (to stop an incoming beer bottle).

The band was usually five to six fun-loving musicians with day jobs. We were a solid set when we played. In fact, we rocked! Felt really good, too. The music we performed, mostly from the early 1920s, was unusual with lyrics that I didn't really understand, but our audiences were thoroughly entertained. I just knew those old numbers had staying power.

I'd started to view music groups like this to be my community of like-minded friends. College had proven more competitive than social. Besides, I don't believe at that age many of us were too confident about putting ourselves out there. Fear of rejection, whether that be someone in a potentially romantic relationship or fitting in with one's peers, was a real thing. As a kid, I used to watch farm animals interact. Like all pack animals—cows, horses, pigs, dogs, cats—we need community. That's part of our basic mammalian wiring. Our chances of survival increase with numbers. But in order to survive, community pack animal behavior also has a dark side.

Think back to grade, middle or high school. Nobody wants to be the weird kid that, for a variety of reasons, someone in the group thinks a "weak link." Kids can be ruthless in bullying a tagged "loser." Why is that? The brutal mindset might actually have evolutionary roots. Consider: In times of limited resources like food, the strongest mammals in the community are usually the ones programmed to survive. And, as group leaders, some of them can be heartless in considering the weak that could jeopardize resources for the rest of the community. Personally, I usually liked befriending the odd kid. I seemed able to do that without being considered like them. Actually, that scenario didn't enter my head. The fact that they looked, acted and/or thought differently was intriguing. Also, in a grade-school scenario, fear can be a motivator for ostracizing. In a potential bully's eyes, they can make themselves look bigger or stronger by picking on someone weaker. In such cases, this immature sentient pack animal isn't necessarily evolved enough to show compassion. *For humans, family values demonstrated in front of youngsters by elders can lay the groundwork for future interactions with others.* I grew up surrounded by kindness. Everyone matters.

If you were rejected by a group as a kid in school, you know what it feels like to be on the outside. It sucks. On the other hand, if you're in a healthy, supportive community, you know someone's got your back. Strong relationships are real confidence-builders. That's why we're programmed to seek them out. I'd seen and experienced this firsthand in my small-town Early years. I know how important it is.

Think Differently

I had a favorite instructor in the MBA program at the University of Minnesota. His name was Dr. Cardozo. He was formerly a Harvard professor that liked to teach using the Harvard case-study method. Every week, students were presented with a pretty significant business problem and given a timeline of various incidents, facts and events that happened along the way. The task was two-fold: determine the real cause (versus symptom) of the problem(s), then assemble a solution.

I felt uneasy in my class; about two-thirds of my classmates were computer programmers from Honeywell, Control Data Corporation, and other computer-based operations in Minneapolis. This was too competitive a situation to be a community. I was on my own. Simply by showing up and studying my peers, the class introduced me to social anthropology. It's where I first witnessed that people usually process information one of two ways. One can either be *pragmatic* (A leads to B leads to C and so on) or *intuitive*. The latter may start with E, backfill to A, then move forward to the end of the alphabet. Intuitives often jump into the middle of a problem and then find their way out. I discovered that's core me.

Earlier, when I'd earned my master's degree in physiology, I had learned the scientific method, the pragmatic approach—so, actually, I had the best of both worlds. I could follow my native programming and get excited about solution possibilities—because intuition is more fun than pragmatism (unless you're a computer programmer). I could then backfill (pragmatically) to figure out a proper approach. Anytime we had a group class project, I would look for pragmatists within so it would cut time to find a solution in half. At our meetings I could throw out possible solutions and then ask, "How do I get here?"

Each week, Dr. Cardozo would introduce a new Harvard case study. The following week he would walk in sporting his blue Brooks Brothers suit, complete with black Florsheim wingtip shoes, look briefly at the class and announce somebody's name. That person would then stand ... alone.

The good professor would approach and announce the challenge. "This week's case study is about a major car brand's manufacturing problems." He would then turn, head to the white board, and over his shoulder ask, "What did you, Mr. or Ms. [insert name here] learn from this case?" As the standing student would begin to spill, Dr. Cardozo would pick up a marker and begin writing down the respondent's comments. He would place his remark on one side of the board, toward the top or bottom, occasionally walk to the other side to write an observed fact or comment there, and then move again. What was most interesting is that he was actually mapping that person's brain by response. All the while we were all staring at the professor's little bald spot.

This process could go on for as long as 20 minutes. The maps were often very one-sided. This would be representative of either the individual's knowledge base, focus (go with what you know) or the depth of that person's thought toward a problem (executive functioning). It didn't take me long to figure out what he was doing, and I was completely intrigued with the whole- brain–mapping exercise.

I couldn't wait for the next class because problem-solving challenges are intriguing and fun. Every week a new person would have to stand up and talk for their time in a barrel while the good doctor performed his task and analysis.

When a student was finished with their observations, she or he would take a seat, and Dr. Cardozo would then open discussion up to the rest of the class. By this point I could hardly contain myself. I was often the first raising my hand, saying, "*There's this. And there's this. And there's an opportunity over here.*" Dr. Cardozo would resume recording comments on the board until it was pretty much full ...

equally across the board. I loved this methodology for problem analysis. It was second nature to me. This was probably the most engaging class I'd ever taken.

Then my day in the barrel came. "Mr. Evans, stand up, please." Nervous, I looked down, heart in my throat. I stood, looked up and found myself staring directly into Dr. Cardozo's face. He'd walked over in front of me. "I can't wait to hear what you have to say about JCPenney's white wars, because if it wasn't for people like you, things wouldn't happen." Then he turned around and walked toward the board. I focused on his bald spot and tried to figure out what just happened. If I wasn't nervous enough to begin with, now I was in shock.

I glanced around at the students in my row. A couple were staring at me with bewildered and incredulous looks. Wow. I suddenly realized, *I really am different.* Up until that moment in *this* class, I had been experiencing what it feels like to be the oddball. Now I know what those poor kids felt like. Dr. Cardozo had never said anything like that in class before, nor did he after that night. But he gave me an amazing gift ... an affirmation *he knew I needed.* Different is *good. Be who you are.*

In hindsight, what Dr. Cardozo did for me that day was incredibly significant. He was telling me I could be confident in myself *even if I didn't have the support of a community behind me.* Scary but needed wisdom. It required me to be bold, which got me places. But it came at a price I wouldn't recognize until later. This making money thing was important. Music had to wait. So I put it aside.... I left my joy behind. I was now *a corporate warrior.*

Dr. Cardozo also helped me discover something else: the beauty in neurodiversity ... *we're all different.* Each and every one of us has a way of doing things. Gestalt describes "the whole [community] being greater than the sum of the individual parts." That's profound. Because we're all different, we're better, stronger, and more capable of finding better solutions to problems. I took it to mean that if you find you don't fit somewhere, you're the one responsible for doing something different, because, in theory, you're not afraid to do so. I dedicated my first book, *Marketing Channels: Infomercials and the Future of Televised Marketing* (Prentice Hall), to Dr. Cardozo.

Being an innovator isn't easy. You have to ignore most of society, because you're quirky. Artists are mostly innovators. At the very least, they're solitary producers. Think of all the things they have to think about to get things done? Wow. I will always love them for swimming against the stream. It's lonely out there. Neurodiversity is powerful in offering resources to many. Unfortunately, labels aren't generally perceived as positive. Often, labels harm.

"But wait! There's more!"

My introduction to other artists, other than musicians, was through advertising. Many of the creatives I'd met had short attention spans. It was hard to keep them on a subject during a briefing; it was harder to keep them focused in a room full of MBAs busy briefing numbers. I quickly learned I was wrong about that latter statement. One of the benefits of ADD/ADHD is the ability to hyper focus. Where their thoughts might appear to jump around in a meeting, once that artist decided what they were going to create, they could then do it and forget about time—being hyper focused—*time stopped. Joy started*! More often than not, what they would end up with would be extraordinary! I still link ADD/ADHD to creativity.

I've worked my entire life, beginning as a young boy mowing lawns, walking through bean fields and bailing hay in northwest Iowa. My official business career lasted only about 25 years. I was good at sales, marketing, designing alternative solutions, and negotiations. On the Myers–Briggs assessment, considered relevant at the time, I was an ENTP (E—Extroversion, N—Intuition, T—Thinking, and P—Perceiving), which worked well for me with people. I earned an MBA in marketing so I could sell bigger products to bigger customers. I was fascinated watching people think, i.e., how do people make choices? Is that an innate or a learned skill? I had become a social anthropologist. Oh, and I read all the high-brow coffee table books on how to be a warrior marketer. They were interesting reads. Ironically, when it came to actually designing a strategy to reach and engage people, I found basic pack-animal behavior to be the most successful approach.

Since I like to do research—another side career—I was good at figuring out what specifically made people tick, learning how they would make decisions. Depending on the subject's age and life experience, it's largely based on the values they learn from their parents and peers as a young person, modified when they hit their 20s and then once again when reevaluated in their 40s. I was fascinated by this thinking process. I even went on to teach it in marketing and business classes at a technical college in Rosemount, Minnesota.

When I started to develop infomercials for the Home Shopping Network in the late 1980s, I was exploiting the fact that I could buy a half hour of television outside Milwaukee at 2 o'clock in the morning for about $50. Ronald Reagan made infomercials legal in 1988, and since I would often have insomnia, I would stay up late to watch shows about exercise machines, spray-on hair, and how to quickly prepare a toasted meat sandwich. I was fascinated with the concept of a half-hour, real-life show about novelty products. To put that time to better use, I designed what I saw as television/longform programming about more complicated, expensive products and services, and, in 1993, I wrote *Marketing Channels: Infomercials and the Future of Televised Marketing*. The book was based on a cable TV show called *"E" Entertainment*. These "high-involvement" products like cars, computers, insurance and investments, cameras, and home appliances required time for research in order to make the best buying decision … or simply avoid a bad one (no one wants to intentionally buy a lemon for a car). For instance, a car channel: Monday night prime time might feature half-hour shows on minivans, each program produced by the brand or manufacturer. Tuesday could be trucks and SUVs. Wednesday, sports cars.

In between the main programs would be news, reviews, and even live call-in shows with brand representatives to answer questions. This "E" programming format would be replicated for all of the product categories.

I was deeply interested in building TV channels dedicated to things you *had* to think about because you feared you might regret making a bad decision. I figured a car channel, a computer channel, and an insurance and investment channel would be a solid alternative smart people would watch in the wee hours of the morning rather than the latest diet fad infomercial.

Oh, I got the Home Shopping Network job by sending a handmade, six-page, Macintosh-produced brochure on the concept of high-involvement, considered-purchase products and service infomercials to their programming department. Within two weeks they flew me out to Maine to meet with some key people on location, which was more like vacation. The next week they flew me down to Florida to meet with the owner, Roy Speer. Later that same week they offered me an enormous amount of money that almost tripled my salary as an ad guy. Dad was proud. Looked like I was on the road to Florida, but that was not necessarily good for me, though there were some flashy, amazing highlights that were appealing.

In 1992, I gave a speech and presented my marketing channels concept at a national infomercial gathering at the Waldorf Astoria in New York City. I was sandwiched between the ABC and NBC networks, which, if I remember correctly, struggled to make sure they said positive things about the medium. At the time, infomercials were considered trailer trash by most networks—but they'd gladly take money for the empty time slots in the early, wee-morning hours when they felt no one was watching.

I boldly announced to my audience of infomercial producers that my publisher had allowed me to give a free copy of my book to whoever had an interest in my big idea. I genuinely had a manuscript fleshed out and an agent in mind.

At the end of the presentation there were three lines in front of the dais. ABC had two people, NBC had one, and I had everybody else in the room. The third person in line pulled out a business card, raised it to his eye level (so I couldn't grab at it) and asked, "Who is your publisher?" The card read Simon & Schuster. I coyly asked, "Who are you?" We smiled at each other. He said, "If you don't have a publisher yet, talk to me." When we spoke a few days later, he connected me to the book acquisition people at Prentice Hall. The book came out in 1993 and sold somewhere between 6,000 and 8,000 copies. I'm told that's a business bestseller. That adventure took me to another level.

Best part about the book was it got me some notoriety and put me on the speaker circuit. For the next few years, Denver-based Liberty Media was pushing their 500-channel universe as the next (possibly interactive) evolution in cable programming. In owner/innovator Dr. John Malone's universe, a TV cable box could feature seven to 10 news channels, 15 more of "what-already-exists" channels, and 300 channels of movies to be named later. Conferences of cable operators loved what

3. College, Career and Crash 39

Mom, Dad and me in the early 1990s.

I had to offer because *it was something new and advertising dollars were attached*—capitalism at its best. At cable conferences nationally, my audiences numbered between 50 and 3,000 people. And I got paid handsomely, which made Dad even prouder.

I also learned that putting a fresh, new (capitalistic) idea in book format was a great way to be discovered. I received a couple of job inquiries during this time, one for $170,000 a year (Denver) and the second for $250,000 (LA). Dad was thrilled. Then, concurrent with the uptick, I experienced a brush with cancer (mid-40s). Coincidence? The latter discovery changed my perspective some, but not enough, and not for long. I told myself everything was fine—but suddenly I recognized that working on things that were quickly forgotten made me feel hollow. Maybe there was more to life? When the bright and flashy Internet came along in the early 1990s, I got distracted (again). But this time, a real paradigm shift began.

Alan Weiner, a friend of mine, worked for the Gartner Group—a premier high-tech think tank that helped large corporations navigate uncharted mine fields. Alan called me out of the blue and said, "Come to Chicago and meet me at the McCormick center. I have to introduce you to somebody." I did as Alan instructed and showed up on a Monday morning. The McCormick conference center was packed with bright, shiny displays, colorful signs and banners, and huge billboards of brand names like Cisco, Adobe, and Microsoft. Most, however, were companies I'd never heard of. This was the Consumer Electronics Show at it biggest and best. And yes, it was quite a show. Clearly a gold rush was on, and these were folks that supplied the shovels, pans, clothes, and food for the miners.

Alan marched me past the dazzling displays to the far end of the conference center. Over there were plain tables with simple displays. Nothing fancy. We walked up to one table called Netscape, at which point Alan was literally bouncing with excitement. "You've got to meet this guy!" he said. He took me behind the display where we found a young man facing a computer, head down, typing. Alan announced, "Craig, I want you to meet Mark Andreessen. Mark, show him what this thing can do." At that point, the inventor of Netscape, the first mainstream browser, gave me a hands-on walk-through of his creation. I didn't know who he was then, but I sure did later. I'd stumbled onto this newfangled thing called the Internet. Mark showed me what it could do. Alan and I then dreamed about what it—and we—were going to do.

When Mark finished, Alan was jumping up and down, saying, "Do you know what this means?!" "Do you know what this means?" Alan felt we no longer needed television studios. "People can put all sorts of programming online, on a website. And other people can access it 24 hours a day. There will be some costs but they're minimal compared to setting up a television studio." Right again. Hmmm, maybe this is a better way to skin and sell cats.

That's the first time I can genuinely say I saw a paradigm shift in motion. Up until then, I didn't know what it meant. And I quickly shifted my focus from televised marketing channels to websites. The operating theory was that once people needed information, they would look for it on their own. This fit nicely with my description of high-involvement, considered-purchase products and services. Overnight, I became a warrior website developer.

In the early '90s, I took a job with a small but aggressive family-owned advertising agency in Minneapolis, Minnesota, as director of their interactive department. Talk about right place, right time. Within a few months we were designing five-page, $30,000 websites for small, aggressive businesses that *got it*." Eventually we landed larger clients, like 3M, Minnegasco, our local gas supply company, Artic Cat, and the 12th largest bank in the United States, U.S. Bank. One year we joined 26 vendors all shooting to win the Peace Corps account.

We were a *band of warriors* inside the company. Finally, I was a part of a small community in business that was similar to what I knew growing up. All of the benefits of community were there: open sharing of knowledge, division of labor, protection and security, social support, and resource sharing. As a result, we *rocked*! We could literally finish each other's sentences ... and then laugh as a group of *friends*!

Since we were all getting along so well, one time we decided to try to guess each other's Myers– Briggs personality type. We each took a piece of paper, and next to a list of everyone's name, we wrote their four letters. Instantly I knew why our community worked so well. These programmers were almost all INTPs, quiet, thoughtful introverts. Plus, they all could convert an intuitive solution to a pragmatic approach. With me being the ENTP, the one to throw out solutions knowing they could not only understand them but also improve them on the fly. Like my study teams in college, we were unstoppable. Together, we won almost all our battles, landing business including the 26-vendor shoot-out for the Peace Corps project.

Approaching 50, I found I was growing weary of the rat race. Sure, it was exciting—but Time wasn't Stopping and Joy had pretty much left the building. I couldn't remember the last time I'd played music, or smiled, for that matter. After leaving the ad agency (lured away for more money), once again I was a lone warrior. And being able to trust others, based on the competitive nature of the business, was exhausting. The writing was on the wall: this scarred and battered warrior was done—it was time to turn in my spear and shield. I found myself daydreaming of small-town Early and of the community and relationships I so missed.

Capitalism: Man's Economy

Man's economy is *getting more for less*, whether it's products and goods, services, even employees; everyone's gotta make a buck. I did very well for the first part of my career. I was tasked with learning how people think, how people make decisions. Prior to social media, I would craft messages that would flood the airwaves with insignificant messages that might influence somebody to make an appropriate decision and favor buying the brand I was promoting. I was also good at keeping costs low when buying media, so when consumers did buy, it was a positive capitalistic—a.k.a. "earthly measurement"—scenario. And I was paid well for my participation, but there was nothing in there about helping others, especially the needy. In fact, empathy was pretty much absent everywhere I was operating, but so was music. There were no time-stopping joy-rushes, and I wasn't a part of any community. Yes, I was paid well. I thought that was the goal. But at the end of the day, there was no rejoicing or celebrating with others. In fact, in my business there were no others. Where was my community?! Suddenly, I started feeling really, *really* lonely. What a hollow existence I'd been creating. Dad had recently passed. I missed his reassuring voice. I was lost and homesick. I thought of Mom ... and I cried.

I threw out my business books and picked up my old philosophy books from college. I'd always loved the big thoughts. *Maybe we are down here to learn ... and serve.* Mom did it selflessly through music. And if I really was to reach millions of people with important life or personal messages, I wasn't drawing water from the right well. Something had to change.

Back in Early, I had learned from my time with the elderly neighbors, the Zimmermans, that if I have a *real, significant* conversation with *a few people*, I can communicate *much more effectively*. Longevity and wisdom have taught me that positively affecting or contributing to another's life might be the whole reason we're here. So, if I really want to change the world, instead of *broadcasting to many*, maybe doing it *one person at a time* is the best route. If it's within a healthy community, word of mouth does the rest. As any seasoned advertiser will tell you, that original way of promoting any thought is still the best.

Communities are set up to foster relationships. For those within, communications happen on a more frequent basis, leading to more understanding and efficiency, which builds trust that promotes more bonding among individuals. I didn't know it yet, but within a few years, traditional music would show me *firsthand* how a community makes all this happen.

At this point, my life had turned south—straight south. After decades on the road to making money, I'd been away from an already-troubled marital relationship. My life was unraveling, which was something, no matter how hard I worked or how creative I needed to be, I couldn't fix. I'm going to spare you the gritty details of what happened, but the end game was bleak. All that time, travel, work, and effort cost me my family and my home. Would I do it differently next time? Well, 25 years after the fact, I'm actually not too sure I can answer that … yet.

As painful as it was, as one door closed, another opened for me—and it was to a place that I'd forgotten was even there.

4

Life Interruptus: My Hero's Journey

Movin' Out, Movin' On

We can pretty well establish that by the age of 50, I was tanking. In more detailed terms, my attitude was one of being depressed, on the verge of despondence. I could find no escape from my personal or my professional dilemmas. The Eagle Scout was unable to land ... anywhere, on anything, and feel good about it. Seriously, I was in a world of hurt.

One Thursday afternoon while I was sitting at my soon-to-be vacated desk, because 400 of us late-40, early-50-year-old, well-paid execs were being let go, I made an audacious decision. I knew I was in need of a change, something so far removed from my daily life and known surroundings that I could escape my situation—even if it was for only a moment—and breathe. My counselor was worried about me. My pastor was worried about me. My mom had Alzheimer's, and I was now worried about her. I needed to find a distraction.

In moving out of my house, I discovered something I'd forgotten from a previous and happier time. I looked under the bed and found my long-lost instruments ... my bluegrass banjo, my wonderful guitar, and a three-ring binder of my own music. These happy, comfortable old friends hadn't left me; I'd left them. Without thought, I knew instinctively it was time to become reacquainted. Boy, that was a good move.

In thinking about how I'd return to playing music, I decided not to play my loud bluegrass banjo. I was wanting to be happy, but not *that* happy, so I started looking into alternative banjos. I'd enjoyed seeing Stringbean and Grandpa Jones on the TV show *Hee Haw*. I liked the sound of those banjos but didn't know much about them. One day after work, I drove down to the Homestead Pickin' Parlor on Penn Avenue in Minneapolis to pick up some banjo CDs. Figured this might be something I could do to get my head out of my troubles. Besides, learning something new always refreshed me ... and learning a new musical instrument sounded especially good.

I picked up 10 CDs by all the major open-back, clawhammer players of the day: Cathy Fink, Ken Perlman, Frank Lee and the Freighthoppers, Dan Levenson and the Boiled Buzzards, Art Rosenbaum, David Holt, Dwight Diller, and more. I listened to them all, repeatedly. I have to admit, listening was not only a relief but hearing that pleasant, well-played, happy music also actually buoyed my spirits. I took that as a win, a confirmation that I was on the right track. I listened more, tuning into not just the excitement of the sounds but also the techniques. Some sounded very repetitive, almost too busy, ringy. Others were more open and flowing. Even others showed versatility in playing phrases differently to add variety. I was developing a critical, discerning banjo ear right out of the gate.

I was using my internal level of delight or joy as my guide to whom I would ultimately pick as my teacher. Whose play made me feel the best … not just sound the best, but to ride the joy-noise I was making? Dwight Diller had two tracks on his *Just Banjo '99* CD that knocked me out of the park: "Turkey in the Straw" ("and a haw haw haw") and "Arkansas Traveler." Even as I type this, I'm getting goosebumps simply thinking of those tunes. I could get lost in the way the banjo's melody would float within his strokes. Everything was working in his playing style. That's what I wanted to sound like.

Sitting at my desk, I looked at Dwight Diller's website and found his phone number. I called him. Dwight answered in a gruff bark.

"Hullo?"

"Is this Dwight Diller?"

"Yeah."

"Dwight, if your Lansing, Michigan, class this weekend isn't full, I'd like to register for it. Do you have room?"

"Dunno."

"Okay."

Pause.

"Call the guy organizing it."

"Who's that?"

Phone drops.

I wait.

Still waiting.

Phone picks up…

"Call this number and see if there's room."

Gives me the number.

"Okay. Thank you."

Click.

Not a confirming, warm-fuzzy conversation. When I called the number, I spoke with Dwight's workshop host and found out there was a single opening left. I took it. I asked where I could find a nearby hotel. He told me his daughter was away at college, and I could stay in her bedroom. Remarkably kind offer. There was "trusting a stranger" in there, and I hadn't seen or felt that for a long time, so I accepted the gift.

Next day I took off work and drove the 11-plus hours to Lansing, Michigan, arriving around 7, when the sun was almost down. The house was in the country. I located a heavily wooded lane and drove up to a two-story log cabin in the pines. It looked warm with lights shining from the windows.

The parking area was filled with a few cars; most were next to a building with a large, open, sliding door. It was lit from within and, once I got closer, I could hear talking inside. I took my banjo in with me. I found myself in a machine shed with 11 other folks in chairs facing a workbench at the front of the room. A gray-headed old man was telling a story until I interrupted him. I walked quickly and silently to an open chair, looking down, trying not to establish any eye contact. Didn't work.

"You. *You*! Who are you?" bellowed the old man who turned out to be Dwight.

"Me?"

"Yes, you! Who are you?"

"Uh, I'm Craig Ev—"

"Sit down!"

"Okay."

I quickly sat and pulled my banjo case in front of me. When I glanced up to my left, a lady with a smirk on her face was looking back at me over her shoulder. I read it as "Ha, looks like you're going to be the class stooge." It wasn't meant to be hurtful but a lighthearted acknowledgment of me being late. Too bad she was next proven to be right.

"*You*. What's that you got there?"

"What? This?"

I held up my banjo case. "My banjo."

"I know that's a banjo. What kinda banjo is that?!"

"Uh, it's a bluegrass banjo. It's all I ha—"

"Bluegrass?! We won't be playing bluegrass here!"

"Yes, I know, but it's all I ha—"

"Here, you play this."

Dwight sprang outta his chair, walked back and handed me the very banjo, the Lo Gordon Cedar Mountain, that he'd played on *Just Banjo '99*. I was stunned to be holding it! This was the banjo with the amazing voice he'd played on that CD!

"*You!* Do you play that bluegrass banjo?"

"Well, I did, but—"

"How long did you play that bluegrass banjo?"

"Uh, 10 years or so…"

"No notes! You won't be playing no notes on that banjo. You'll mute the strings. No note playing."

"Okay."

The lady on the left was smirking again, so I let it go and smirked back. I'd already been beaten up enough over the past year. This guy was nothin'. Dwight was already back into the story he was telling when I had walked it, so I tuned in—and that proved life changing. Time stopped.

As a young man, Dwight had been angry, the product of a rough childhood. His dad ran a beer parlor, and he didn't get much positive attention. In poverty-stricken West Virginia, Dwight had learned to fend for himself, his bravado bolstered by booze. He'd been thrown out of the Navy, diagnosed as manic depressive (bad label) and then found religion. Not being one to pass up a good notion, he pursued and succeeded in becoming a Mennonite minister, until that too was ended. I don't know about that, but here he was in front of his evening congregation of 12 pilgrims telling the story of *how the music found him.*

He told this story many times over the years; it was his standard intro to understanding traditional music—the way the old-timers played it. The music was precious to him. It was to be revered and played properly. Dwight considered himself one of the keepers of the old-time tradition. You can read that story in his own words later on in this book, included in Part II: Talking Old-Time Community. By the time he was a few sentences into his story, he was in tears. This wasn't just leaking a bit at the edges, he was sobbing. Sobbing! You could have heard a pin drop.

The story was him telling how some old folks, those that could least afford it, took him in and saved him. For the first time in his battered life, he'd been genuinely loved on, cared for. It was easy to see him as the oddball outsider, defensive, argumentative and prickly. But these old people looked past that and genuinely listened. Like the Zimmermans that showed me attention in my childhood, these old people genuinely cared. They included Dwight in their community. *That kindness changed his life.* It was there he began to learn their music. He took the gifts, and the love and the music and trust that came with it, *and made it his life's purpose to share their stories ... and their love.* Music and concern for others couldn't be separated in his mind. As he would say, "I don't have to like ya, but I do have to love and teach ya, so pay attention." Dwight was gruff, but his heart was pure. He'd found his mission in life: *To pass along love ... the love he found in the music and community.* Life changing. *Not lost on lost me.* I was now a part of that community, *feeling the same love.*

There are more stories to that whole weekend, but the good news is that *I got it.* I mean, *I learned how to play the clawhammer stroke.*

I popped out of the daughter's bed early on the last day, grabbed Dwight's Gordon banjo that he'd entrusted to me and ran out to the machine shed to practice. With my left hand muting the strings, I started repeating the sound of the right hand "throw" or clawhammer stroke that Dwight had been teaching us for the last day. And there it was! I couldn't believe it, so I repeated it over and over.

Two hours later Dwight came sauntering out the front door of the log cabin in the same clothes he'd been sleeping in for three days. He looked up. "Dwight! Come here," I shouted. He gave a startled jump and squared his eyes toward me, glaring. I went back to looking down, working on my throw. A few moments passed, and I looked up again. There he stood, still glaring.

"Dwight!"

"What?!"

"Come here!"
"What for?!"
"I think I got it!"
"Do you…"

He lowered his head and started toward me. He walked straight up to me and stopped about six inches from my nose. I looked up and there he was, clearly in my space, glaring at me. I first saw his wide-open blue eyes. They weren't angry as much as they were wild. He was looking *as if he was expecting something miraculous.* I also noticed he didn't have any wrinkles around his eyes, just these two, wide-open, pale blue headlights.

Apparently, I'd paused too long on his appearance *"Play!"* he barked.

So I did. I started the throw. I did it again and again. I played for what seemed like minutes, but I'm sure it wasn't that long. Time stopped. I did breathe through it.

Suddenly, in a very quiet voice, Dwight spoke. "That's remarkable. Most folks work on this for at least three months, some a year, before they get it. You got it in three days! That's remarkable!" Still six inches from my nose, he then pointed his index finger in my face. "That's the *Lord* speaking through you, and *don't* you forget it!" He turned and walked away. I stopped playing…. I was weak in the knees. If God had ever spoken to me in person, I'd just met Him.

Dwight Diller in 2000.

I'll never forget that moment. I knew this man loved me, and he taught me all he knew. We didn't always get along, but we had some precious moments later on. When he was young, the older people had taken him in *and given him a new life*—and *that's what he'd given me.* Through Dwight Diller, I'd been introduced to the traditional music community. That's what the music and community is … and does. And I'd so missed it after leaving Early, Iowa.

The Lansing workshop provided me a new experience, much of which I couldn't appreciate yet because I was not able to really play, but I was given the key to escape my mental prison … simply *learning to play a new instrument*! I also felt a part of that community of 12 pilgrims learning to master a new challenge. We were all in it together. My God, I'd missed community.

And time stopped when I practiced. I could forget about everything stressful and only focus on my hands, the sounds, and the rhythm in my head. The rumble of the instrument through my legs and midsection was equally part of it. Everything was connected and operating smoothly.

I'd play and listen to my sounds, then listen to a CD, then play and practice again. There was comforting satisfaction in the discipline. I was actually living in the moment … moment to moment. Hours *flew* by, and in them, I was in a different place, a learning space, a refreshing place. I wasn't experiencing what I'd call joy yet, but it felt good, and I was rewarded to keep up the routine.

Here's what was going on behind the scenes in that scenario:

- The benefits of music are many: Young or old, music is really good for the brain. By listening to, learning or otherwise experiencing music, one can learn faster and function better. It helps improve focus and concentration, which can be beneficial for those with attention deficit disorders (ADD and ADHD). By engaging multiple areas of the brain at once, music also improves memory and cognitive function.
- Music is also good for mood regulation and emotional states! *Listening* to music can help reduce stress, anxiety, and depression, and it can improve feelings of happiness and well-being. Music therapy has been used to help people with various mental health disorders, including schizophrenia and post-traumatic stress disorder.
- Music has the power to bring people together and facilitate social bonding. It can help form communities and relationships as individuals come together to share their common interest in music.
- *Dancing* to music improves one's physical health as well as our coordination and movement skills.
- *Playing* music hones our timing and coordination and the accuracy of finger placement.
- *Creative expression*: Music can provide an outlet for creative expression and allow individuals to explore their emotions and experiences in a unique way.
- Music has been used in spiritual practices for thousands of years and can be a powerful tool for promoting feelings of peace and connection to the Divine.

The real hero here is our amazing mammalian brain. *Neuroplasticity*, defined by Webster's as the ability of the brain to form and reorganize synaptic connections—especially in response to learning or experience or following injury—keeps us young regardless of our age. An old dog *can* learn new tricks. Talk about a mood elevator. I saw almost immediate results from my time with Dwight. Upon my return from Lansing, within three months I was playing with and for others in public. Within a year, I'd joined a band. My melancholy moments were fewer as the endorphin rush of learning and moving forward was increasingly filling my days. I discovered I was smiling again.

Now I needed more places I could play music, and I needed more friends, so I went looking for them ... and found a *community*.

It all started with me wanting to be happy. According to the Harvard Happiness Study, strong, quality relationships and close friends are key. Positive attitudes and a focus on one's growth and development are also important. Finally, keeping yourself in good physical and mental shape contributes to a happy, satisfied perspective on life.

I didn't know it yet, but I'd actually started on my happiness journey at the bottom of the Harvard Happiness Study findings—*personal growth, positive attitude*—and successfully worked myself up to the top—*strong, quality relationships*. Here's how that transpired.

Being excited about playing a banjo and looking for others to share music—which is good for learning and memory, mood regulation, social bonding, physical coordination, creative expression and spirituality—I was off to a great start.

Finding another person to play music with, I started to not only build my own personal music circle but I plugged into the others as well. Pretty soon, we were all hitched up in a traditional music community. This became a tribe, of which I was a member.

The Minnesota Bluegrass and Old-Time Music Association (MBOTMA) was just what the doctor ordered. A bunch of mostly easy-going, fun musicians that loved to camp, enjoy a casual jam, and didn't pass judgment on who you were, where you came from or the position you were in. If you joined a circle, it's "Welcome! Let's play!" Pretty soon I was participating in Saturday morning coffee house jams with new friends, and on Thursday nights, I was listening to others play at Dulono's, the local dive bar. There *was* a "scene," and I was an active part of it. But there was more to be learned.

Now, once in a jam circle, I had to experience that *it really isn't about you, how well you play, how expensive your instrument is, anything superficial*. It *is* about the tune—like, what can you bring to it? How well can the three, nine or 20 of us in a circle play it? If there are two banjos, maybe it needs a guitar or a bass to fill it out. Treating the tune with reverence isn't present all the time, but I have found that serious musicians enjoy the music that much more *when you really play it well*. That became my goal. I've since found the mindset to be true wherever I play. I noticed I was really happy playing music with others.

> *"When the student is ready, the teacher appears."*
> —Buddhist Proverb

When you're caught up in something, as in "going with the flow," you follow the path as it appears. That's fine, but sometimes, if you look around, you can see even more beauty as it passes by. In this case, I started noticing how often people were smiling ... laughing. Sure, they were pleasant, but this smiling and happy thing was new. It was also contagious. I heard myself laugh a few times and, at first, it sounded foreign, like somebody else was laughing. I quickly got past that hang up. Besides, "when in Rome…"

I took a closer look at what was going on around me. This tribe of musicians seemed to share a number of common values. I first noticed how they loved sharing creative moments in nature (camping). Knowing that community fosters these opportunities and relationships, they would walk around the campsite seeking others to jam. In that setting, it's totally fine if that other is a stranger. They would be welcomed because many of us were once like them.

Between playing tunes, they would talk about and acknowledge that musical experiences are life-time "highs," *transcendent moments*. Within them, one can experience being completely "in the moment." *Time stops and joy starts.* Everything in the universe seems to align, to come together, to make sense, to reach a state of physical and emotional perfection. Indeed, in these deep-in-our-soul moments, some can sense *communing with the Divine*. All this happens through feelings, without words. One look at another musician's eyes can tell you they're sensing it, too. And for those of us that have been there, we can relive the joy of those moments (of euphoria) *just thinking about them.* And there's always the possibility that one can go there again. Every time one opens up an instrument case, a new adventure awaits. The quest never gets old. I guess that's why we all smile—a lot.

I'm now camping and meeting new, interesting members of my music tribe. New tunes and songs are everywhere. There's no limit to what I can learn, only to the time I put in. My moments are getting longer, and I'm starting to find the joy in any scenario I stumble into. I didn't have to think about it. When I put it out there in the universe, and did the work, I found it ... it just happened. And something else happened—some folks noticed *me*. Actually, they were enjoying my music and wanted to share in it.

One of those people was a fiddler named Debbie Sorensen-Boeh. Debbie was a positive, wide-eyed, fun-seeking professional musician that dropped out of a New York program teaching her to play Classical music. It burned her out, having to play music only a certain way. She discovered bluegrass later in life, like in her mid–30s. She had a raucous but sweet playing style and a bawdy, smoky, barroom voice. She laughed and smiled a lot. There was little she loved more than playing with and for folks.

Debbie's day job was working at nursing homes. She played often, and not just for funerals. She loved to put on square dances for the homes' residents, even those in wheelchairs. I'd often get a last-minute call inviting me to play with her at a square dance where up to 20 or so people, most over 80, would show up and dance, smile and laugh. It was contagious. I could *not* get enough of it. I was seeing the joy and feeling what others in that community were enjoying in the moment. I could now put faces to what *Time Stops. Joy Starts* looks like. And in settings like this, it's everywhere.

4. Life Interruptus

Debbie Sorensen-Boeh and me playing for the Afton Apple Orchard crowd about 2005. I'm still doing it, 17 years later.

> *Student: "Master, I'm discouraged."*
> *Master: "Serve others."*
> *Student: "Master, I'm troubled."*
> *Master: "Serve others."*
> *Student: "Master, I'm lost."*
> *Master: "Serve others."*
> —Buddhist proverb

Deb and I played together every time we could. We didn't need an audience; we'd build it. Busking, playing in an open space for folks walking by, became a favorite pastime. Yes, occasionally someone would throw a few bucks in our strategically placed hat for tips, but *we were putting music out in the world*. Those within earshot responded with smiles. I found I was happily living off that rush. Often, I'd picture Mom playing for people back in Early. *In all the pictures I have of her performing, she's smiling.* Can it really be that easy? Yes, it can, as you'll see later on in this book. People that play this music smile—a lot. Watch for it, wherever they're playing, from Carnegie Hall to Clifftop to the corner of Broadway and Fourth Street East next to the St. Paul Farmer's Market. Music is good for people, and it needs to be shared liberally.

Music was filling me up. I wasn't the suffering, hollow shell of a human being anymore. I was feeling better, working out, eating right, and caring for myself. Music had given me a voice and a presence again. The Harvard Happiness Study determined that strong relationships with close friends is critical to one's happiness as well as overall health. I was feeling that satisfaction blossoming daily in my new relationships.

And rather than working long days for quickly-forgotten capitalist needs, I was now making people smile, if even for only a moment. That was a satisfying return. Besides, it was now *about* that moment of *making their time stop for their joy to start*. I decided I needed to step out even further, so I joined some bands.

Yes, this added a more formal structure than I was used to, but it also opened the door even more to joy. Playing well with others, and having people appreciate it, is a rush.

In 2003, I met up with Singleton Street, a singing and playing husband and wife team accompanied by an accomplished bass player and singer. They loved bluegrass, gospel and old-time music. We set out to change the world—and from my seat at the table, for the next 10 years, we did!

> *"In times of Darkness, the enlightened become craftsmen and teach them various skills."*
> —Lao Tzu

A few years later, in 2005, I formed another group, the Eelpout Stringers. We were first a bunch of jamming buddies. We had so much fun playing together, we thought we'd be a band simply "because it was fun!" The 'Pouts lasted 12 years. The joy we experienced playing square dances for weddings, street events and community gatherings could not be beat.

My bands were my new community, and together we made it our goal to not only entertain people *but also to move them*. Music can do that, especially if the

Singleton Street CD (2004). What a delightful group of human beings. For 10 years we presented the joy of music to our audiences throughout the Midwest (they're still doing it)! From left: me, Sherri Leyda, Chuck Leyda and Jimmy Newkirk.

4. Life Interruptus

The Eelpout Stringers in 2019. Whether it was a tale of lost love from the Civil War or a square dance tune, we delighted in sharing the emotional and physical energy of traditional music. Yee-ha! From left: Nick Rowse, me, Karl Burke and Loyd Mitchell.

singer or players have experienced the messages within the music. We played festivals, bars, weddings, funerals, country clubs, coffee houses, and living rooms. Each was as important and as special as the last. It never got old. Time stopped. The Joy was in the moments of poignant songs and the laughter at the conversation between numbers, as well as the compliments or stories people would share after the show as to what the music or lyrics meant to them. Our "conversations in the language of music," the instruments and our voices, were to bring joy.

Since those first days, every time I step up to play, my dear, sweet mom is with me in spirit, nodding and saying, "Yes, yes. That's what it's all about it. The Divine is in there, in the music. Share it." Dwight Diller would also talk about the importance of sharing. Before I left Lansing, he turned to me and said, "Now, as I taught you, *you* teach others to play. What you learned you need to share with others. It's important." My next step was to teach others how to play the banjo, which I continue to do.

I found myself wanting to go deeper in my new passion. My busy brain kept posing questions both *historical* (what is this banjo thing all about—i.e., unknown history/curious artifact, creative/artistic medium, science in how it works) and *metaphysical* (why do so many "different" people seem to be drawn to traditional music and its supportive, loving community?). Because I needed to learn more, I came up with an incredible, once-in-a-lifetime project. Again, sorry ... background first.

"A journey of a thousand miles begins with a single step" (Lao Tzu)

A few years into my exciting new quest to find myself—the *real* me—after my meltdown over the moral shallowness of capitalism and the disastrous consequences of my decades of blind allegiance, I needed to learn more about my newfound community, its friendships, growth opportunities, and where the music might take me. The magic was there, I never doubted it ... and it felt both honest and right to explore. But I was looking to dive deeper. Along about that time, I'd been dating an artist, also newly single, who was on a similar quest for truth and light. She was further down this road than me, and that made for great conversations.

DeAnne is a painter, a teacher, a camper, and a seeking pilgrim with a positive attitude and a quirky sense of humor. She's also kind. She's a mom to two, the younger an amazing human being on the autism spectrum. I'm convinced there is no deeper love and dedication than that found in a parent wanting the best opportunities for their offspring. DeAnne had all these qualities and more. She's a beautiful, old soul. DeAnne would become my spiritual partner and soulmate. After a four-year courtship, as we wanted to make sure, we set out to be each other's life partner, dedicating ourselves to support and grow the other's creative, spiritual soul.

My talented, wonderfully supportive wife, artist DeAnne L. Parks, in 2004.

Back to the story. I was about to turn 60. DeAnne knew me well enough to know I'm not into things, but I am into experiences, and I'm constantly wanting to learn. When she asked me what I wanted for my 60th birthday, I told her I wanted to learn more about open-back banjos ... what makes a good one? And why would someone want to build one, anyway? I told her I'd like to travel across North America and meet maybe a half dozen builders, just to ask them some simple questions. She said, "I think that's a great idea!" God, I love that woman. My 60th birthday present to myself was about to become my greatest life adventure.

In 2011, I announced my intent on BanjoHangout.com—an online community of about 30,000 or so banjo-lovers back then. Today it's well over 100,000. I told folks, if they had an interest in my findings, I might take along some cameras and record our conversations. Within a few days I had close to 50 people sign up—which meant I had to get serious about doing this right.

I signed up for a couple how-to-film-a-documentary classes, bought some used equipment off Craigslist and eBay, practiced interviewing a few folks and was off. My first 19-day trip to the East Coast and parts of Canada took in 11 builders. Then I realized I was being a bit too compulsive. But the electricity I was feeling was amazing, and I couldn't get enough of being with these happy, delightful people who were so excited to be talking about what they did for a living.

This excerpt is taken from my Old-Time Conversations Documentary presentation to the American Folklore Society in 2020.

Craig: I wanted to learn firsthand about what we call the open-back banjo. Why would somebody today want to make it? There's very little money in it. Besides, it's a weird combination of art and music and history and science. I wasn't thinking about thoughts like that back when I started out filming people in this music community. I wanted to know how people were building banjos. Boy, did I get a lesson on our species, but that's only a part of the story.

As a former career marketing executive, I had to study how people make decisions. We're a very complicated species, and we're far from logical. When filming my subjects, I wanted to make sure that I followed the scientific method, and I'd asked similar questions throughout all the interviews. I'd start with something simple like "Why do you build a banjo?"

Here are their answers.

- **banjo builder Jeff Menzies:** Banjos for me are a medium and a creative outlet. When I first started, I didn't think this would keep going. I thought it was just an obsession that would pass, and I would mature and grow up.
- **banjo builder Kevin Enoch:** When I worked with my dad doing carpentry, I was always the guy that wanted to do the more intricate stuff because I love the challenge, especially in staircases, all the compound miters and all that stuff, getting everything to fit.
- **banjo builder Brooks Masten:** Seems like since the day I put my hands on a banjo, my life took off.
- **banjo builder Mark Platin:** I'd never started out wanting to build banjos. I don't know that I chose it, and I'm not sure it chose me. We simply said, "This works. Let's try this for a while. Banjos have been very, very good to me!"

Banjo builder and excellent player Jeff Menzies. The artist in Jeff sees the banjo as a physical, artistic medium. His creativity is inspiring as well as playful.

Left: Banjo builder Kevin Enoch. Kevin's eye for detail is amazing. His banjos are treasured for their craftsmanship, especially his inlay work. *Right:* Banjo builder Brooks Masten. Whether he's building or playing, Brook's joy is contagious. You can sense it in his instruments.

- **banjo builder John Bowlin:** Couldn't afford to get one, so I would build it. I remember I came home with a block of wood for the neck, and I had a pocket knife and a rasp, and my wife said, "You can't build a banjo. There's no way. How can you do that?" I said, "Well, why not? Other people do it."
- **banjo builder Lo Gordon:** If I wanted to go fishing, I built a fishing rod. If I wanted to go hunting, I built a bow. As a kid, if I wanted to go row-boating, I built a rowboat. When it hit me that I was going to play banjo, I went out and got a kit because I was so hungry for it. I had to have it.
- **banjo builder Pete Ross:** I was trying to undo a cultural injustice by bringing these things back to life and putting them in front of people. They did not like it when I started making banjos in art school. Some of the faculty had a real problem with it. They were threatening to flunk me, all sorts of stuff like that.

Craig: Are you obsessed with banjos?

- **banjo builder Pete Ross:** Yes.
- **banjo builder Doug Unger:** Engraving, which is sort of my specialty, is so technically hard to do. You have to do what you do with painting. I think the American painter Whistler said, "It's done when there's no evidence of its doing." You have to make something that's technically demanding to do look effortless. If you don't, then its beauty is lost. To make it look effortless,

Banjo builder Mark Platin. Mark's legacy is as an innovator and as a teacher. Many of his apprentices also went on to become innovative builders.

Banjo builder Lo Gordon. Another innovator. His company, Cedar Mountain Banjos, continues to evolve under Lo's son Tim Gardner's creative eye and hand.

Banjo builder John Bowlin. John's premier offering, the John Bowlin 1865 banjo, is a standard for those that want to experience what a banjo was like during the minstrel era.

> it takes years of practice and coming to grips with how to do it. That's what I try to do.

Craig: How do you want to be remembered about your banjos?

- **banjo builder Mike Ramsey:** Probably as the Johnny Appleseed of banjo building, making people happy.

Banjo builder Doug Unger. A recognized artist in many mediums. Doug brings his tasteful eye and meticulous skills to banjo building.

Left: Banjo builder Mike Ramsey. The Johnny Appleseed of banjo builders. Sure, he loved making great banjos, but his humor and love of community endeared him to all. *Right:* Banjo builder Greg Galbreath. Another Leonardo da Vinci type. No challenge is too big. And whatever he does is done incredibly well.

- **banjo builder Greg Galbreath:** My wife Cindy and I really try to tie it all together. The banjo and the banjo-making, the old-time music and where we live. That's part of our philosophy of life. To live simply, work hard, live life, and have fun. And tie it altogether in a nice package.

Craig: How do you feel when you watch a video of somebody playing one of your banjos?

- **banjo builder Chuck Lee:** I'm looking to see if they're having a good time. That's why I build each one. I think if people weren't having a good time, I'd find something else to do.
- **banjo builder Will Fielding:** The

Banjo builder Chuck Lee. If you could put love in an instrument, Chuck could list it as an ingredient. And that's how they're made.

only thing you can do with banjos, or any musical instrument, is make music with other people. As far as I'm concerned, that's like the best thing that humans do.

Look at all the reasons these people build banjos. Some are simply the "build-it-to-understand-it" types. Where another sees the banjo as a medium—the instrument being more than a piece of art, it's something you can actually *play*. A second artist enjoys incorporating meticulous and difficult art *into it*, like engraving. A third artist activist is correcting a social injustice by bringing banjos back to life. "Being noble" doesn't begin to touch this builder's motivation.

Banjo builder Will Fielding. Will saw the beauty and so much potential in just about any piece of wood. The simplicity in his banjos, highlighting the woods, makes them objects of art. Gone too soon.

Carrying on a time-honored tradition is mentioned by those that really study who has built fine instruments before—and their handiwork is still performing today or the improvements they brought to the craft have elevated the instrument. All of these builders know they're providing a tool for musicians to use and genuinely feel *most rewarded* when a customer is happy. Nobody is talking about how much money they're making. Sure, they can make a living, but the reward of doing what they do, *as seen by the community and players within, is far greater*!

Now that you've met and experienced a few of my amazing traditional music friends in the community, I'd like you to meet even more.

I finished the Banjo Builder series in 2014, but I was a long way from finishing what had started as a birthday lark. I was fascinated with not only the artists' stories but also with the connection between the music and the community. It seemed you really couldn't separate the people from the music, from the instruments, and from the greater community where it all was celebrated. Gestalt works like that, with the whole becoming greater than the sum of all the individual parts.

Smithsonian Folkways had called me early on during my Banjo Builder filming and asked to save these precious stories for posterity because nobody had filmed this level of a music community before; where you could see how—at *this moment in time*

Traditional Music Community Documentary Series *by Craig R. Evans*

SERIES 1
Conversations with North American Banjo Builders

Interviews with today's roster of extraordinary artists and craftsmen that build remarkable instruments.

*Acquired by
Smithsonian Folkways Recordings - 2014*

SERIES 2
Conversations with Old-time Performers

Interviews with those musicians who have dedicated their lives to passing on the flame of traditional music.

SERIES 3
Old-time Conversations

Interviews with folklorists, ethnomusicologists, violin and guitar builders, Old-time music publishers and more.

Three Documentary Video Series Dedicated to Preserving Stories, Music and the Community Surrounding Traditional Music.

Over 180 interviews with instrument builders, performers and teachers of Traditional Music, the thoughts and findings of historians, folklorists, ethnomusicologists, retailers, festival goers, players and more, including a volume dedicated to black performers and historians.

Series 1 Featuring

Volume 1: Bill Rickard, Jason Burns, Jeff Menzies, Greg Galbreath, Pete Ross, Bart Reiter, Lo Gordon & Tim Gardner, George Wunderlich, Mike Ramsey, Will Fielding, Chuck Lee, Kevin Enoch, Doug Unger and Jim Hartel.

Volume 2: John Bowlin, Greg Deering, Bob Flesher, Patrick "Doc" Huff, Brooks Masten, Jason Mogi, Chuck Ogsbury, Mark Platin, Jason and Pharis Romero, Bob Thornburg, Colin Vance and Banjo Hangout Founder Eric Schlange.

Volume 3: Greg Adams, Laurent Dubois, Peter Szego and Friends Banjo Collection Tour, Bob Winans, Bob Carlin, CeCe Conway, Jim Bollman Banjo Collection Tour, Kevin Fore, Ulf Jagfors, Taj Mahal, Dwight Diller, Adam Hurt, The Tombigbee River / Gum Tree Canoe Music Video.

Volume 4: Patrick Heavner, Jeff Delfield, Jeff Kramer, Randy Cordle, David Ball, Glenn Carson, Mac Traynham, Luke Mercier, Ken LeVan, Dan Knowles, Noel Booth and Wyatt Fawley.

Series 2 Featuring

Volume 1: Rayna Gellert, Chris Coole, Rebekah Weiler, Howard Bursen, Mac Benford, Walt Koken, Clare Milliner, Lukas Pool, Seth Swingle, Stephen Wade, John Herrmann and Dwight Diller *(from Volume 3 of the Banjo Builder series, courtesy of Smithsonian Folkways).*

Volume 2: Joe Newberry, Ken Perlman, Laura Boosinger, Steve Arkin, Frank Lee, Michael Miles, Mary Z. Cox, Arnie Naiman, Mark Johnson, Dan Gellert and Adam Hurt *(from Volume 3 of the Banjo Builder series, courtesy of Smithsonian Folkways).*

Volume 3: David Holt, Brad Leftwich, Art Rosenbaum, Reed Martin, Brad Kolodner, Richie Stearns, Paul Brown, Terri McMurray, Steve Rosen and Chirps Smith.

Volume 4: Cathy Fink, Jay Ungar, Molly Mason, Evie Ladin, Jane Rothfield, Rafe Stefanini, Clelia Stefanini, Clarke Buehling, Jody Stecher, Kate Brislin, Bruce Molsky and Dr. Alan Jabbour.

Series 3 Featuring

Volume 1: Greg & Jere Canote, William Seeders Mosheim, Erynn Marshall, Carl Jones, Tas Philp, Beverly Smith, John Grimm, Jan Bloom, James Leva, Matt Arcara, Dan Levenson, Dean Robinson.

Volume 2: Phil Jamison, Tony Klassen, Zachary Hoyt, Wayne Erbsen, Dr. Ronald Cohen, Dr. Bill Malone, Jeff Place, Dr. Neil Rosenberg, Barry Sholder, Dale Fairbanks, Carl Arcand, Donna Hebert

Volume 3: Kaia Kater, Sparky Rucker, Rhonda Rucker, Don Vappie, Leyla McCalla, Jake Blount, Dom Flemons, Earl White, Tim Brooks, Dr. Steven Lewis.

Volume 4: Jean Horner, Nathaniel Rowan, Dr. Bob Childs, Roger Treat, Ryan Navey, Bob Anderson, Clifton Hicks, Mike Chew, Amythyst Kiah, Dakota Dave Hull, John McCutcheon.

Opposite, and above: Traditional Music Community Documentary Series by Craig R. Evans, 2011–2019.

on the timeline of traditional music—everyone and everything works. Saving the conversations for posterity is exactly what I also wanted. It was never about money. An artist talking here. I gave them the films. They've since asked for the rest of my collection.

I went on to complete four DVDs of old-time performers and teachers, with an occasional banjo builder thrown in (they happened to be on the route to another old-time performer). There are close to 60 of them total now.

The old-time performers and teachers, like the instrument builders, *are* making a living, but more importantly, *they are sharing their gifts to make the world a better and happier place.* You could see the pride they feel in teaching another person how to play music, in essence giving them the ability to use their gifts *for life*. Peacemakers are also among them, interested in telling stories through music, where words can often fail. Musicians employing their teaching gifts speak in at least two languages: one reaching your mind, the other speaking to your heart and soul. If you watch my films, you will see more smiles per minute than any other group of people you know. Like the banjo builders, they're happy in their souls.

The last series, Old-Time Conversations, takes in even more of the above, plus makers of other instruments and historians and authors to provide more context to the tradition and communities we adore. All are generously sharing their gifts for us to use in appreciating our Time-stopping, Joy-filled moments. Making a living is important to them, of course, but in their sharing of themselves and their gifts, they're getting back even more: *love*.

I thought maybe I was finished at that point. *Not!* I was missing the wonderfully exciting conversations I'd been having with these folks. Their joy fills me up. Besides, I wanted to hear from a few more builders, performers, historians, and authors. Then I started the third series, Old-Time Conversations, where I began interviewing interesting traditional music community members, regardless of what they did, and gathered them up into another batch of DVDs. I also included the everyday players and festival goers. Clifftop, also known as Appalachian String Band Music Festival, was new to my world in 2015, and its effect was immediate and profound. Wow! You'll see what I mean later on in the book.

Part II

Talking Old-Time Community

"Beware of looking for goals: look for a way of life. Decide how you want to live and then see what you can do to make a living within that way of life."
—Hunter S. Thompson

Conversations ... knee to knee with my guests. Just like a music circle. Great way to meet and learn about someone new. No wonder I now consider them all my friends.

The following are film transcript excerpts from the original "Conversations" between Craig R. Evans of the Old-Time Conversations Documentary Series and luthiers—the banjo builders—old-time performers and teachers, and old-time historians and authors.

These positive stories are true as recorded. Thanks to finding a supportive community, these artists have experienced what they term productive, satisfying careers … and found friends for life.

Discussion of the interviewee's history and experiences with the music and community are complete. Shop tours have not been included due to relevance to the subject of this book. And musical segues and performances are also not included for an obvious reason (this is a book).

Welcome to the old-time community! These people are not only the subjects of my films but they are also my friends, kin, peers, and soulmates. Many are friends at Clifftop, a microcosm of what the Southern Appalachian traditional music community is today—at this moment in time!

As you're reading excerpts from the transcripts of these Conversations, I want you to notice something about the people being interviewed. They're genuinely happy. Can you see it? Hear it? Feel it? Trust me, it's there! They're happy for many reasons, most of which you'll recognize if, while you read, you listen closely to their words. Things like this: *I really like what I do. I like building, playing, teaching, helping. I like the people that are a part of this community.*

These people are kind. They care for others. Tradition is important to us all (humanity). And they all feel responsible for passing it along. I love being a part of this group of people. What a great way to spend *my* time.

Most of the pilgrims in our tribe seek others to celebrate what we know to be helpful, uplifting, and true—and we share it in its native language … music. We commune through playing and losing ourselves in the moment. *Time Stops. Joy Starts.* It's contagious, fulfilling, refreshing, and satisfying. And at Clifftop, we do it for up to nine days. It's so powerful; experiencing the emotional high carries me for the year.

One more thing. You don't have to go to Clifftop to find happy people like this. Consider learning how to play an instrument and join a jam or two *where you are.* You'll find them, or they might find you. You've got nothing to lose but loneliness and poor health. Everything else comes with the package, including smiling. What a deal!

Craig to banjo builder Brooks Masten: If somebody picks up one of your banjos 50 years from now, what little bit of you will still be inside that banjo?

Brooks: Well, there's a little bit of my blood in most of them because I always cut myself in some way.

Craig: Is there a message in there? Is there a message in a bottle from you to them as they're playing your banjo?

Brooks: [Laughing.] Sure! "Get out of the house! Go play some tunes! Drink a beer!"

Look, I even cut myself during an interview.

Banjo builder Brooks Masten. Good nature runs in his blood.

INSTRUMENT BUILDERS

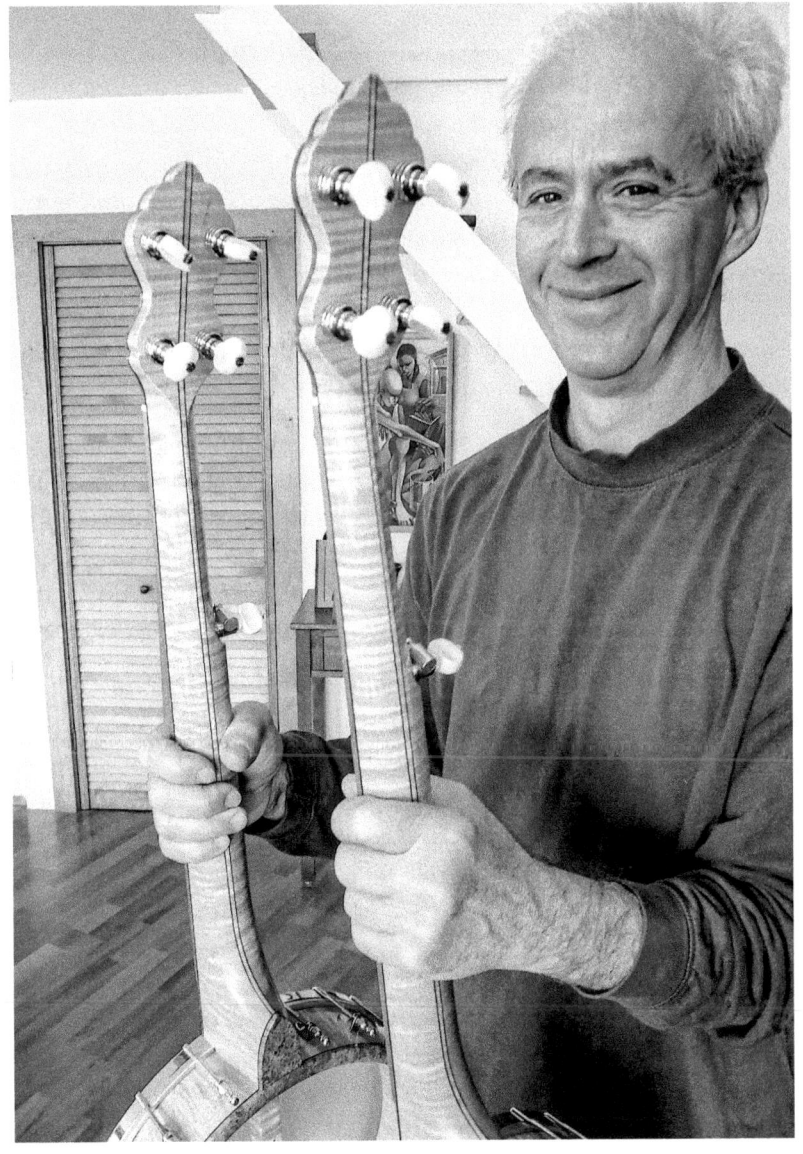

Will Fielding, one of the best builders of this era.

5

Bart Reiter

Haslett, Michigan, 2011

"A primary motivation for me is always to be self-employed, my own boss, independent, have a lot of freedom, come and go as I please, wander around the country on a motorcycle, or wander around in the woods.

"I work five hours a day."

"You make a stack of necks, stack of bodies or pots, rims, and then bolt them together at the end. It's wonderful. It's a perfect product for a small production, small shop. The finished product fits in a box, and UPS will take it wherever you want it to go."

"The house has been paid off for a long time. The truck's paid for. The motorcycles are paid for. Everything's paid ... no debt."

Bart was one of the first of a group of banjo-building peers that all started at about the same time (Bart Reiter, Kevin Enoch, Chuck Lee, Mark Platin, Mike Ramsey). Bart would call up new guys and pass along the names of his suppliers to help them get started. He would tell the others, "There's enough business for us all here."

Bart Reiter finished his luthier career after making 5,012 banjos. Exactly 5,000 have serial numbers; the first 12 were unnumbered prototypes.

Old-Time Community Role: The *Benevolent Businessman*. Yes, Bart is an amazing builder. Yes, he practically wrote the book on how to batch-build banjos. Yes, he holds the records for most banjos made. But every Christmas season, he builds wooden toys for children from underprivileged families. He also plows driveways for the elderly and delivers groceries to shut-ins. Bart has a heart of gold.

Craig Evans: You found banjo building to be a good way to make a life and make a living?

Bart: Oh, yeah. Yes, the house has been paid off for a long time. The truck's paid for. The motorcycles are paid for. Everything's paid ... no debt.

My wife made me a beautiful sign for the front of the building. Within a couple

Bart Reiter. Successful in business. Good neighbor to all.

of weeks, the tax assessor saw that and started sending me a personal property tax bill for all the machinery, so I took the sign down.

Craig: What I want to know is, how come your banjos are such a bargain?

Bart: I price the same as the competition, maybe a few dollars less. They get a real good banjo at a real fair price. And that's that.

Craig: Bart, I am absolutely delighted to be sitting here with you today in Haslett, Michigan. How many years have you been making banjos?

Bart: Since maybe '77, '78, when I made my first banjo. It is sitting on the table in there.

Craig: You actually started off making guitars, though, right?

Bart: That is correct.

Craig: What was your inspiration to move over to banjos from guitars?

Bart: The guitars I made in the evenings and weekends while I was working at Elderly Instruments in the repair department hung on the wall of the store, and no one bought them. I'd been making reproduction necks for old Vega banjo pots. One of the sales clerks suggested I make banjos, open-back banjos. They didn't have enough open-back banjos, new or used ones, so I gave it a try. That was 1982, during the bad recession that put Arthur Smith and Great Lakes Banjo companies out of business.

No one was manufacturing and wholesaling a dowel-stick banjo, so I gave it a try. I picked the brains of David Nichols in New York and a few other people, made a couple of fixtures for my machines to cut parts quickly and accurately, took a week off and made a half a dozen banjos, and took them one at a time to Elderly. They sold very quickly, within hours or days—and it's been like that ever since. Everything I make is pretty much sold before it is started.

Craig: You're very much an independent proprietor. You had a couple of mentors to get started. What did you use as a basis? How did you come up with the first designer template for your banjos?

Bart: Since I've been making repro necks for old Vega pots, I made my own rim and stuck pretty much the same necks in there. They're Vega copies, knock-offs. There are a few shortcuts, like the way the Vega veneer comes into the end of the fingerboard at the bone nut. I save some time doing it a little differently, but some things are better. My neck has an adjustable truss rod in it.

Craig: How did you find banjo building, compared to guitar building?

Bart: I loved it. Besides making flat-top guitars, I'd also made electric guitars and gotten into a limited production of making Fender copies, necks and Strat, Tele bodies, that type of thing. Banjos are very similar. You make a stack of necks, stack of bodies or pots, rims, and then bolt them together at the end. It's wonderful. It's a perfect product for a small production, small shop. The finished product fits in a box, and UPS will take it wherever you want it to go.

Craig: You initially got into building banjos because you saw a need, and you now filled it.

Bart: Yes. It's no fun building the guitar—and watching it collect dust for six months while it does not sell. It's much more exciting to make a banjo and have it sold right away. Happy customer, that type of thing.

Craig: About how many banjos do you think you have out there today?
Bart: I've made 3,500.

Craig: You're making banjos full-time.
Bart: I work five hours a day.

Craig: You found banjo building to be a good way to make a life and make a living?
Bart: Oh, yeah. I have everything I ever imagined I'd want.

Craig: When you're building banjos, do you think about the end user at all?
Bart: A little bit. I've got a pragmatic view of the whole thing. As a consumer myself, I know I'm very frustrated and depressed when I buy something and it doesn't perform as it's supposed to or it breaks and you can't get a part. You've been through that. You're so frustrated that you're about to sit down and cry. I don't want anybody to have to go through that. I want the banjo to need very little maintenance and repair. I want the person to be happy and really get a lot of use out of it, especially considering what they paid for it.

Craig: Does a banjo touch you emotionally at all?
Bart: My whole life at one point was music, but I've developed different hobbies. A primary motivation for me is always to be self-employed, my own boss, independent, have a lot of freedom, come and go as I please, wander around the country on a motorcycle, or wander around in the woods. There's 30 acres behind my banjo shop, and sometimes, I get sick of sanding or breathing lacquer fumes, and I'll go for a walk and see what I find.

Craig: You've spent your whole life up here in Haslett, Michigan, haven't you?
Bart: Pretty much, 50 years. I'm 57. My parents brought us here when I was seven. I do like this place. There's nothing here. You saw downtown, there's a railroad track and a couple old shops, and a little strip mall. That's the beauty of it. There's nothing here—but a nice place to live.

Craig: What has the banjo done for you and your life?
Bart: It's made my life very good. It made a lot of friends, the people I've met in business, other banjo makers, my suppliers, my vendors, and, of course, banjo players. Everybody's been good to me. Never received a bad check. People respect me.

Craig: Would you do anything different?
Bart: Anything different? I wish I knew way back then what I know now. I wouldn't have worked so many hours. Now I can work a few hours and make a dozen banjos every month. It used to take me a long time.

Craig: Now you're enjoying life.

A cat saunters across the table in front of both Craig and Bart.

Bart: Yes, I can get rid of that cat if you want.

Craig: No, I love the cat. The cat's fantastic.

Bart's pretty banjo.

Bart: I can throw her out in the yard. She's used to it. I rescued her from my parents' barn when she was a little tiny kitten, so she adores me.

This is the first banjo I ever made. It's got a new head on it. The head broke in 1977, maybe '78.

Craig: Is this what started your special or your standard?

Bart: There was no such thing then. No. The first neck I made as practice so I can make a good repro neck to go on a Tubaphone. Tubaphone No. 3 style would have had the flowerpot in the peghead. I didn't do it on this one, but it had a heel carving. That's a butchered heel carving. The first one was close but not quite.

Craig: That's right. You were learning.

Bart: It's 33 years old. The neck is still absolutely, perfectly straight. It's still set up exactly the way it was.

Craig: That's the way it's supposed to be.

Bart: The day I made it.

Craig: What's the other one you got here?

Bart: This is a nice one. This is a pretty one. Just got the straightaway Vega Whyte Laydie No. 7 inlays. It looks like I had a sharp graver when I did this one, though. Lines are rather fine, with incredible carving. That's a winged cherub. Ron Chasey of Colorado did that. At the time, he lived in Athens, Ohio. People I know went to college together in Athens, Ohio. Kick Stewart, Bill MacDonald, Ron Chasey, Dave Hostetler. Dave plays drums in a jazz band.

Craig: Their influence on you is very strong.

Bart: They supported me. They encouraged me. All of this hardware is made in Ohio or Montana by the Stewart-MacDonald company. They've always given me a good price, a good deal. I think I might be their best customer now. I buy about everything there. Of course, the wood is from the local sawmill. There's a large operation on the other side of town. Mark Platin was always very nice to me. I used to call him to pick his brain when I got started, and I must have been incredibly annoying, but he was always patient and friendly.

Craig: Now, I've heard a rumor about you. When you say you look at a banjo, you see something. What do you see?

Bart: Oh, I see a cart full of groceries, maybe a full tank of gas.

Craig: You and Mike Ramsey are buddies for a long time, right?

Bart: Yes, we're good buddies, birds of a feather. We like the same things.

Craig: Yes, I know. When you guys aren't building banjos, you're riding bikes.

Bart: Riding bikes and drinking whiskey.

Craig: What's the worst part of banjo building for you?

Bart: Sanding. Sanding, sanding, sanding. Sanding wood, sanding lacquer.

Hand-carved wooden car. A Christmas gift from Bart.

Sanding, sanding, sanding. Sanding is essential if you want it to look pretty and have a nice finish. This is an unhealthy business. It's all the dust. I've got a big dust collector here for the machines. Blows it out into the swamp. That thing will suck your hand in. I've got an air purifier. I've got masks. I certainly have a very nice lacquering room, but still, it gets through. The next day, you still blow black junk out of your nose.

Craig: What's your favorite part of building a banjo?
  Bart: Taking the check out of the mailbox.

Craig: How many more years you want to make banjos?
  Bart: I was going to make 5,000, which would take me another nine years, but now, I've adjusted that. I think I'm going to make 4,000 and quit. I'm at 3,500, so looks like 500 more. I'll be done in five years.

Craig: Aren't you going to miss it?
  Bart: Not at all. I will still keep my shop here. I love to putter around and make things and fix things. I like putting new handles on shovels and hammers. I like making toys and giving them away.

Craig: Who do you give your toys to?
  Bart: Oh, anybody.

6

Patrick "Doc" Huff

Dallas, Oregon, 2011

"We had a big family, and my father did everything, and he expected that you also knew how to do things—and put responsibility on you to do that."

"I went into the military in Vietnam, and I volunteered as a medic towards the end of the war in my time in Vietnam. I made a decision to go into medicine. I figured I could do that."

"When there's something I really want to do, I don't necessarily put it on the shelf. I do it."

"In all the years I played music, I never found the right banjo for me; a few had too much edge on them. I was interested in wood-toned ring banjos because I'd heard about people making them. Then my first banjo was actually three banjos, very complicated ones, because I couldn't do just one. Somewhere inside me, I knew I was going to build banjos."

Based on his somewhat impoverished childhood, Dr. Huff has a lifelong commitment to working with underprivileged families.

Dr. Huff provided medical services to people in Africa, South America and other developing countries. He took his banjo with him when he traveled to these places. Music facilitated his understanding of the people and facilitated their trust in him. Dr. Huff also found an unusual use for a banjo string.

Dr. Huff retired from medicine to be an artist and build banjos.

Old-Time Community Role: The *Polymath*. Dr. Patrick Huff is a banjo builder, he's an inventor, he's an architect, and, as a doctor, he serves those needing medical assistance worldwide. Dr. Huff is a modern-day Leonardo da Vinci. He can design and build structures large and small from scratch. From very humble roots, after serving as a medic in Vietnam, he returned to his childhood community to continue serving others medically. Beyond his love of people, he loves music. He also loves wood … and the banjo. With an understanding that extends far beyond most humans, he uses that knowledge to bridge language barriers when traveling to Third World countries to provide medical services. It's easy to smile around this guy. Fact is, he smiles most of the time. The world needs more Dr. Patrick Huffs.

Doc Huff: When I started out, I'd been living in the cabin, and I got this notion to build a tower, and to this day, we call it the tower.

Craig: What was the interest in a tower? Is that part of your background?

Doc Huff: No, I have no idea where it came from. I had this inspiration. I had the classic primitive tools, a broad axe, a draw knife, and a hand auger. I was starting out in medicine and wasn't making a lot of money, and I wanted to do it.

Craig: So you're an artist?
Doc Huff: Well, I try.

Craig: I have to admit, this is mighty impressive.

Craig: Doc Huff of Dallas, Oregon, I can't tell you how delighted I am to stand here today and talk to you about banjos.
Doc Huff: Great.

Dr. Patrick "Doc" Huff. The best of humanity. Just happens to build banjos. Coincidence?

Craig: Now, first thing is that you are legitimately a doctor. You are a doctor of medical science, and you've practiced for about 20 years up here. You're a native of Oregon, right?
Doc Huff: Yes, sir.

Craig: Another thing I've noticed about you is that you are a jack of all trades. You can do amazing things. You build houses, you build banjos. Where did that ability come from? Was that a part of your family growing up?
Doc Huff: Yes, very much so. We had a big family, and my father did everything, and he expected that you also knew how to do things—and put responsibility on you to do that.

Craig: What was your dad's job? What was his trade?
Doc Huff: He was a logger.

6. Patrick "Doc" Huff

Doc Huff's hand-built home. Typical of how he quickly acts on an idea, Doc says, "I had a notion to build a tower."

Craig: Now, did that inspire a love of wood deep in you?

Doc Huff: Yes, and he loved wood as well.

Craig: Had you always wanted to be a doctor?

Doc Huff: No, I didn't know what I wanted to be. I went into the military in Vietnam, and I volunteered as a medic towards the end of the war in my time in Vietnam. I made a decision to go into medicine. I figured I could do that.

Craig: I know that you came back here after you graduated from college with your degree, and you practiced for 20 years.

Doc Huff: I had a genuine commitment to work with underprivileged families.

Craig: You continued to do that, and as a physician, you've gone around the world.

Doc Huff: I went to Sudan, Rwanda, Zaire, South America, Central America, and Mexico. It was a lot of work.

Craig: What did that teach you about people?

Doc Huff: People are the same everywhere. They have the same passions, desires, needs.

Craig: Did that affect you?

Doc Huff: Yes, you develop a love for people, no matter where they're from, who

Doc with a musical friend in the 1990s, when he was part of Doctors Without Borders.

they are, what color they are. I used to always carry my banjo wherever I traveled to, which was very interesting. In southern Cameroon, I was doing this medical work at a hospital with no electricity, no running water, and I had this lady who had a prolapse uterus. In doctor talk, the only way to repair that is to go into the abdomen and tack the uterus to the posterior aspect of the anterior abdominal wall. Which meant you also had to have non-absorbable suture, which you don't have in that environment. You're lucky to have thread of any kind. I pulled out the first string of my Nylgut set of banjo strings and threaded it through the straight needle. It worked beautifully. When I shared the story with the owner of Nylgut, he sent me 400 D strings.

Craig: Wow! Now we have a whole new application for Nylguts—surgical sutures. How important was music to people in all these different countries you visited?

Doc Huff: Very important. It connected them.

Craig: Where does the banjo come into this?

Doc Huff: I went to a local grange hall where they had a dance, and an old-time band was there. At that moment in time, I made the conscious decision that I'm going to learn this music.

Craig: I am blown away by how, when you put your mind to something, you go out and you learn it, and you become maybe not necessarily an expert overnight, but you continue to improve on it. I mean, look at your buildings around here, and your banjos that we're now going to talk about. Even the bridges that you build for banjos. Are you consumed by these passions, and that's what gets you into it?

Doc Huff: When there's something I really want to do, I don't necessarily put it on the shelf. I do it.

Craig: Okay, so you heard banjos, you liked the sound of banjos. When did you decide to build them?

Doc Huff: In 2003.

Craig: What caused that? Were you looking for a different sound?

Doc Huff: Yes. Frankly, in all the years I played music, I never found the right banjo for me; a few had too much edge on them. I was interested in wood-toned ring banjos because I'd heard about people making them. Then my first banjo was actually three banjos, very complicated ones, because I couldn't do just one. Somewhere inside me, I knew I was going to build banjos.

Craig: How did you learn?

Doc Huff: I had one book on banjo construction, and it really wasn't that helpful, and I built intuitively.

Craig: That's another thing that seems to be a theme that I'm finding about you. The journey, the learning, you were constantly finding situations to put yourself into so you could learn.

Doc Huff: Yes.

Craig: You are dedicated full-time now to building banjos?

Doc Huff: Yes, sir.

Craig: What to you is the perfect banjo?

Doc Huff: The perfect banjo is all about playability, the right scale length, the right set up, the way it feels, and added bonuses are that it sounds sweet.

Craig: How many banjos have you made to date?

Doc Huff: Including the ones that have been burned or never really made it—167.

Craig: One of the things that I know, based on this love of wood, is that when you traveled internationally, wherever you went, you investigated wood and brought wood back. I can't wait to show our viewers the cache of wood that you have around here.

Doc Huff: Color and appearance are important—and tone—and I've been combining a very dense wood with no air in it with a very porous wood with a lot of air. This is a doctor thing for me. Structure is related to function in the body and in banjos. If you need to move somewhere with the banjo sound, you have to think about cell wall structure. Some wood has strong cell walls and air inside or between the cells. The very dense wood throughout the pot will typically give a bright sound.

Craig: If it's too porous?

Doc Huff: It'll be dead. You can put the sound wood on the top of the pot, which is the tone ring, and that captures the energy from the head to the bottom part of the pot. I use the porous woods with a lot of air in them that are like little mini air chambers, little echo chambers. In building banjos, the only thing I can say about the process of learning to build is *intuitive thinking*. Constantly thinking about what you're doing, and why you're doing it. Everything is its original journey. I don't use templates, I don't have a book of procedures, because I want to think as I'm building. It also builds the creative process, because the way you did it three times ago may not be the best way. Every day in the shop, I learn something new, and I attribute that to not doing procedures.

Craig: Where do you start? Somebody calls and says, "I want a banjo"?

Doc Huff: First is the discussion we have. I like to have an email documenting what you like about what kind of music you play, what kind of sound you like, and it always ends up with your favorite colors.

Craig: Favorite colors?

Doc Huff: Yes, because we have a nice palette of wood.

Craig: Do you do one at a time?

Doc Huff: Yes. If I'm building a banjo, I like to put my energy into that banjo.

Craig: Your fingerboards are unique.

Doc Huff: The thing that people notice first is usually the frailing platform. I always beat my thumb up on the side of the neck when I'm frailing up in this sweet zone. You need to have the scoop if you're going to play up here in the first place. Then I actually designed my first frailing platforms after my thumb. I have a big thumb with a little curve in it. I've now tempered it down so it's a little more stylish. This gives them the opportunity to play up the neck and have a little aim. It requires a lot more work.

Craig: I love that detail.

Doc Huff: This is also part of the palette that I didn't really talk about. I have a lot of fretboards. I probably have more fretboards than I'll use in the next three or four years.

Craig: I want to show people your woods. Show me your caches of wood that you've got around your shop.

Doc Huff: Sure. You ask about a favorite wood.

Craig: Yes.

Doc Huff: I have to say this is one of them; it's called bubinga. There's a story here. When I was in the bush in Africa, a young pygmy guy told me to come see his brother who had yellow fever, and so I see him in his little grass dome leaf hut. Sure enough, his eyes are yellow, and his liver is down to his iliac crest, and he's got yellow fever. His brother brings him a cup of bright yellow tea. He had scraped the cambium off of this tree and made a tea out of it. Well, I asked him to take me to the tree then because you always have to know about traditional remedies, and the wood, bubinga, turns out to be one of the sweetest tonewoods that I've found for a banjo.

Doc Huff: I put together every banjo right over here. When I put the strings on, I'm careful not to make a sound 'til the right moment. And then, it sounds a little silly, but it's like the birth of that banjo. I listen to it, and then I tune it up. To date, with every banjo I've made, I get this childish "This is the best one yet" feeling. Then I come over here to this stool and sit down and play. Occasionally you'll find a very old banjo that was really a nice banjo. That banjo didn't necessarily have a lot of inlays or any one thing, but you hold it and it feels great. You look at it, and it looks beautiful. That's the kind of banjos we want to build. We want these to be the ones that will be found generations from now, and people will say, "Wow!"

7

Pete Ross

Baltimore, Maryland, 2011

"They [the faculty] did not like it when I started making banjos in art school."

"I was trying to undo a cultural injustice by bringing these things back to life and putting them in front of people."

"My quest into the history of old-time music is in part because of sensibilities coming from the punk rock scene, which is anti-elitist, anti-corporate. I was looking for a place in American music where it was uncorrupted by the marketplace. The punk scene was folk music by design. Folk music happens when people don't have another option. That's how we think of old-time music originally, and that's what really had me plunging into the history. That's how I ended up making banjos."

Following some early-in-life interests, Pete is now considered a paleontologist/archeologist of the banjo's structure and history.

Pete is a former punk rocker, now obsessed with banjos.

Old-Time Community Role: The *Egalitarian*. Pete partially chose art as his career to re-present a past injustice. The banjo is his Exhibit 1. Pete is serious, thoughtful, fair, engaged and passionate. He is one of the most intelligent and multi-faceted people I met on this adventure. His work makes a statement different from all other builders. And all of his banjos are meticulously and accurately constructed … because the truth matters. This man cares deeply.

Pete Ross: They did not like it when I started making banjos in art school—some of the faculty had a real problem with it. They were threatening to flunk me, all sorts of stuff like that. They didn't like the idea of art that was functional as well.

I was trying to undo a cultural injustice by bringing these things back to life and putting them in front of people.

Craig: Are you obsessed with banjos?

Pete: Yes. It's not quite as all-consuming as it was when I first got into it. It drove me nuts that I couldn't have a time machine to go hear a banjo from 1800. A

Pete Ross. Follows his life's passions. Lucky for us players!

childhood interest of mine, and I'm still obsessed with it, was paleontology. I still love dinosaurs. When I was recreating these historical instruments, I tried to put myself in that paleontologist mindset. They'll find a small part of a whole animal, and they'll look at similar animals and similar fossils, and they'll assemble the whole animal that way.

I feel like I was doing that a little bit with historical instruments—I would have an image. Well, it's a little hazy, but then there's a written description from some other time and place, but it seems like they're talking about the same instrument. I'd pull all these together, and then, just a little bit of deduction…

Craig: Pete Ross of Baltimore, Maryland, thanks for taking the time to talk to me today about banjos. When did you start, and how many years have you been building?

Pete: I think I started building my first banjo at some point in 1991 when I was in art school up in New York. Then I had an apprenticeship in Mississippi with Scott Didlake, and I haven't stopped since then, so it's about 20 years.

Craig: Okay. Art school in New York. Did you think about something like a banjo before you went to art school?

Pete: Not about building them. I was becoming interested in the banjo's history by then.

Craig: What was your first exposure to a banjo?

Pete: I worked at a record store, and by total chance, I put on a record without even thinking about it. It was the *Altamont: Black Stringband Music* album that had just come out in about 1989, and I put it on, and three tracks in … a lightning bolt hit me. It was that exposure.

Craig: Oh, my gosh. It changed your life.

Pete: Yes, that's right.

Craig: What kind of music were you doing prior?

Pete: I was a total punk rocker.

Craig: Guitar, drums. What did you do?

Pete: Guitar.

Craig: Coming out of the punk rock community, are there parallels between punk rock and traditional music?

Pete: My quest into the history of old-time music is in part because of sensibilities coming from the punk rock scene, which is anti-elitist, anti-corporate. I was looking for a place in American music where it was uncorrupted by the marketplace. The punk scene was folk music by design. I like to say it was the music by the kids, for the kids—the kids talking about things that were important to them, creating their own identity. Folk music happens when people don't have another option. That's how we think of old-time music originally, and that's what really had me plunging into the history. That's how I ended up making banjos.

Craig: How does that translate into a banjo?

Pete: I was trying to make an object that made clear the complexities of our culture—the relationships between different groups, different racial groups, were not what we thought they were. Banjos come from Africa. It's a shock to people, and it changes your idea of how, basically, rural white people and rural Black people interacted. To a lot of people, when they see a banjo, it goes right along with a rebel flag. And you'd think of these groups as being opposed to one another. I wanted to make an object that said, "Guess what? Things are more complex."

Craig: When you're building banjos, what are you trying to achieve?

Pete: Well, it depends what I'm doing. Some of the ones I make are historical replicas. I'll begin by looking at an early image or in descriptions, so that has a different set of objectives. Other times, I make players' instruments.

Craig: Beginning to end, how long does it take you to make a banjo?

Pete: That's a hard question. I'm not really sure. I've been really careful almost to not time myself because I'm afraid to see how little I'm paying myself per hour.

Craig: How much a consideration is tone as you're building these?

Pete: When I'm making the ones that are banjos for modern players, I do think a lot about tone. When I make a historical recreation, I let the instrument materials and the historical sources I'm working from create the tone.

Craig: How many banjos do you think you've built so far?

Pete: I've never numbered them.

Craig: 200?

Pete: Probably.

Craig: Besides making the political statement, is this something you're dedicating yourself to?

Pete: Yes, I jumped into it for those historical, political, and high-art reasons. You get involved, and you get curious about making something this way or that way, and it becomes an end in itself.

Craig: Do you have a favorite model you like to build?

Pete: The favorite is whatever the newest idea is.

Craig: Where did you grow up?

Pete: Wheaton, Maryland, a suburb right outside Washington, D.C.

Craig: Okay. Your dad was a college professor, mom was a teacher. Was the music in the house classical?

Pete: Right.

Craig: Why punk for you?

Pete: It was another moment where I basically was recruited at the scene, and I knew I'd found my people. All the music I like hurts your ears a little bit, from the squawky 20th-century classical music, to the punk rock, to my favorite old-timey music … it's really noisy stuff.

Craig: What contribution do you think the banjo has made to society?

Pete: It's the instrument that made African music audible to European Americans. I believe it is the genesis instrument of American music. This is where everything came together in the birth of our unique culture in this country. There's like a list of begats with modern popular music going all the way back to that moment when European and African instruments and music met via the banjo.

Craig: Twenty-five years from now, when people play one of your banjos or hold it up and look at it, what piece of you remains in that banjo?

Pete: I'm trying to make a statement about American culture. It's exceptional in the world because of our multicultural history here. When I started making these, I didn't think anybody else was making them. I had come to realize that none of the originals had survived. When I started corresponding with people, it seemed then like there were about six people in the world interested in this history.

Right after graduation, I took a long trip with my former girlfriend, and we went to Galax. When I told Clarke Buehling I was going to be making this trip, he said, "Well, you're going to be in Jackson, Mississippi. You should really go visit Scott Didlake." He sees it not only as making an instrument but a mission, a cultural mission. He had Lou Gehrig's disease, and he's dying. When we got to Jackson, I went to his and his wife's apartment. I had the last banjo I had finished in New York with me. He looked at it, and he put me in his shop right away.

We were in Jackson for only two days. My girlfriend was visiting her grandparents. I was at Scott's the whole time. I hardly saw her family. The second day when I was leaving, his buddy, Richard, followed me out and said, "Scott's been trying to find an apprentice, but he hasn't had any luck. But now that he's met you, he thinks you're the guy. He wants you to come back." When I returned to New York, he started trying to [convince] me over the telephone. Yes, we'd have these long, long conversations every night.

I packed everything up and moved to Jackson, Mississippi, and lived on his couch. Some days, when he was feeling pretty good, he'd come into the shop and teach me a lot more about hand tools. Some days he was too sick to get out of bed, and we had a little wooden school desk next to his bed. Basically, I would take templates that he had, and I would mime how things would be assembled, and I'd write down notes. Some weeks after this, he said, "Okay, you've got it, you've got it. You understand." We initially all got this history from Dena Epstein's book *Sinful Tunes and Spirituals*. It's our core source.

Pete: I get a lot of museum orders these days. This one is actually for Jeff Menzies. We're good buddies. He provided me with this gourd that he had sent over from Africa. That's going to go on this [picks up neck]. I call it the Monde Banza. I've taken a lot of measurements from African instruments—radius, fingerboard, frets. I've made two of these now. This is a third order for one of these Mondes that have pickups in them.

I don't know who these people are that play these banjos, but I'm getting the feeling that world music people are getting into some of this stuff instead of only people from the old-time scene. These two are going to be next. They will have more of a minstrel-like 1840–1850s style banjo neck with classic peghead that everybody loves. It's my take on a Boucher banjo.

I try to reproduce every little accidental scratch in places where the original tools chattered on the neck, and there wasn't a nut … and I deduced that it was a leather thong holding the strings down.

Craig: This is so cool as to who you are. You're an artist, you're a musician, you're a craftsman, and you're a historian. This whole paleontology thing, it's your approach.

Pete: Yes. An exhibit was being put together in the musical instrument museum in Brussels. They had already commissioned a couple of instruments from me for that exhibit, including one that was based on the "Old Plantation" painting. It's very similar to the Haiti banjo. The curator of this museum looks at the instrument I made them and the Haiti banjo, and she says, "This is remarkable what you've done." I said, "I put together the historical evidence. I'm already making this instrument!"

8

Zachary Hoyt

Piercefield, New York, 2017

"Some people come here [St. Francis Farm] because they're interested in learning about organic farming kinds of things or working at the sawmill. Some people come here more during the day or whatever just to sit by the pond."

"Our first mission is to live an alternative to the consumer culture ... and to do so in a sustainable way. Then beyond that, do whatever outreach we can in the time that we have to put into it."

Zach is a perpetual student; his artistry and skills emerged through creative problem-solving of daily maintenance issues on the farm. He rents space in the evenings to build instruments.

Zachary is seven feet tall.

Old-Time Community Role: The *Humanitarian*. Zack selflessly works in a humble, back-to-the-earth community helping people find nature, spirituality and themselves. In his spare time, he volunteers to help the homebound or the elderly with needs like installing wheelchair ramps. In his personal time, Zack builds his banjos and violins which he sells at cost-plus to make sure everyone that wants one can own one. He is a gentle, peaceful, happy giant, with a heart always for others.

Zach walks up to my car. I struggle to make sure my sound equipment is on.

Craig Evans: Test one-two, test one-two.
Zachary Hoyt: Good morning.

Craig: Clearly you were ready before I was ready.
Zachary: I'm not quite ready yet. I was going to go in and wash my hands. I should probably wash my hands before I shake yours.

Craig: That's fine. It's nice to meet you, Zach.
Zachary: It's very nice to meet you.

8. Zachary Hoyt

Craig: This is St. Francis farm.

Zachary: Yes.

Craig: Why do people come here?

Zachary: Well, some people come here because they're interested in learning about organic farming kinds of things or working at the sawmill. Some people come here more during the day or whatever just to sit by the pond.

Craig: Who supports it?

Zachary: Some of the money comes from donors, but a third of the money comes from selling lumber. The whole budget is pretty small, about $16,000 or $17,000 a year keeps the farm going. We learned how to do what we need to with what we have or what we can make work.

Zachary Hoyt.

Craig: What brought you here?

Zachary: Well, my sister brought me here to some extent. We came in 2001; she was looking for a place where she could combine agricultural work, and a spiritual practice, and community life all in one place. I was looking for more opportunities to work and to learn to do things. I would have liked to volunteer with Habitat for Humanity because I was very interested in construction and carpentry kind of work. My mother was also interested in what we were doing, so we all came out here in 2001 when my sister was 19, and I was 15.

Craig: Well, give me a walkthrough. Where do you want to start?

Zachary: The sawmill is right here, and then the chickens are around back. We got the sawmill in 2007, and it really changed a lot of things.

Craig: What kind of wood do you harvest here?

Zachary: Mostly hardwood, a little bit of hemlock and pine, but most of the woodlot is hardwood. That's what we sell, and then we use the softwoods for building things around here. We grow some shiitake mushrooms on logs. The sugar house is right behind you where we make maple syrup in the spring. Those logs on the rack are going to be making mushrooms soon.

They have little pins on them, and the little bumps you can see coming out of them are going to grow into mushrooms over the next two or three days. You soak the logs in water, and then a week later, you get some mushrooms. We don't have a rooster, but we have some hens. They have the yard where we put things to make compost, and they kind of scratch it up.

Things are winding down a bit. The potatoes are dying back, and we'll be digging them up soon. The garlic and onions have already gone inside and the tomatoes are starting to run down. But the snow peas are still going great, and the kale and all that.

This is where we raise rabbits. They are kind of hyper and afraid sometimes.

Craig: What do you do with rabbits?

Zachary: They are food. We eat them, I'm sorry to say.

Craig: I was afraid to ask. Well, it's kind of another white meat.

Zachary: Yes, it's very much like chickens except the bones are in different places.

Craig: How many total acres is the farm?

Zachary: It's 180 acres. Over 100 of it is real woods, and then some of it is kind of hedgerows. For years we were selling hay, but this year we decided we would give it a rest for a while.

Craig: What is your motive for doing what you do?

Zachary: Our first mission is to live an alternative to the consumer culture … and to do so in a sustainable way. Then beyond that, do whatever outreach we can with the time we have to put into it. We do small things. I build wheelchair ramps occasionally for the local agency that provides them, and we send vegetables to the soup kitchen in Lacona about five miles up that way.

Some of the livestock at St. Francis Farm.

Zach in front of the barn.

Craig: You clearly have incorporated it, though, because your demeanor is one of a person at peace.

Zachary: Oh, well, that's very kind of you. I'm never sure if I'm doing the very best thing I could be doing or the right thing that I ought to be doing or whatever. But I figure as long as I'm doing as little harm as I can, and trying to do something good sometimes, then that'll be good enough.

Craig: The hardest thing you have to do is to look at somebody and say "be normal."

Zachary: Yes, I know. Being normal is not a thing I've been good at, even at the best of times.

Craig: We all have characteristics unique to ourselves. For starters, you're seven feet tall.

Zachary: Yes.

Craig: Does that run in your family?

Zachary: To some extent; my father is 6'6, my mother is 6'2. I've gotten to the point where I can't remember very distinctly anymore what it felt like to *not be as tall as I am*.

Craig: When you went to school, were you constantly asked, "Do you play basketball?"

Zachary: I get that question. I was homeschooled. I didn't get it at school, but even now, I am asked that a lot. When I had turned 15 in the spring before I came out to the farm, there was a guy at the Quaker meeting we attended in Maine. He was in a wheelchair, he had post-polio. He was involved with American Friends Service Committee; they would have meetings in Philadelphia he would have to go to. His wife got tired from having to go down to Philadelphia with him every other weekend or whatever and push him around.

A couple of times I went down with him. Once it was during the basketball playoffs. As I was pushing him around in his wheelchair, people were constantly asking me if I played basketball. Now my friend was only about four feet tall, and in a wheelchair—and he starts telling people that no, I was his coach when he played basketball.

Craig: I want to go into your background a bit. You grew up in Maine. You said there was music in your house? Was it Mom or Dad, and what did they play?

Zachary: Yes, well, they didn't play music, but there was recorded music—the radio, records, tapes, folk music, classical music, we listened to Garrison Keillor's *Prairie Home Companion* radio show from as early as I can remember.

Craig: Who were some of the artists on *Prairie Home* that caught your attention?

Zachary: Pat Donohue has always been my favorite, I don't know why, and Robin and Linda Williams, I always loved them and the Hopeful Gospel Quartet, which of course included them.

Craig: Garrison.
Zachary: Yes.

Craig: You were homeschooled all the way through high school?
Zachary: Yes.

Craig: Did you go to college?

Zachary: No. My mother was the one who did the homeschooling for the most part, my father did some, but he was a professor teaching chemistry at a college. He was gone a lot of the time, but my mother said she was more of a reference librarian than a teacher. It wasn't the kind of school where we have a curriculum, and you sit down for a certain number of hours, and you do a little bit of this and a little bit of that.

She tried to balance out so that we also learned the things we didn't want to learn like math, as well as the things we did want to learn like history and that kind of thing. But if we had questions, she would help us. Rather than just saying this is the answer, she would help us learn, like, how do you go to the library and find out what you want to know.

Craig: I heard you mention when we were walking around earlier that you have been able to learn to do many extraordinary things here with tools and equipment being on the farm.

Zachary: I always had a knack for how things work. When I'm working with a tool or driving a tractor or whatever, it's like the whole thing is part of me. I can almost somehow feel with my body what's happening throughout the whole operation, and in a way that I don't with people or animals.

Craig: When you're working with your banjo, did the tools help facilitate your…

Zachary: Oh, yes. When I'm holding a drill in my hand, it's like the drill is part of my arm. I thought that was how everybody related to machinery, and I know a lot of people relate that way to people.

Craig: This is interesting because when you talk to people that play instruments, the instrument becomes their voice in the language of music. In playing that instrument, it is a part of them. It sounds to me like that same analogy applies for you when you pick up a tool to build a banjo.

Zachary: Yes, and I get the same feeling when I hold the instrument. I haven't spent as much time playing instruments as I have working with tools, so I haven't become as comfortable and fluent in that language as I have with tools.

Craig: When you decided to build musical instruments, what came first, the desire to work with tools, the desire to work with wood, or the desire to build an instrument that gives you a voice in a language called music?

Zachary: The desire to work with tools, and work with wood, both came at a very young age when I was maybe five or six. Then the desire to build instruments came in my early teens when I became interested in music. Music had always been played around the house, but then I really began to pay attention to it in a different way.

Then I had the desire a long time before I had the ability, unfortunately. I started out building a mountain dulcimer. The first one I built successfully was when I was 18. I built one when I was 14 or 15 from a *Reader's Digest* book.

Somebody gave me a book that had a dulcimer plan, a harp plan, and hammered dulcimer plans, so I built all those. Then for my birthday my mother gave me a book by Roger Siminoff, *The Ultimate Bluegrass Mandolin Construction Manual*, and I was really intimidated by it. It took me months and months to build that first mandolin.

Craig: Oh my gosh, I would think. You jumped right into one of the most difficult instruments possible.

Zachary: I had already built the dulcimer so I had some basic understanding of how to put in frets, but it was carving the archtop and the arch back.

Craig: When did you get to banjos?

Zachary: Well, I got my first banjo in 2005 when I was 19. It was a tenor banjo I bought at the flea market. It was all in pieces. Then I built a five-string neck for it that winter. It was a very primitive five-string neck, but I could learn to play, five-stringing on it to some extent. Then I built my first real banjo in 2009 into 2010, and then got into it further from there. With all the instruments, I would build one, and then I would put it up for sale, and start building another one. The ones that sold are the ones I kept making more and more of. That's how I ended up making more banjos than anything else.

Craig: How many banjos have you built to date?
Zachary: 57.

Craig: Oh my goodness.
Zachary: 58. I'm just starting out, but I'm having fun with it.

Craig: What year officially did you start?
Zachary: I completed the first one in 2010. Then in the last 12 months, I've built about 24 or so. It's ramped up quite a bit over the years. It seems to go in waves—I think it was 2014 when I sold more fiddles than banjos for some reason. Then most of the time I sell more banjos than fiddles. I don't understand how that comes about, but—

Craig: You're making fiddles too now?
Zachary: Yes, yes, and guitars and mandolins and I've made a cello. I know it'd be smarter to stick with one thing and learn to really do it well, but I'm always tempted by the new thing, the new skill to learn. That's always true, even beyond instrument building. That has always lured me … as learning to use a sewing machine or learning to weld or learning to make pie crust, whatever it might be. I always figure the more skills I can learn, the better chance there is of being able to do whatever needs to be done.

Craig: What time of day do you make your banjos because you're busy working on a farm?
Zachary: In the evening. From 6:00 or 7:00 in the evening 'til 9:00 or 10:00, depending on the day. Monday to Saturday, usually, is when I'm in the shop, and occasionally, if we have a rainy day. This year, I've been doing once a month where I'll rent the shop for a day. I pay the farm $100 for the day, and I work in the shop instead of working at the sawmill or whatever else is needed.

Craig: When you start to make a banjo, what is your goal?
Zachary: First, to make a banjo that sounds good. Second, to make a banjo that is easy and comfortable to play, and that's durable. Then looks, I'd like them to look nice, but I don't do anything ornate. I haven't ever gotten to the more decorative end of things, although I admire a lot of the work of people who do.

Craig: Do you have an endgame plan for your banjo building?
Zachary: I would hope someday perhaps to be able to do it full-time. I don't know if that's realistic or not, but it's something to which I aspire. I figure I won't be able to do heavy work forever, and at some point, it'll be something I can do when I'm too tired or my knees or my back are too far gone.

Craig: This beautiful place is where you've worked for many years with pigs and goats and chickens and rabbits and beautiful, beautiful gardens, what of this place comes through you and now goes into your banjos?

Zachary: A sense of expedience or practicality that things have a function and a job they do. The banjo makes music, and if it looks good, then it looks good. If it doesn't, it doesn't.

Craig: It does what it's supposed to do.

Zachary: Yes. What brought me into this kind of life was joining the Quaker meeting in Portland, Maine, when I was 13 or so. Then I met the man who I mentioned going to Philadelphia to push in his wheelchair. His name was Bob. I used to go to his house one or two days a week and work for him because he knew how to do almost everything, mechanical work, home repair work. He'd been a clock repairman and repaired jewelry in his younger days.

He was a great teacher. He had these buckthorn bushes around his front door, and I was trying to trim them with the electric hedge trimmer. He said, "No, don't cut the cord. That's the most important thing." Of course, I did. Then I got to learn about how to change fuses and how to splice the extension cord and all sorts of great stuff.

Craig: You also mentioned Bob introduce you to Quakers. Is there any part of the Quaker philosophy that you've incorporated into your life?

Zachary: Yes. Yes. We began going to the Quaker meeting, and he was there. That's how I met him. The Quaker method is to sit in silence and to reflect or meditate or whatever the word is you would use. We still do that every day from 7:00 to 7:30. On weekdays, we get up and do our chores, and then do that before we have breakfast, and it makes the day go so much better.

I learned so much from him. That made it possible for me to be here and be able to do the things I need to do—not only learning specific skills, but learning how to do with what you have, and figure out a way to get done what you need to do with the resources at hand. That's flowed into my instrument building, as well as the rest of my life here.

9

Bill Rickard

Aurora, Ontario, 2011

Bill Rickard is a successful, genius mechanical designer. In his career, he designed machines that built machines.

Bill suffered a severe, life-altering motorcycle accident. He healed mentally and physically, thanks to his music community friends playing next to his hospital bed during his recovery.

Since Bill could no longer play a banjo, he decided to begin building them full-time, making machines that could serve as his left arm.

Making people happy through music and banjos is Bill's primary motivation.

Bill is also proud to represent what disabled people can do to change the world.

"You can do anything. It doesn't matter what you're given or what you've got. If you want to put your mind to it, I really believe we can do anything."

Old-Time Community Role: The *Inventor*. As a problem solver, Bill is peerless. When he was no longer able to build banjos due to his injuries, he employed his incredible mind and invented new, better processes. He actually raised the bar for all builders with his inventions. But he didn't stop there. He began building improved products such as tone rings and sophisticated tuners for the industry. Through his ever-present smile, what Bill clearly demonstrates is optimism, perseverance and stamina. Bill is yet another incredible human being that just happens to like banjos. So grateful to share his tribe.

Bill: I'm a guy, the glass is always half full. I got into this as a rehab and it just pulled me out of the darkest hole I think I've ever been in in my life. I don't think about being disabled. I just think about a different way to do things. This is banjo heaven here, Craig.

Craig: I appreciate that!

Bill: Look at this. [Chuckles.] This is all banjo stuff.

Craig: Bill Rickard, this is a delight! I have waited so long to finally meet you in person. I'm in your shop, I'm looking around at all these pieces of banjo ware and I guess you and I share the same sense of excitement about this instrument. Tell me how you first got interested in banjo.

Bill: Boy, I started playing banjo when I was probably 16 years old. I needed a banjo, so I built it. I came from that kind of family, started playing bluegrass music, which was three-finger style, and played probably the time I was probably about 28, 29, and then because of corporate stuff, I gave it up. Then, 48 years old, I was in a record store one day and saw a record or a CD by Chris Coole and brought it home and played it. I saw Merryweather Records on the back and gave this guy, Arnie Naiman, a call and he put me onto Chris Coole. I think it was that afternoon I was taking lessons and playing two hours a day again. It literally took my life over.

Craig: Something else happened in your life that changed your perspective on things.

Bill: I had a very serious accident in 2002. I was in Italy on a business/holiday-type trip, and I'd been riding motorcycles all my life. In fact, used to race sidecars at one time, and the first day I got in Italy, I was coming down a really nice road, sunshine, and I caught out of the corner of my eye, a white truck came over the center line and he got me head-on. I went down the road, got tremendous road burn, I guess to say, and burned the left side right off me. Took my arm off on the spot and took my leg off.

Somebody was there that had a cell phone stopped immediately, called an ambulance. They airlifted me to a university hospital in Pavia. Two days later I woke up, they told me that the first surgeon had gone home that night and found his 20-year-old son had been in an accident and hit a man on a motorcycle, which was me. It was just an unbelievable story.

Bill Rickard. Bill loves a good challenge. Then he surpasses them.

Craig: I know there was a period of time after that that you were pretty discouraged.

Bill: Well, naturally, if you play banjo every day and you get into the playing banjo and the people that play banjo, you get very connected naturally. I couldn't play anymore and I was just devastated. I contemplated taking my life. It was that bad mentally. And one day I woke up and just thought about, here are all these people that had come in the hospital to play for me. People I didn't even know. In fact, turned up at Sunnybrook Hospital here in Toronto and I'd come out of it. I was drugged up at the time, and there'd be somebody in my room playing a fiddle or playing a banjo. That really impacted me!

I decided that I would try to build a banjo. I'd always built instruments when I was in part of my 20s and I took a shot at building a banjo and built Chris Coole's banjo. It was a surprise for him. Took on an inlay job I wouldn't have done with two hands. I guess it was to prove to myself that I could still do it. It took me about a year and I finished this banjo and gave it to Chris and I realized at the time, you can't build one banjo, you got to build more.

So I started making all these parts, as you can see around me, and it just took off. It's, as I say now, it's a hobby or rehab thing I got into that literally got totally out of control. That's the best way to put it.

Craig: Knowing what the banjo has done for you and your life when you're making these banjos, are you thinking about the end user?

Bill: Oh yes, definitely. When you create an instrument or so, lots of the parts in an instrument I really think about. I think possibly, it's very likely, somebody a hundred years from now is going to be sitting in their kitchen playing this with some guys just like us and have a lot of fun. A lot of really good fun. If you can believe that, that means a lot to me.

Craig: Are you in this business for the money?

Bill: Oh geez, no.

[Laughter.]

Bill: You couldn't make money doing this? No, this is a passion.

Craig: Making people happy, satisfied, is your primary motivation?

Bill: Yes, definitely. The majority of banjo builders, I know they all laugh when we talk about money. You make a living doing this for sure. You're sure not going to get rich, but you'll be very, very wealthy in the end.

Craig: Well, the fact that people are going to be playing these things a hundred years from now, how many things can you build today that are going to have that sort of longevity? And every time somebody plays it, you hope it brings joy.

Bill: Yes.

Craig: In building your banjos, is it more important for you to honor tradition or to try to push the boundaries?

Bill: I do both. I tend to follow traditions in building banjos, but I'm still on the edge because I'm doing something different. I've been in the automation business all my life, so I applied what I did for a living to my situation. The necks are all carved on a CNC router. They're threaded on a CNC router. The parts I make are all done on CNC equipment, which they didn't have in the 1800s. A good example would be if you look at the edge of the fingerboard on this particular neck, it's not finished yet, but the frets are in and there's no tang hanging under that fingerboard.

Craig: That is as smooth as a baby's bottom.

Bill: That's the only way you could do that is on a CNC router; you can't do it any other way.

Craig: A lot of your machinery, you have it set up that you can actually operate it yourself.

Bill: Yes, right.

Craig: How does that work?

Bill: My left hand is that vise in the corner. I just put an air motor on it with some gearing, so it operates very smoothly, and it uses a foot pedal. It opens and closes it. First thing I did when I recovered from my accident and figured out I can't do this with just one hand, I built this left-hand device. This is like my left arm and it's really neat. It's just a standard metal device I bought and we put an air motor on it.

There's some gears in here, so it doesn't slam open and closed. If I've got a fingerboard in my hand and I wanted to do something, I'd basically take this and I place it in the vise. See, it moves nice and slow and this is solid. Now I can cut, I can file with my right hand. So this machine is my left arm.

Craig: You pushed the pedal on the floor there?

Bill: Yes, I got an air pedal. I can also set all my frets in there one at a time. When it's stabilized in the vise, I can nip frets with my right hand. People wonder how I do it. Ninety percent of what I do, I do here with just one hand.

Craig: How many machines do you have set up with these devices?

Bill: Oh, they're all over the shop.

Craig: That's fantastic.

Bill: In a little while, I'll show you how I build my rims. It's a one-armed rim-rolling machine I built.

Craig: So you can do a whole banjo all by yourself?

Bill: Oh yes, no problem at all. Well, it takes time. My brain's still working at old speed, which used to be I could do one in a day. Now it takes me four days, maybe. So I certainly can't move as fast.

Craig: When did you in earnest start building banjos? What year?

Bill: I really didn't get into it full until about 2006. It took off and that end up being seven days a week.

Craig: How many banjos are you building a year now, do you think?

Bill: I'm guessing 60 to 70. I could do a lot more if I wanted, but you got to remember I do parts too.

Bill: We could talk all day, Craig.

[Laughter.]

Craig: Yes, we could.

Bill: I love this stuff. I'm really happy I can still do it.

Craig: 100 years from now, somebody's going to be playing one of your banjos. What do you want them to know about you?

Bill: I'd want them to say, "Wow, this is a Rickard banjo. This was built with somebody that was disabled." I think that's a powerful message. You can do anything. It doesn't matter what you're given or what you got. If you want to put your mind to it, I really believe we can do anything.

Craig: How many more years do you want to build banjos?

Bill: All the rest of my life.

Craig: Okay.

Bill: Yes. If I can go out of this world doing this, I'll be one happy guy.

Craig: I think you're already a happy guy. You'll be a happier guy.

Bill: That's right. You got it.

[Laughter.]

10

William Seeders Mosheim

Dorset, Vermont, 2011

Will was born to a family of multi-medium artists. His father taught him how to build fine, crafted wood furniture.

Will is not a *traditional learner.* Will's education included alternative programs to realize his gifts.

Today, Will is successfully employing his talents and passion:; music and banjo building.

Old-Time Community Role: The *Gifted Prodigy*. If you're born into a family of extremely talented artists, the bar gets set very high. So, early on, this gifted prodigy started climbing the creative ropes. As his furniture-making skills excelled, he decided to take a different, more difficult route and create musical instruments. Today, Will's banjos are among the finest *ever* made. And he continues to push his creative bounds. If perfection can be achieved, my hunch is Will *will* get there first.

Craig Evans: I just pulled into the home of Seeders Banjos, and it's not quite a home, I'm calling it a compound.

William: We call it the Compound or Dorsey Custom Furniture. My father's furniture shop, he's been in business over 30 years now.

Craig: How did he get into furniture?

William: He took the slow way in. He started out as a logger, then he went to carpentry and then finish carpentry. Then he slowly started making standalone, finished fine furniture pieces.

Craig: What kind of furniture do you make?

William: It's hard to pinpoint. I started building what my Dad makes. He's made almost every style of furniture. There is everything from kitchen cabinets, tables, chairs, pool tables, fine cabinet pieces.

Craig: Why don't you give me a quick tour of some of these buildings. This is really impressive.

William: Great. Well, let's start over behind you here. This is my brother's metal shop. My older brother Sam is a metal worker. He does mostly fabrication. A little bit of blacksmithing, but mostly grinding, welding. He makes a lot of railings, and also does a lot of work for my father's business. They collaborate a lot.

Craig: Are you guys all artsy like this?

William: Yes, I'm coming from a pretty artistic family. This next little building is my father's finish room. And here is a rare glimpse of a piece of furniture that I made years ago. I stopped making furniture for my father about three years ago when I took my banjo business full-time.

William Seeders Mosheim. A beautiful mind playing and building beautiful instruments.

Craig: How old are you?
William: I'm 32.

Craig: When did you get serious about building banjos?
William: I got serious about it around 2010. The third one is the first one that I sold. It was a really interesting, unique banjo too, because it was ordered from me by two really close friends of mine who had a son who was turning four. He was enamored with me playing the banjo. They wanted something that he could play as a four-year-old but also grow into.

Craig: [Laughs.] How do you do that?
William: At the time, I really knew nothing about banjos, being in southwestern Vermont, I was very isolated from banjos and the banjo world. Thanks to the Internet, there's a lot of photos out there these days. I started looking around and I found these banjos called piccolo banjos and pony banjos.

Craig: Sure. Yes.
William: I took that idea and I developed my own version of those banjos. I built this piccolo pony banjo for him that he could play as a four-year-old and grow into. Just this last year, that kid turned nine, and I built him a full-size banjo. He's still playing and still enjoying the banjo.

10. William Seeders Mosheim

Craig: William Seeders Mosheim, thank you for sitting down with me today to talk about banjos. Just driving in here today, the beauty of Vermont, the beauty of these trees, the beauty of the wood … it's overwhelming. I can see why you're here.

William: [Laughs.] Thanks for coming, Craig. It's great to have you here.

Craig: I have to admit, following you on social media today, the pictures you take specifically of your inlay and the fine details of your banjos are amazing. It's clear that you understand wood, and you understand how to put things together.

William: My father's been a woodworker for longer than I've been alive, so I grew up in his wood shop. Some of my earliest memories are sitting in his shop, sanding a piece of wood, playing with chisels. When I'm six to eight, nine years old. I have little chisel scars on my hands that go back beyond my memory. It's part of me, and his shop has always been right next to our house. This compound that we're in now is the second location of his business. We were in Arlington, Vermont, where the shop was 10 feet from the house. When he is not in the wood shop making furniture, designing furniture, he's doing pottery, he's painting, he's working on his house. He's always creating something.

Craig: Are those also skills that you've picked up?

William: As far as the broad realm of artistic creativity, I would say I picked up that a lot.

Craig: What are some of the philosophies you've picked up about wood that apply to your banjo building?

William: Wood is an amazing organic material. You can work with black walnut your whole life and every piece is a little bit different. You can work with maple, and cherry, and mahogany and all sorts of different wood. There's just too many to count. Each one has its own character, and each its own soul and its own voice. Growing up, immersed in that, it becomes second nature. I see a piece of wood and I say, "Hey, that would make a great neck. Hey, that would be a great fingerboard, or these two really complement each other well, and they can speak for you in a lot of ways."

The other accents that you put to that, mother of pearl wood inlay versus shell inlay versus metal inlay or details, can also add to that voice or that mood that you're trying to create.

Craig: Let's follow down the music track here. Was there music in your house growing up?

William: There was a lot of music in my house growing up. Nobody was a musician, in particular. My mother dabbled a little bit with guitar when she was younger. I never played it when I was a kid. My father was the same. He always talked about learning how to play instruments, always wanted to learn how to play instruments, but never did. I was the first one in the family to pick up music. When I was around 10 years old or so my father—I'm not really sure of the story behind it—but he ended up with an electric guitar. It just sat in the corner of the living room, and I'd knock it over occasionally as kids do.

One day I just picked it up and I started playing it. I next picked up the book that he had with it, and I started teaching myself. They saw me doing this for a week or so straight. They said, "Wow, you're really interested in this?" I said, "Yes, I think so." They took me to a music shop that was local here in just next town over in Manchester. I walk in and I see an electric bass, and I said, I want to play that. In middle school I was already playing somewhat professionally. I was really serious about it. I was a quiet, shy kid.

Craig: Are you sitting in your room just listening to, like, John Coltrane? [Laughter.]
William: Yeah. A lot of [Charles] Mingus. [Laughter.]

Craig: Are you making money at this point?
William: A little bit, definitely. As a middle schooler and a high schooler, it's good money. You make $50 or $100, and it felt really good to feel like I was pursuing something that was worth pursuing.

Craig: Banjo. Where did the banjo come in?
William: Oh, the banjo didn't come in for many years after that, so I grew up with a lot of early country music, a lot of Bob Dylan, Grateful Dead. I didn't hear a lot of banjo. That music didn't come into my life until my 20s or so. It's funny, too, because in high school I actually borrowed a banjo from a friend, a good friend of mine's mother. Looking back on it I now know that I was a Bart Reiter banjo, and I borrowed it from her and it sat in the case in my music room for six months. I never took it out. I was intimidated by it. I had an interest in it, but I didn't know what to do with it.

I was playing punk rock at the time. I was playing loud, angry music, but for some reason I was drawn to these acoustic instruments and I had no idea why. Right around that time I started playing music with an old friend of mine. He was playing his acoustic guitar. He was singing more, and he was learning folk songs and old country songs. The two of us started playing together, really not knowing anything about the music other than what we'd heard growing up. Mostly Waylon Jennings, Merle Haggard, Old & In the Way ... that realm of music.

Slowly through that we started up a band and we found bluegrass, and I started learning the traditional styles of banjo playing. Shortly after, I started teaching myself clawhammer and just took off from there.

Craig: Learning clawhammer, did you have a teacher?
William: No. I'm completely self-taught on the banjo.

Craig: Cool. Before you got into banjos, what were you doing?
William: I was working for my father full-time. For about five years. I was making all furniture.

Craig: Did you go to school for that or just learn from your dad?

William: No, I've learned completely from my father. I very quickly became the guy in the shop that he gave all the really meticulous, fussy [laughs], challenging projects too. I would never trade that for anything because I got to build some amazing pieces of furniture. Stuff that I look at now. I say, "I built that."

Craig: If you make a dresser, and you make a banjo, clearly you've made two completely different things. What's so intriguing about a musical instrument versus a beautiful piece of art?

William: As functional as furniture is we're sitting in chairs that we made, and we're eating off of tables that we make. As functional as that is there's something about a musical instrument that is very different because it can give a voice to somebody that plays it. It can create something to dance to, it can create something to sing to, it can create emotion. Having control over how that can create those sounds is quite an amazing process. The relationship that people have with their instruments is also something that you don't often find with a piece of furniture.

Through my father's business, I also did a lot of antique repair, so I picked up a lot of the repair chops through that.

Craig: What made you decide just to build banjos full-time?

William: It was a slow evolution. We can take it back a little bit. Through high school I was struggling a lot. I actually, I never went to college. I barely even went to high school. I went to an alternative program at our local high school that was for at-risk kids of dropping out. It was designed for kids like me, honestly, that were intelligent, but just struggled with that traditional classroom setting.

I've always loved to learn, but I don't learn just being lectured at and being told what to do. So they took me out of that traditional classroom setting and said, "What do you want to do? What do you like?" I said, "I like to create, I like to draw, I like to play music." They said, "That's what you're going to do. You're going to play music, you're going to do art. Here's the other work you have to do. You've got to get done. But the majority of what you're going to do is play music and create art."

Craig: Oh, my gosh. What an incredible confirmation.

William: It was pretty amazing.

Craig: This school just sounds awesome.

William: It's called the Target Program at Burr and Burton Academy.

Craig: Do you mind if I drill down on that a bit?

William: I've spoken about it quite a lot.

Craig: Oftentimes with creatives, not just people that build banjos, but with creatives, there is some sort of, if you want to call it, a learning constraint. They don't all learn in traditional patterns. They're really kinesthetic. They want to feel it. Or the attention span is short. Some people call it ADD, other people can call it a creative mind. There's dyslexia, sometimes things that are backwards or forwards. Were any of those things conditions that you have, that you've learned to adapt or learned how to work with as strengths?

William: Oh, completely. You name it, I've been labelled ADD, depression, anxiety. Over the years, I've learned that it's not really those labels. It's who I am. It's not being able to fit into a box. I can hyper focus on things, but I can easily get distracted and run down this other path for hours and hours while hyper focusing on that other path.

Craig: The beautiful thing about this school is when they recognized, they confirmed the fact that what you have is a gift and not a constraint.

William: I didn't know where I fit in the world. It gave me this really unique perspective on life. What the path of my life could be.

Craig: Because *if it wasn't for people like you, things wouldn't happen.* Thank you for sharing that. [Laughter.] What year did you start making banjos?

William: 2009.

Craig: How many have you made to date?

William: As far as full banjos go, I am just about to finish number 47, but I also do quite a number of necks for old rims. I've built a number of guitars as well. That puts the instruments I've made over 50 at this point.

Craig: What's the most rewarding part of it to you?

William: I think the whole process is the most rewarding part … I love so much of it that it's hard to pinpoint exactly one thing that I love because it's the process of creating, it's the process of designing something.

Craig: What is the biggest reward in building a banjo?

William: Handing it to the person that I'm building it for, or hearing back from them and they say, "This is exactly or more than what I could have ever dreamed for." It's knowing that they're going to create music with it. Whether that's professionally or just in their own living room for themselves, knowing that I met or exceeded their dreams of what that instrument could be is quite an amazing feeling.

Craig: As you're building a piece of furniture as you're building a banjo, what part of you do you put into that creation?

William: The part of me that goes into all my work is my eye for detail, my meticulous sense of nature. The analytical, engineering brain that I tend to have. These few teachers that I really have a lot to thank for pulled that creative element out of me. They said, "This is who you are, this is what you do, this is your voice in the world." These instruments will, hopefully, outlive me in a lot of ways and keep creating music.

Craig: 50 years from now. Do you see yourself doing what you're doing right now?

William: I think with who I am, music and creativity will always be part of my life, and I don't think I will ever be able to separate the two.

PERFORMERS AND TEACHERS

Clare Milliner and Walt Koken. A delightful musical combination with historic results.

11

Rayna Gellert

Swannanoa, North Carolina, 2015

Rayna was drawn to the music and surrounding community early through family. Rayna started playing classical violin at age 10 (fifth grade).

"When I was in high school, I was secretly noodling [old-time] a little bit. [Laughter.] Just a little bit, though, because it was so scary. I can't even describe how intimidating it was to me. I was listening to it like mad. I can say, though, the moment when I was like, 'I have to do this. I just have to get over it and do it,' I was listening to Greg Hooven when I was 17. I heard that and just freaked out. I was just like, 'Oh my God, what is that? [Laughs.] I want to make those sounds!'"

"I went to Clifftop when I was 15 and met all these great people. That to me is a really important part of the story because it was my connection with those people and my desire to connect with them more that kept drawing me into playing."

"I just had this moment where I was like, 'Oh my God, the world needs more music. I can totally do this! I can give my energy to this. It's okay for me to say this is what I'm doing as a career because music does actually change people's lives and it's a completely worthwhile thing to do full-time.'"

"I'm endlessly moved by the connection that music creates between people."

Old-Time Community Role: The *Virtuoso*. Born to a music filled home, a fiercely independent artist must choose whether to follow the norm or to make their own way. Thankfully for all of us in the old-time community, then second choice was Rayna's decision. But it seemed the bar was intimidatingly high … until the joy of the music (versus competitive shadow) won her over. She had to make her music. And in doing so, she recognized how it made the world a better place. What better career could one choose?

Craig Evans: Rayna Gellert, thank you for sitting down to talk to me about old-time music. I have looked forward to this day for so long because I am a huge fan. You bring such a style to this. You bring such a joy to how you play. Thank you for being a part of this community.

Rayna: You're welcome.

11. Rayna Gellert

Craig: Where did you first hear your music and where did you first decide this is something you wanted to do?

Rayna: I have a lot of early memories of music but not a specific moment where it's like, "Oh, and that's the first time I heard—" I mean, Dan [Gellert] was playing constantly. He and my mom, Jen, they had a string band when I was a kid. They would play music around the house, the two of them. Then, of course, just all the records that they were into listening to. It was a pretty immersive experience.

Craig: What was that music? Was that traditional music at that point?

Rayna: Yes. It was all traditional music. Not all old-time. There was a lot of blues and Irish traditional music and some more folky stuff. My mom listened to some folk singers and stuff like that.

Rayna Gellert. Prodigy plus. Bringing beautiful sounds to a world in need.

Craig: When were you drawn into it? When did you first start playing, and what did you play?

Rayna: Well, I was always drawn into it. I was always fixated on it. I have two older brothers and they both went through that teenager phase of, like, "Oh my God, my parents are so dorky, play dorky music." I never went through that phase. I always just thought it was super cool and wanted to be around it and loved all their music friends and wanted to hang out with them. My musical story is that I was too intimidated by Dan to play old-time music when I was a kid. I knew I wanted to play old-time music, but I was scared to try. He's such a force. When I was 10, in fifth grade, everybody started an instrument.

When it came time for me to choose an instrument, I chose violin because I knew that I wanted to play the fiddle, but I was scared to play old-time music at that point, so I did classical, which is something Dan doesn't do. Even at that age, it was like, "I'm going to play the fiddle someday, but I'm not ready yet." [Chuckles.] Then I did classical music through fifth grade through graduating from high school and was pretty serious about it. I had a private teacher that I really loved. She was 45 minutes away in Michigan. This was in northern Indiana where I was growing up, and the whole drive to my fiddle lessons, there and back, I was listening to old-time music.

Craig: I've got to ask, though, are you secretly playing it? Are you trying it out with your classical music?

Rayna: When I was in high school, I was secretly noodling [old-time] a little bit. [Laughter.] Just a little bit, though, because it was so scary. I can't even describe how intimidating it was to me. I was listening to it like mad. I can say, though, the moment when I was like, "I have to do this. I just have to get over it and do it," I was listening to Greg Hooven when I was 17. I heard that and just freaked out. I was just like, "Oh my God, what is that? [Laughs.] I want to make those sounds!" I went to Clifftop when I was 15 and met all these great people. That to me is a really important part of the story because it was my connection with those people and my desire to connect with them more that kept drawing me into playing. I wanted to be able to have the musical communication with them that I saw them having at Clifftop.

Craig: High school, you're playing classical music. Time comes for college. What'd you decide to do?

Rayna: I applied to IU Bloomington and I applied to Warren Wilson College. Went on a visit down here at Warren Wilson with my mom and she was just like, "We got to figure out how to get you here," because she just saw it. They gave me a lot of really great financial aid, so it wound up being doable. I knew there was a lot of music and dance down here, but I had no idea that I was landing in the middle of such a vibrant community of old-time players.

Craig: Can you talk about that experience?

Rayna: Yes. It was magical. I already had it in my head, like, "I'm quitting classical music. I'm going to play old-time music. I'm going to be hundreds of miles away from Dan. I'm just going to figure this out. People do this!" Meeting all these great musicians. The first old-time musician I met locally was Phil Jamison because he teaches at Warren Wilson, and he hosts an old-time jam session on campus. I went to the jam session with my fiddle. I thought I could try to learn some tunes. Really quickly, I made a bunch of great full-time music friends in the area.

I was a freshman in college. I didn't have a car. All these sweet people would drive out to campus and pick me up and take me to music potlucks. It was amazing. It was really just immediately this sense of being welcomed into this really fascinating community of wacky people who love old-time music and—

Craig: Wow. It literally was a total immersion for you. You were in it all the time?

Rayna: Oh, yes, and I got completely obsessed.

Craig: Music major?

Rayna: No. I was a women's studies major. In college, I was bouncing back and forth between being here, during the school year, and then going back to Indiana in the summer. I think the first legit dance gig I ever had was because my fiddle-playing friend Rhys Jones invited me to come and play some dances with him. We would play together a lot when I was back home.

Craig: When did you decide to perform and what was the motivation to perform?

Rayna: I mean, it's part of playing music in general. That was actually one of the things that I was writing to my teacher about. I used to get so incredibly nervous about performing classical music, like, horrible stage fright. She would say to me, "Well, you like this piece, right?" I'd be like, "Yes, it's beautiful." Then she'd be like, "Don't you want to share it with people?" I'd be like, "Well, uh, kind of, but, uh."

Then when I started playing old-time music, it was a completely different thing because I got that. I got the sense of, like, "Oh my God, this tune is so cool. You have to hear it." It didn't feel like it was about me. It was really about just sharing music that I was excited about. I just wasn't scared of performing it, but I also just feel like in the old-time community, it's like, "Oh, there's this thing going on. You should hop up on stage, play a couple tunes." It's just so casual. It wasn't like I made a decision about that, about just getting on stage and playing stuff. It just came up.

I feel like a real gift that I have gotten from growing up with Dan is a sense of *the music just comes through you*. Obviously, Dan has a totally amazing and completely unique style and unique musical voice, but I never got the sense that it was something he was trying to do. I feel like that's something I absorbed from him. It's just that *you get out of the way of the tune*. And that's a good place to be coming from if you're going to get on stage.

Craig: Do you have a reverence for the tune?

Rayna: Oh, yes, absolutely. I don't know. Certainly, there's a place to just bust down or the way you play for a square dance and just channeling energy and just having it be like "Woo." I suppose as a professional musician, I have sometimes wound up playing music that I don't feel entirely reverent about, but most of the time I'm lucky enough to get to play stuff that I do feel really reverent about. To me, it's, like, otherwise why would I want to share it with an audience? [Chuckles.]

Craig: Now you've played lots of square dances. How did something like the band Uncle Earl happen?

Rayna: That's quite a ways after.

Craig: What's in between?

Rayna: I got out of college and wanted to stick around the Asheville area. I started doing odd jobs. I moved into Phil Jamison's old house. Was renting from him and his family, which is actually an important part of the story because Phil and his family gave me really cheap rent and that is a key element of me actually becoming a professional musician. Low overhead. Yes, I was doing odd jobs. I was working for a stone mason in Black Mountain who I knew through old-time music. I was cleaning hotel rooms. The first thing I recorded was *Ways of the World*.

Craig: Yes.

Rayna: I think I was 23, not that long after I'd gotten out of college, and John Herrmann, my banjo-playing friend John Herrmann, was like, "I think you should record an album." I was like, "Really? Huh." He just kept after me about it and was like, "No, really. I think it'd be good for you to do that. You play some cool tunes and you've got people around here that you play with." He's like, "Everyone would do it for free." Just put a plan together to record.

Paul Brown came over and set up a mobile rig in the Kittredge Theater at Warren Wilson, just on the stage there. Just in the course of a weekend, we recorded this whole thing. Paul charged me way too little. None of the musicians charged me anything to play. If that's not a testament to a supportive community, I don't know what is because that was a game-changer for me. That was a huge part of the reason that I wound up being a professional musician. Right after I graduated from college, I went up and helped John Cohen catalog all of his negatives and proof sheets and I just lived with him for five weeks.

Craig: Oh my gosh. How did you score that?

Rayna: John had this big thing he had to deal with and he didn't have loads of energy at the time. He was recovering from cancer and he had this idea that he was going to be able to just set me in his barn with all of his stuff and have me deal with it, but it turned out that the way it was, it was just kind of a mess, and he actually needed to be involved with this process of organizing everything.

I had this absolutely mind-blowing experience of just sitting with John Cohen and looking through every image he had ever taken and having him talk about everybody in the pictures and when things happened.

Craig: Do you have a story you could tell?

Rayna: There were all sorts of magical things. There was a wonderful experience of loving these photos of Mike Seeger and his first wife. There were these images of this party and she had a pipe. She was smoking a pipe in these pictures. I just was freaking out about this woman. I was like, "Oh, my God, John, who is this woman? I love her. I want to hang out with her." He was like, "Oh, you know—" and he was talking about the context of this party and that was Mike's first wife.

And then, completely crazy, the next day, we were down in Manhattan and we were walking down the street and she appeared. She just walked up to John. My mind was so totally blown. I was like, "Oh my God, you're that woman from the photograph." I couldn't even express to her. I was like, "I'm obsessed with you. You're awesome." She was like, "Great. Okay. Anyway, nice to see you John." I was like, "What are the chances of that happening?" I mean, he's still a very dear friend.

My first real pro gig was an accident, really, which was with Ira Bernstein, a great percussive dancer. He used to do these really big European tours doing this one-man dance show. He's used a few different fiddlers for these shows, but at the time, he was using Ruthie Dornfeld a lot and she couldn't do this one tour and so he was looking for someone who could play all these different styles of music and I was like, "Well, I can't. I don't know how to do that." He was like, "I think you can learn."

I basically had this moment of, like, "Yes, totally, I'm going to do this," just because I wanted to go to Europe. I'd never left the country. In the end, what happened was Ira just hooked me and Ruthie up. We just hung out and she taught me all the material for the show. I got this act together and go on this tour. And in order to go on that tour, I wound up having to quit all the odd jobs that I'd been doing. I came back and it was like now do I get more work or do I look for gigs? I started trying to look for more gigs.

Craig: How old are you at this point?
Rayna: 22, 23.

Craig: Yes.
Rayna: Then I wound up joining the Freight Hoppers on guitar, and I didn't play guitar. Once again it was like, "Here, learn how to do this." [Laughter.] I was like, "Ahh." Not long after I started playing with them, we played MerleFest. I just didn't have the calluses for it. I remember sitting backstage soaking my fingers in salt water because they were just throbbing. I was in so much pain.

Then, yes, I was floating around doing random things and the Uncle Earl thing came up, which that band already existed. Again, it was a situation where their fiddler couldn't make this one weekend of gigs, so they asked me to come out and play. I was like, "Oh, sure, I'll do that. That sounds fun." I did that and then they wound up asking me to join the band. I really wasn't sure because it wasn't an old-time band, and I was really such a profound old-time geek. I wasn't sure it was going to satisfy me because it wasn't hardcore. But I just really connected with them as people and wanted to spend more time with them. That was a really important thing for me to do because—

Craig: How many years was that?
Rayna: I was active in that band for five years. I did leave the band in 2008.

Craig: What'd you learn from that experience?
Rayna: I learned so much from the whole Uncle Earl experience. A huge part of it for me was letting go of my own ideas about what old-time music was.

Craig: What did it become to you?
Rayna: I still personally have my own ideas about, as my dad would say, what's idiomatically correct. I know old-time music when I hear it. I actually never, ever referred to Uncle Earl as an old-time band. I referred to it as a string band, and we did some old-time music, but we did so many other things. The thing that was important for me was that it was an experience of genuine collaboration with other

people who were coming from different musical places than I was, and I couldn't expect them to care about the same things I did. We all had different priorities as far as just aesthetically, our priorities were really different.

It was a super important experience of working with people who had different aesthetics than me and embracing that instead of being like, "No, you're wrong."

Craig: How did you balance that with the reverence for the music or did that problem ever pop up?

Rayna: Oh, it would pop up sometimes. Every once in a while, I would actually say something like, "No, we're not going to do that to that song" or that tune. "Sorry, you guys." Because my relationship with this music is so personal, it's associated with home and family for me. Prior to Uncle Earl, I felt like people doing things with traditional music, like changing it, modernizing it, purposefully making it their own, I saw that as an ego trip. I saw that as people saying this is not good enough as it is. I need to do something, spiff it up somehow. That was how I interpreted that.

Because of my experience in Uncle Earl, I saw that you can be completely reverent about the source recording and the traditional context and aesthetic and also do something else with it, and those are just two different things. It's not saying this is worthless and this is cool. It's saying, "Hey, look, here's something else that you can do with the same material and it's not negating anything." That was a lesson for me because previously I really saw it as being dismissive of the source or the aesthetic of the original version.

Craig: Yes. Somebody finally said it the appropriate way that it makes sense. You're not being irreverent in "it's traditional music, leave it be." You have the right to do creative things. You said it so well. Thank you for doing that.

Rayna: That's the move from feeling protective … like I had to protect something that was endangered to instead feeling really open and free about it and trusting that the music is going to be okay. There's so many people who care about it and love it, that there are always going to be different ways of interacting with it. To just trust that process and not feel like it's my job to police it in some way has been a load off my mind.

Craig: When you go to Clifftop, when you go to jam with some other people, it's a new way of approaching the conversation of the tune. And when you allow other people to creatively explore, it's that trust factor that you mentioned. We all trust each other with this. Oh, that was so eloquent. You're really good at this.

Rayna: You're such a cheerleader.

Craig: What do you want to do now? What's next?

Rayna: Well, I was a professional musician for years before I actually decided that I wanted to be a professional musician, if that makes any sense. I really did just fall into it, and I kept thinking it was going to dry up and I was going to go to grad school or something, but I actually had a moment when I made the decision about it.

We were at Telluride and Gillian Welch and David Rawlings had a set there. It was watching their set. I was so bowled over by the power of what they were doing with just voices and guitars. I realized that it was worth devoting your life to perform music. There was some part of my brain that wasn't fully valuing it even though, obviously, I value music immensely.

I just had this moment where I was like, "Oh my God, *the world needs more music*. I can totally do this. I can give my energy to this. It's okay for me to say this is what I'm doing as a career because music does actually change people's lives and it's a completely worthwhile thing to do full-time."

The old-time aesthetic has really served me well as a musician in other contexts, accompanying singer-songwriters, or sitting in with a rock band ... all these different contexts. Yes, I mean, old-time musicians are used to doing pretty simple, straightforward stuff and so there isn't this sense of "When's my solo? When's my moment to shine?"

I'm perfectly happy to play a drone through an entire song if that's actually the thing that serves the song best. I feel like my sense of what it is to be on stage is different because I am an old-time musician. It isn't about "And now, let me share myself with you." Right now, I've started playing music with my husband, Jeff Keith. We're doing a tour in the UK next month. I've gotten into teaching in a way that I never was so into it.

Craig: How so?

Rayna: I used to go, "Well, okay, I guess I'll try to teach some people a tune." I didn't think in a terribly profound way about teaching. I feel like I'm so much more into it now than I used to be. I get so much from my students now and learn so much every time I try to teach somebody something. Just this year, I've already had a couple incredible week-long workshop experiences.

I taught at the John C. Campbell Folk School and had this transcendent teaching experience. Then, just a couple weeks ago, I was over in the UK at the Sore Fingers Week. Again, I had an amazing group and amazing week of basically learning from my students. It was really so cool. I'm endlessly moved by the connection that music creates between people. I could have done a lot of other things and I'm sure it would've been fine, but I feel really lucky that this is what I've gotten to do.

Craig: By the way, is that your grandfather's fiddle?

Rayna: Great-grandfather's.

Craig: Wonderful.

Rayna: Yes. Dan's grandpa's.

We actually don't know a whole lot about this fiddle, but it was my great-grandpa George Steiner's. I've shown it to a few different fancy violin people and they haven't been able to identify where it's from. There's no label, but around turn of the century, Czech or German or possibly Hungarian. He was Hungarian. That's what I've learned. Dan used to play this one, and when I got serious into classical music, he was like, "Oh, you should probably use this. It's better instrument." Then, of course, I ran off with it and started playing old-time music. At one point, he did say something to me about it, like, "Ah, I never should have given you that fiddle."

12

David Holt

Asheville, North Carolina, 2015

As a college student, David developed a lifelong reverence for early traditional music performers. He spent time learning from them, photographing them, and, later on, featuring their music and stories in radio and television productions.

David received degrees in art and teaching. He started the Appalachian music program at Warren Wilson College in 1975.

David was a *Hee Haw* TV show regular—and frequently appeared on the Grand Old Opry.

David has won four Grammys at the time of our filming. He is also a non-stop student and promoter of traditional music.

"I really love the people, I really love the culture, and I really love the music. There's something powerful in this music that you can't put down in words. It's a force of nature. This music is a force of nature!"

Old-Time Community Role: The *Promoting Producer.* It's one thing to be talented on your own. It's another to complement a troupe of performers. And it's even better if you can assist older, age-challenged artists continue their exemplary careers. David did all that (and has the Grammys to prove it). But David produced even more, saving and documenting his peers' stories and history along the way. And if that wasn't enough, he taught his skills and shared his knowledge with others. Some saw it as entertainment, and others have gone on to continue carrying the flame of his legacy by giving back to the community he so deeply loves.

Craig Evans: What are some of your favorite memories with the music?

David: Being on stage with Doc Watson, and we're playing "Shady Grove" and looking over, he's really whooping the harmony. He's playing harmony to me, playing the lead, and the timing is absolutely perfect. This is like, "Oh man, this is it. I'm in heaven right now."

I love these guys—being with Roy Acuff and Grandpa Jones, and hanging backstage at the *Hee Haw* show, and telling jokes and stories and then singing something. These are guys I'm reading about in books, and they're my buddies. I was like, "God, what more could you want?"

Craig: David Holt, thank you for sitting down to talk about old-time music. I consider you the ambassador of folk traditions. You have done so many things that not only talk about the beautiful history this music is, but you've brought present performers to other people, and you're providing for the future by doing the shows you're doing today to document this incredible music.

David: It's a lot of work, but it's fun work. I love doing it.

David Holt. Studying, saving and making musical history.

Craig: You've spent your life doing it, too, so I know it's your calling.

David: Yes, it's definitely a calling.

Craig: I'd like to find out more of your history today—the things most meaningful to you. Where would you like to start? How about something as simple as when did you first hear the music?

David: I would say the first time I heard some quirky odd music was when my dad and granddad played the bones, which had been passed down in my family. Now these guys were engineers and lawyers. They weren't musicians. We had a pair of bones made by my great, great grandfather during the American Civil War.

To have my dad and my granddad sit around doing this was, like, "Wow, what is that?" Of course, I had to learn, because it was the '50s when I was a little kid. It was songs like "How Much Is That Doggy in the Window?" I didn't care anything about that. But that older stuff really interested me.

My uncle played a little bit of fiddle, so I heard that. I grew up in Texas. We moved to California when I was 10, grew up around Pacific Palisades. I went to high school there and college in San Francisco. Now this was the beginning of the hippie era, and so there was lots of music. My neighbors were people like Jimmy Hendrix and folks like that. They weren't famous at all.

What happened to me is I dropped out of college to see if I wanted to teach elementary school and got a job at a private elementary school. The very first night I was there, I was being put up in the school building. Some guys came out of the blue and jumped me for no reason. They didn't know me, but I guess it was against the school. It was a liberal school. They broke my jaw, and almost killed me. I just turned 21. This experience made me realize that life is short, and you better do what you want to do.

I didn't really know what I wanted to do, but one of the teachers there had a 78 RPM record collection with a lot of old cowboy songs. One was Carl Sandburg singing "I Ride an Old Paint," which really got to me. He had Carl Sprague singing "Bury Me Not on the Lone Prairie." Somebody told me that Carl Sprague was still alive in Texas, not far from where my parents were living. They had moved back to Texas when I went away to college. So I went to see him. Now I'm 21, and Carl Sprague was in his 80s. He was the first cowboy singer ever to record. He recorded in 1927. He started the western part of country western music.

I thought this was so incredible. He was so nice and showed me how to play the cowboy lick on the guitar. He showed me how to do that tongue-thumping-type harmonica playing. I said, "This is great. I gotta learn more about this."

I went back into college in Santa Barbara and met a buddy named Steve Keith, who's a wonderful clawhammer banjo player. About the same age, Steve and I started getting together. I was started playing the guitar. I'm about 22 now. We went to see Ralph Stanley at a concert at UC Santa Barbara—about 30 people attended.

After the show, I got really excited about his clawhammer style. If you've ever seen Ralph Stanley do that stuff, he learned from his mother. It is like flying and just kicking. I went up to him afterwards, asking, "Where can I go to learn that?" There were no books or DVDs or anything like that in those days. He said, "Oh, well, you need to go back to Clinch Mountain where I live or Mount Airy. There's a lot of music there. Galax has a lot of music, and there's a lot of music in Asheville," he said.

It was the summer of 1969, and Steve Keith and I got into my old pickup truck and we left Santa Barbara. We traveled all through the Southern mountains for three months. The whole summer we were going from one fiddlers' convention to another, meeting old timers. I realized the banjo, the clawhammer-style banjo, was a magical tool that opened up this world. We would go see these old mountain people in between the fiddlers' conventions. People would say, "Come stay a week with us." We thought they were being nice, but we'd go stay a week with them.

Anyway, it was like the clawhammer banjo was this magic thing. They hadn't seen that style in years. Their grandparents played that style, but everybody now was playing two-finger or mostly Scruggs' style. Steve would take out his banjo, and he would start to clawhammer and people would say, "Come on in." It was magic. I said, "I want to learn that. Man, I gotta have some of that."

This was 1969. If you think about it, there was Hobart Smith who was the older guy who could really play on the banjo—play all the notes you wanted to hear. Ahead of us was somebody like Tommy Thompson. He was taking the tunes and playing them pretty much like the way the fiddlers played them.

I watched Steve real closely, and he showed me the basic lick. Then as we went around the Southern mountains, I recorded this stuff on the tape recorder, and then tried to do it myself. I love the banjo because you can play these gorgeous melodies like "Forked Deer" or something like that. My goal was to add as many of the notes as possible without losing the drive and the rhythm. If you start losing the drive and the rhythm by having too many notes, then cut back. This style was, in a way, being invented in those days.

Craig: What was your major in college?

David: I have degrees in biology and in art. Then I went back for a fifth year to get a teaching credential.

Craig: Did you ever use your degree?

David: No, much to my parents' consternation. I use the art all the time. Now I'm actually doing art, but I do it in designing album covers and stuff like that for myself. I used the biology because I love nature. I taught in college. I started the Appalachian Music program at Warren Wilson College in 1975.

Craig: Laura Boosinger told me some wonderful stories about attending your classes. She talked about how, if you had an interest in something, you developed classes around your interest.

David: That's true.

Craig: The beautiful thing about that was when you taught, you taught with passion because you were learning at the same time you were helping other people learn.

David: Laura was one of my star students. Still is. Great lady, great player, great singer. I had a class in the history of country music, and I took them down to see the Opry. As I was watching, I was thinking, "Man, this is so boring." Grandpa was pretty much the only guy still kicking that was playing a lot of old-time music, but they didn't have him on the show that I saw. When I got back home, I called Hal Durham, the manager of the Opry. I said, "You need to have some old-time music on the Opry." He said, "I'd like to, but I don't know anybody that plays anymore."

I said, "I do." He said, "Come on down and show me what you can do." My friend Anne Romaine said, "If you go down there, don't put on blue jeans and a shirt or something. You get dressed up the way you're going to be on the Opry." I bought a white suit and a white hat and had a pretty banjo made like that. I went down there and really tried to make an impression, and he loved it.

I was born in '46. Now I was on the Opry in 1980. Then *Hee Haw* called me shortly after the Opry. All that happened right in the early '80s.

Craig: What was it like working on the cast of *Hee Haw*?

David: It was fun. You went for the week. If I was being used, it was usually in the four banjo players, the four harmonica players, and this opening of the second half of the show. The rest of the time, I could hang around to talk to people. It was great to hear their stories because this was really like a little family.

Craig: You're living in Asheville by this time, right?

David: Yes. I came here with no intention of making a living, and I fell in love with Asheville. At that time there were hundreds of musicians around here. Old guys and girls that were born in the 1800s. I was like, "Man, I've just stumbled on the Lost World." I had no intention of making a living—but I wanted to learn this stuff. There was an old fellow named Byard Ray who really took me under his wing. A lot of people did, but Byard would come over every night and play with me, teach me how to shade a tune.

David in his white suit with his pretty banjo, his first appearance at the Grand Ole Opry in 1980.

Craig: Shading. What does shading mean?

David: A fiddle tune would have the basic notes. He would teach me the notes all around it to fill it out and give it some groove. This woman named Martha Ashmire came and wrote an article on me for the *Asheville Citizen-Times*. The article had a big eight-by-ten picture in the paper, with a whole page devoted to my story about a guy coming from California to learn mountain music. That's how odd it was.

Nobody here was really doing that. The article got people calling and saying, "Well, would you come play for my little church group or my school or something?" and I didn't know anything about performing. The public library called, which was my first concert. When I was standing there doing the show, I realized I like this performing thing. It's fun trying to get people to care what you're doing about something that's so old—something they don't even know anything about. It slowly built up.

Craig: I did read an interview about you one time where you talked about how you developed your work ethic, and it involved a conversation with your mother and your brother. You're driving past a field. Do you mind telling that story?

David Holt: I was a little boy. The spiritual home of our family was in Gatesville, Texas, because this is where all the grandparents lived, and I was born there. We were driving back from the grocery store one day. It's August, and we're visiting in Gatesville out in the country, surrounded by cotton fields, thousands of acres of cotton growing. My mother's really mad at my brother and me.

Craig: What did you do?

David Holt: Oh, we went to the grocery store. If you can imagine this, a parent wouldn't buy us the jar of Ovaltine that had the coupon for the Captain Midnight decoder ring in it.

Craig: You still remember that?

David: Oh, I wanted that decoder ring so bad. She wouldn't buy it. We kept asking her for it while going down the road. My mother gets mad real fast. She pulls the car over and says, "Get out of the car." She marches my brother and me up to the foreman of the crew of about 50 Black people out there working, picking cotton. She said, "I got these two little boys who never worked a day in their lives." She's holding us. "Could you put them to work, and show them what hard work really is?"

I guess the foreman said, "Yes, maybe. We'll put these two little white boys out to work in August. Let them see what it's like."

He gave us each a cotton bag. Now, cotton bags are about this big around and about 10 feet long, and he put it over our little shoulders and showed us how to get the cotton out of this thing, but there's stickers all over it. If you don't know how to get in there and get that thing, in no time, your hands are bleeding. We're down there crying, and Mother's up at the car. The foreman sneaks up behind my brother and me because he could see that he was in over his head. He sings out, "There's a long white robe in heaven I know."

From all around us come these beautiful Black voices, singing low, "There's a long white robe in heaven I know. Good news. Good news." I was like, "Wow, we never heard anything like that before," and so we shut up and started picking cotton, doing it the whole rest of that day. At the end of the day, we picked about a quarter of a bag of cotton. He gave us a check for a dollar, which my mother would never let us cash.

Craig: Oh my gosh.

David: She hoped that would teach us the value of hard work, but it showed me the opposite. It showed me that I wanted to be a professional musician and be in the heart of music if I could be, right in the center of it.

Years later, I was telling that story in a concert with my mother in attendance. Now, my mother was a real character, *I Love Lucy*-type gal. She came up after the show. She said, "David, I got to admit something to you. Thank you for telling that story about me, but I had set that whole thing up." She said, "I wanted to teach you boys the value of hard work. I want you boys to learn that, and so I set it up with the foreman, with the landowner." She said, "I didn't know it was going to make you a professional musician." Life is what happens when you make other plans, Mama.

Craig: She didn't regret that, I'm sure.

David: No, no, she was proud, and she loved having stories about her.

Craig: You're in Asheville, and you're performing.

David: Starting to perform.

Craig: You're finding out that you like to perform; what happens next?

David: If you're starting to perform, even now, you either have to play in bars, stay late at night, or play in schools and get up early in the morning. They're pretty much mutually exclusive. Like my friend John McCutcheon said, "Playing for a bunch of school kids is pretty much like playing for drunks anyway."

Craig: That's right.

David: I love kids. Well, gosh, I was at the doctor yesterday, and this young guy, well, he wasn't young, he was 50, he said, "You came to my school and played for me, and that's the reason I play saxophone today." I meet guys and gals like this all the time. I have played live for over a million children at their schools. That's a lot of concerts, buddy.

Craig: It changed somebody's life. The moment you took with the music changed somebody's life.

David: As I started getting gigs, I realized, "I could make a little living doing this." Then, when I had kids, I thought, "I have to make a living doing this." I loved doing it. I found that the way to do it for me was to add a variety of instruments because from then to now, most of the audiences you're playing for don't know anything about the music. They don't know about the history. They don't know about the instruments. They don't know about the sounds. If you can entertain them with those sounds—not in a stupid way, but in a fun way—because I think people like to think. I think a person who is given a new thought is as entertained as a person who's heard a joke. I try to combine both of those things, humor and things that are real.

Craig: You've expanded into many areas. You've put together DVDs on how to play the banjo. On a more spectacular level, you took some of these players national, such as Doc Watson, to talk about old-time music. Can you talk a little bit about how that happened?

David: Well, my first experience, really, except for being on *Hee Haw*, with real episodic television, North Carolina PBS asked me to do a show called *Folkways*. In 1980, I did my first one, and we would go visit not only music people but craftspeople. There's only 30 shows, and they play them all the time. People who are in it, it's made them famous by being in that show because they play it so much here.

Then the Nashville Network started in 1984. Cable was completely new, and Nashville was one of the channels, along with CNN and with MTV. Nobody knew what was going to happen with any of that. I was the representative of the Nashville Network because the press out in California and New York didn't care about country music stars. They didn't even know who they were. They knew who Dolly Parton was, and that was it. I was the guy doing this weird thing, playing the mouth bow and the banjo and the hambone and all that stuff. They liked that. We did 95 half-hour *Fire on the Mountain* shows.

Craig: Oh my gosh.

David: If anybody can ever get that released, it's the most complete documentary of traditional mountain music from the '80s and '90s that there is. CBS owns it, and it's locked up. I hosted the *Riverwalk Jazz* radio show for public radio for 25 years. People are always surprised. "Oh, that's you? Well, I thought you were a banjo player." I didn't play on the show. I was a host and helped write it and told the stories. It ran from 1989 to 2012.

To me, it completely fit because it's what the Black folks were doing in the cities, in the golden age of music, which was in the '20s and '30s. That was the golden age of old-time music, the golden age of classic jazz. It's all right in there together. I'm proud of doing those shows.

And I really love photography. I think that may end up being some of my best stuff because in some cases the photos I took have become the iconic shots. If you look at a picture of Tommy Jarrell, you'll probably find it was my picture.

David: John Hartford was a good friend of mine. Remember I mentioned I was on the Opry that very first time? I had the white suit and the white hat and the banjo? Well, I got up there to play—I was going to play solo. I didn't know what I was going to play. I could do an Uncle Dave Macon tune. You know what? I'm going to play the paper bag because I know they've never seen that. I bet it'll tear them up. The paper bag and the harmonica, this is a very rhythmic number. I'm playing "Lost John."

The next day I called John Hartford, and I said that I was a guy from Asheville, and he didn't know me, but could I come over? I really loved his stuff, and I play banjo. He said, "Sure, come on over." I go to his house, and we were talking. He said, "Man, I was listening to the Opry last night, and there was this guy playing the paper bag. I would love to meet that guy." I laughed and said, "Here I am."

Craig: That's mighty impressive.

David: On this shelf are my Grammy awards. I actually have four, but the one I'm really proud of is this one with Doc Watson, the *Legacy* CD, because I feel like it ended up being Doc's biography. He didn't want a written biography, and I said, "Well, let's speak it. You just tell it the way you want to tell it." We were both pretty excited when we won a Grammy in 2002.

Doc Watson (left) and David Holt in the early 2000s. Two of the greatest performers of traditional music (courtesy David Holt).

Craig: You've set goals for yourself, and you've accomplished them, coming here to Asheville to learn more about the music, becoming a performer, moving into television, continuing to educate people. What motivates you to do this?

David: One thing simply follows another, but I love doing it, and it seems that this is something I know a lot about. I can host a television show, which is a very particular skill—getting up and doing an intro and trying to not look like an idiot. It's a skill that takes a long time to learn, so there's no reason not to use it.

My goals now, I would love to see this *David Holt's State of Music* become a series. That would be great, but if it doesn't, I'm 68 years old now, so the thing is to keep playing because my main mentor was Doc Watson, and I played the last 14 years of his life with him and watched him during the very last few years start to lose some of his incredible ability. He was almost 89 years old, and as I get older, I see that's not easy to do—to keep playing at a high quality 'til you're in your mid-80s, that's something.

Craig: Let's talk about Doc a bit. In the 14 years you played with Doc, what did you learn?

David: Oh, man, I learned to pick up my feet when I walk. A blind person doesn't drag his feet. I learned that looking for really good key-lime pie is a good thing on the road because it keeps you on your toes and it's really hard to find. I learned to pay attention to every note and really listen to the note. Being blind was an asset for Doc in that way. He could never look around to see if the audience was interested in him, so he was completely in the tune.

Even when we would do a sound check, he wouldn't play only like five seconds of the tune and say, "That sounds all right." He'd play the whole dang song and play it with soul, and his emotions were very close to his surface. He was a fierce person, but not fierce in a mean way.

Craig: Intense?

David: Intense, yes. Thing about Doc is, he knew what to leave out or what to put in. I don't think anybody beats Doc, and if you give him a solo, he's not going to just blow you away with his stuff. He might occasionally, but he's going to play something that makes you feel something, and that I love.

Craig: If somebody looks at some of your work 200 years from now, what do you want them to recognize most through the work that you've archived?

David: I really love the people, I really love the culture, and I really love the music. There's something powerful in this music you can't put it down in words. It's a force of nature. This music is a force of nature!

13

James "Sparky" Rucker

Knoxville, Tennessee, 2018

"There's a part of me that's always the teacher. I think if people are informed, they make correct decisions. We have to get better. Otherwise, what's the point of being on this planet if we don't change and make it better?"

Sparky comes from a family of preachers, artists, musicians, and cops. He is a Civil War historian and Civil Rights activist.

"[I teach people to] try and get past the things that hurt you. If you understand it, then you can control it. It's the ignorance of something … it's what makes it offensive and hurtful."

As both a performer and a teacher, Sparky has dedicated his life to teaching people through and about this music.

Old-Time Community Role: The *Peacemaker*. Sparky has always been a teacher. As he says, "If I know it, I want you to know it." Sparky's favorite subject and cause is peace. And his life is a testament to kindness and understanding. He's the best of the best when it comes to being a loving human being.

James "Sparky" Rucker: There's a part of me that's always the teacher. It's my mother—and it's the old saying, "Don't throw the baby out with the bathwater." I began to realize that I have to sift through these things to learn history—because there's always a calling of truth in all of these songs and stories. I found that if I tell the stories before I sing the songs, it takes away the offensive part because people understand where the things are coming from. I think if people are informed, they make correct decisions. We have to get better. Otherwise, what's the point of being on this planet if we don't change and make it better?

Craig: James "Sparky" Rucker, Grammy-nominated musician, historian, author, and storyteller to audiences of all ages. Your venues include the Kennedy Center, Smithsonian Folklife Festival, Mountain Stage, International Storytelling Festival, and NPR's *Prairie Home Companion*. You have dedicated your life to teaching people through and about this music. You're an emissary of peace. I thank you for that, but thank you most for sitting down today to talk about traditional music.

Sparky: Yes, well, don't make my head much bigger than it is, because we won't be able to get in and out the door.

Craig: All right, so life started for you here in Knoxville.

Sparky: Yes.

Craig: Okay, tell me about your mom and your dad.

Sparky: My father was born in a family of 12 kids: six boys, six girls. His daddy was a Church of God sanctified preacher who became the bishop of that church. They started out in Athens, Tennessee, which is about 50 miles south of here. When about half the kids were born, they moved to Knoxville where he started the church. He expanded that church to Nashville and then up into Chicago and Detroit. Then he actually took the church down to Haiti and Jamaica. This is a man that I didn't meet except for the first year of my life. My grandfather died when I was a year old.

James "Sparky" Rucker. A devoted teacher of peace and understanding.

My father, after he came back from World War II, was an insurance salesman for a short time, then he joined the Knoxville police force, where he rose to the rank of captain. I'm very proud of that fact, because when you realize the period of time during Jim Crow, he actually gained some respect in this community. Of course, him being a cop ended up affecting me, because I grew up in the projects until about 14 to 15 years old, and finally, through a GI loan, he was able to build a home. If you live in the projects and your dad is a cop, then you think about that for a while, like hearing, "Your dad is the man that threw my dad in jail."

I'm this shy kid. Most people don't believe me when I say that. I found that most people who have art in their life probably have some of that shyness in them, and art is the way you express yourself. I was a loner, because I didn't have many friends except the nerdy ones. Then I was a Boy Scout. My mother was a homemaker, but she was an artist. I got all of my art from Mom, as well as the permission to do this for a living, even though I'm going to school to learn to do something else. This is what I ended up doing because, as they say, "God didn't close the door without opening a window."

Craig: Was this painting versus music?

Sparky: I was a painter, then fine arts painting. Then I switched to education because people said, "How are going to make a living? You going to sell them paintings?" I was an art education teacher and taught in Chattanooga schools for a while. During the Vietnam War, I was a draft counselor, because I didn't want to have all these kids I'm teaching end up going over there dying on Michelin Tires' rubber tree plantations, guarding those trees. All those kind of war things that are for the rich people to profit from and poor people are paying for it with their lives.

So that's what nudged me into being the person I am. Of course, growing up Black, I grew up in Jim Crow all the way—Jim Crow existed in the South until after I graduated college. All of these things formed me into being the person I became and not realizing that this was what was happening. These kind of things—well, how do you change this world? I look back, and it was partly my father who had a very good sense of social justice, and my mother who was a very caring Girl Scout leader. She knew how to cook and taught me how to cook. She was a teacher assistant while she was still a stay-at-home mother.

I was one of the lucky ones in the projects as I had both parents. I knew I was loved. I knew that there were people who'll protect me and had this big family on my father's side. Like I said, all these aunts and uncles, they were all sort of musically inclined singers in church. I had a little bit of prestige in my family because my dad was a cop. In fact, one funny thing was that my father would get phone calls in the middle of the night about some problem. He'd say, "Well, that's not my jurisdiction...." Their reply: "Well, you're a cop, ain't you?" They knew he was the one they would depend on. I started realizing that I had parents who took care of other people.

Every Christmas, my father would load up these boxes of food that he would take around to certain families he knew didn't have any money and no Christmas dinner. He would be there for them. As a kid, seeing this kind of thing, I'd realize, "Wow, you have to take care of the people around you. You have to take care of this community that sustains you." That's what it's all about. As I always say, why are we here if we're not here for each other? Working in the Chattanooga school system, and being this draft counselor at the same time, got me into a lot of trouble, because this was at the time when everybody was for the war in Vietnam, saying, "You're not a patriot because you don't want to support this war." I was drafted five times from age 18 to 27.

I found ways to say, "Wait a minute, if I'm going to put my life on the line, and if I'm going to fight for something, it's going to be a reason I want to fight, and not because you want me to do it." When I found myself not being able to work anymore because I was in trouble from all the draft counseling I was doing then, for a time, I worked as an advocate for a social-change workforce, something called the Council of the Southern Mountains. This job took me into coal country. All of a sudden, I'm trying to use the things that I've learned as a Civil Rights worker to try to help poor white people up in eastern Kentucky and southwestern Virginia.

This ends up being even scarier, because these people know I'm there trying to help them to get black lung recognized as a real disease, as well as helping the people who were trying to get unions into some of these non-union mines. People were dying. People were getting shot. All these people saw was a Black man living in their area who doesn't have the respect to jump off the sidewalk anytime a white person came through. I'm thinking, "What? I'm up here trying to help these people, and all they see is a Black man they're wanting to threaten."

It was a scary time. Then, I was like, "Well, what else can I do?" A friend who had moved up to Canada called, saying, "Why don't you come up and play some folk music? I got you a week-long gig at a place called the Ting Tea Room up in Winnipeg, Manitoba." That's how I started doing this for a living.

Craig: Tell me about the music from your family.

Sparky: Yes. Both Mother and Father sang in the church choir—my father because that was his daddy's church. He and his brothers and sisters were all wonderful singers. Oh my God, I wish you could hear them singing. They were so good. In fact, they were the children's choir. Then after my grandfather died when I was a year old, they started having these memorial services for him the first Sunday in May every year, with people coming from all over to honor him and talk about what he had done to build up the church. I would hear all this music.

Then, as I got older, they started letting me be in the choir, too. My mother had a wonderful alto voice. My father had a wonderful, window-shaking bass voice. In the mornings, when he would be getting ready to go to work, he'd be in there shaving, you'd hear him singing all these gospel songs. Then you'd hear Mom all of a sudden start with the harmony. This is the way I grew up, hearing all this music. When my wife, Rhonda, and I record, we add voices to the recordings. I get to do all these sounds that I hear in my head, all the harmonies and things like that, so when the recording goes out, people hear the way I'm hearing it in my head.

When I was about 11 years old, I talked my parents into buying me a guitar, a little plastic guitar, but it was a real guitar. It had a little device that fit over the fretboard that you press a button and it would make the chord. It was kind of like an autoharp kind of thing. One day, that thing broke. I had to actually learn how to play the guitar. When I started doing this for a living, my father was upset because he'd spent all this money sending me to college. In 1964, I was one of the first Black undergraduates to go to the University of Tennessee.

This was during the Civil Rights movement. I was learning to sing freedom songs, and that's what got me into doing the old slave songs—and introduced me to the blues. My father was upset because he'd spent all this money for me to get my degree. "Now you're going to throw this all away? You're not teaching?" My mother said, "JD"—that's what she called him, James David—JD, why don't you come and watch him play?" She talked him into coming to a concert at the Laurel Theater. My father was sitting there, and Mom said he leaned over to her and said, "He's good, ain't he?" After that, every time we played in town, he'd be sitting in the front row and always requesting one song in particular that he wanted me to do.

Craig: That was?

Sparky: It was "Tramp on the Street," a song from the '30s, talking about that Lazarus was only a tramp that day.

> Only a tramp was Lazarus that day.
> He would lay down at the rich man's gate.
> He begged for some crumbs from the rich man to eat.
> But they left him to die like a tramp on the street.

It goes on…

> He was some mother's darling, some mother's son.
> Once he was fair, once he was young.
> Some mother rocked him, her little darling to sleep.
> But they left him to die like a tramp on the street.

Then it goes on talking about Jesus being born, but they killed him. It's a wonderful song. My daddy really loved it. He had never heard that song until he heard me singing it, and it ended up being one of his favorite songs.

Craig: I'm curious. I want to connect a thread. From the time you went to Winnipeg to the time you came back, you went from Civil Rights to the Civil War to some degree. Is there a way to connect that? Is there one connection? Tell me how that worked.

Sparky: In one of those projects that I lived in, we didn't have many toys. You played outside a lot. I would dig and play in the dirt and stuff. I started finding these things that I thought were bullets that my father had used; then we found out that were Minié balls. The project had been built right along the Confederate siege lines of the Civil War's Battle of Knoxville. Because of my understanding of history, and knowing how important the Civil War was in terms of changing things for African Americans in this country, I began to become a Civil War historian.

In fact, somewhere in my collection I still have the first book my mother bought me as a kid, a little picture book, *History of the Civil War*. When I first started touring, it was mostly playing old-time blues. It was through the Civil Rights movement that I met people like the Reverend Pearly Brown, who was a blind street singer from Americus, Georgia, who taught me how to play slide guitar. A guy named Babe Stovall was also on some of those tours, the Southern Folk Revival Project tours. He was the New Orleans blues man.

When I started traveling as a folk musician, that's the kind of music I played. I had been playing rock and roll, electric guitar all through high school and into college. Then in the Civil Rights movement, you have the acoustic guitar, you're singing the slave songs, the freedom songs. I started making that connection in my head—had Lincoln not signed that Emancipation Proclamation, and the Union army not freed all those Black men who joined the Union army, where 200,000 Black men fought to save this union, I realized, "Wow, that was a contribution to saving this country." I'm proud to say 40,000 of them came from Tennessee.

Rhonda and I beat Ken Burns by about six months on starting to do these Civil War songs because I first started doing things on the Buffalo Soldiers. While traveling out West, I started seeing how they had fought it certain places and helped to expand the country going West. I had talked Rhonda into playing with me, and she would wear some things expressing some of her Native American roots. I would dress like a soldier, learning some songs from that. Then we received a call from the battlefield at Petersburg. Somebody had heard about us and said, "Do you guys do any music and stories on the Civil War?" Rhonda was getting ready to tell him no, and I said, "Wait a minute. Ask him how much time do we have."

We had six months to get it together. I said, "Tell him yes, we can do it." This was about six months before Ken Burns' *The Civil War* show came out. The Civil War became something we were able to add to our shows. We have Appalachian programs, something on storytelling, and something on telling the history of the Civil Rights movement.

We had a thing called the "Blue and Gray and Black and White," telling the story of the Civil War from both the North and South, from both Black and white perspectives, to see how it affected everybody.

In the '60s, we celebrated the centennial of the Civil War—a hundred years. Well, I realized that in my grandfather's church and in my uncles' churches, there were these old Black people down in the front pew, some of them in the "amen corner," and people would say, "That's Sister Saffert. She used to be a slave." Then I started realizing the Civil War was not that long ago. The wounds are still fresh in people's minds. We have to tell the story, and we have to get past this thing and understand the pain that it inflicted on us. That's why today we're still having the political things, saving those statues, and all these kinds of things. Close to a million people died in that war. It's part of our psyche, especially down South.

I say to all my Northern friends, "They lost." They can go to the sites and point out where their grandfather, great grandfather died in that war. It's still real to them. I said, "The only way we're going to heal from this thing is if we explore it together." We have done family research. I've been able to trace my family back on both my mother's and father's sides, to people who were slaves. My great grandfather, Daniel Rucker—because Rucker's such a unique name, I went into McMinn County, where my father's family came from. I found only one man named Rucker down there who owned slaves, and this helped me narrow down where the name had come

Rhonda and Sparky Rucker. The best of musical educators.

from. Then I found out that that man died intestate—he did not leave a will. They had to list all of their property, including the names of all the slaves. I found my great-grandfather as a five-year-old boy in that listing.

Craig: Wow.

Sparky: Yes. On my father's mother's side, her name was Eliza Cunningham Fore. We had done research before all my aunts and uncles died. One of the oldest aunts, the one that nicknamed me Sparky, because when she saw me at six days old, she said, "Oh, look at his eyes. They're so sparkling." Because I was a junior, my nickname became Sparky. I think she knew that down the line I was going to become a blue singer—and it'd be a great nickname.

Craig: It worked.

Sparky: I think her name was Fore or Ford or something like that, and everybody else said, "Don't pay attention to her, she's got dementia." As we were down there looking through the graveyards, we found Eliza Fore, and all of a sudden, I realized, "Oh my God, that's my great-grandmother." We were able to get a picture of the tombstone from that. On my mother's side, her people had always talked about the fact that my great-grandmother on that side, her father had been the slave master. Her name was Harriet Carter, and she always told her kids that they were Virginia Carters. I don't know if you know how significant that is, but Robert Lee's mother was a Virginia Carter.

She would always say, "Don't you ever forget that you are a Virginia Carter." She named her kids after people who had connections to that family. All of a sudden, I start realizing why so many people on that side of the family looked white. Their father was the slave master. Having that ancestry from both sides, and people have been slaves, and people who've been slave owners, gives me a different perspective on things. I know that lately in this country, the descendants of both slaves and slave owners are starting to have these family reunions together on plantations because it's helping them to heal. They're also learning more about their families because the histories are so intertwined.

Craig: Right. You've been performing for 40 years now.

Sparky: Actually, it's closer to 50. We have to update our website.

Craig: When did you decide you needed to include messages like these in your programs?

Sparky: I think, Craig, it goes back to having been a school teacher. I've never stopped teaching. If I know it, I want you to know it. I told you I played rock and roll, played in a lot of bands. Well, when you're doing that, you stand on stage, and you play song after song after song. People are dancing and singing along, but when I went out as a solo performer, I started realizing I was wearing myself out because I had been just playing songs—so I started talking between songs.

Part of it was to try to explain to people why I thought the song I was getting ready to sing was important. I have found that ballads come from actual historic things that have happened. It was the way people passed stories along, back during medieval times. The minstrels that went from village to village would bring the stories with them, and later on, people started printing these broadside ballads. They were like protest songs. "The king, evil King John." In this country, it's different. The ballads that sprang up from American culture, most of them were written between about 1875 to about 1900. Things like "John Henry," "John Hardy," "Stagger Lee," and "Delia."

Craig: "Jesse James."

Sparky: "Jesse James." All these things came from the period of time that basically was when the Industrial Revolution was happening, and people were seeing their lives change. And so they started wanting to know the stories about things before everything had changed.

Craig: I want to back up to the bit about ballads, because for all their romance and all their history, oftentimes as we go back through ballads, especially English and Irish ballads, we are introduced to values from that period of time that are offensive by today's standards—things like the violence and the misogyny. Then when we go through minstrel music, it's reintroduced in the form of either racist or stereotypical stereotypes. When you approach a piece of music and some of these values are present, how do you approach it? I mean, what is worth saving, and what is worth rejecting, and if you reject it, how do you reject it?

Sparky: It's interesting you should mention minstrel songs because one of the classes I teach at music camps is the history of the minstrel. The minstrel shows because, number one, they were not all blackface minstrels. Every disenfranchised group did minstrel shows. There were Irish minstrel shows, poor white minstrel shows, and Pat and Mike Jokes, they were the end men in the Irish minstrel shows—like Bones and Tambo were in the blackface minstrel.

Craig: How far do you take it with minstrelsy? I mean, we have something like "Turkey in the Straw," an American icon for music, that has horrible…

Sparky: It's Jim Crow, this is where the old Jim Crow laws came from.

Craig: How do you approach something like that?

Sparky: Well, once again, when I'm teaching the classes, we talk about the politics of it. We talk about the songs or talk about … *this was offensive, this is why they put this in there*—and we'll actually sing the song. I'll sing them in the class, because I want people to hear it. I want them to see, but this is what survived from it. This is what became vaudeville—and what became the stand-up kind, the two comics of Abbott and Costello kind of things, which was originally part of the minstrel show. The minstrel show started out with a group of people sitting in a semi-circle with Bones and Tambo, Mr. Interlocutor, the only guy in whiteface, sitting in the middle, and he was the straight guy.

He was also a target for Bones and Tambo, because while they were making fun of Black people, these two were making fun of this white guy in the middle. Then I realized that everybody was kind of being lampooned. Then they would close the curtain and get ready to do a farce or a travesty in the background, but they had to have something to entertain. They would call this the "olio," when these two people would come out, usually Bones and Tambo, who would tell jokes back and forth, once while they were changing the stage, and then they would open up and that would be the rest of the show. I wanted people to understand this is how the entertainment industry in this country developed.

I mean, people loved Bing Crosby, but part of his shtick was doing blackface. Sure, I'm offended by that, but what's weird about it was that Black performers became minstrel performers who had actually blackened their skin. They were Black men imitating white people who had been imitating Black people. I mean, talk about a screwed-up system, but people need to know this. This was one of the reasons I decided I wanted to teach a class on this. Once again, try and get past the things that hurt you. If you understand it, then you can control it. The ignorance of something is what makes it offensive and hurtful.

Craig: If we don't talk about it, we don't learn.

Sparky: Yes, we don't learn a thing, and we keep making the same mistakes over and over again.

Craig: Who's entitled to talk about it?

Sparky: That is something people have asked me, and I say, well, that's one of the reasons I decided to do these classes because I know that white people can't teach this class.

Craig: What could a white person do?

Sparky: Well, there's certainly things that they can talk about in terms of their own culture. They can talk about the whole exploitation that, because especially these people, these nativists now keep saying, "I want my country back." Well, that's what I hear all my Native American friends saying. They want their country back, too. To understand what we did to the native population and where we did it, we did it in Australia, we did it in Africa. The people complained about this whole thing recently—talking about the "blank-hole countries." I said, "Do you realize that Europe colonized Africa, arrested its natural development, and when colonialism was finally thrown off, these people still had to go through the whole evolution?" That's why all these things are happening right now, because they're trying to go through what Europe went through centuries before when they were trying to work things out. You have to understand you are the reason that those countries are like that. Once again, if you teach people history, it makes it easier for them to understand and untangle the problems.

Craig: I think we would both acknowledge that if change is going to happen, it has to happen with us. We're the first level of how it happens. If somebody is at a festival, if somebody's at a Civil War reenactment, if somebody's at a Saturday morning jam or something like "Turkey in the Straw" comes up and somebody says, "Hey, I just heard a song called 'Zip Coon,'" and starts to sing it. What are people to do in that scenario?

Sparky: Instead of reacting … let me back up. We performed a concert in this county we're living in now, back about eight years ago. After the concert, this guy, who I'm sure would never vote the way I would vote, came up to me and said, "I want you to know I agree with about 95 percent of what you said."

I said, "Wow, my friends don't agree with 95 percent of what I say." I realized that's because people respect our music. I'm always constantly surprised when we perform in bluegrass-type situations. People see us, they love our music, even though maybe in their minds, they're wondering, what's that Black man doing with that white woman up on stage?

They love our music so much that they get past that. Because they like my music, and like me as a person, I found I can pull them aside and say, "You do know that what you just did offends people." Because I can do it that way, as opposed to getting angry at them, saying, "How dare you sing that 'Zip Coon' song," they'll listen to me.

Craig: But you did it one on one.

Sparky: Yes, it's because of the one-on-one thing—and not embarrassing them in front of a lot of people. If you attack somebody, their natural reaction is to try to react to what I just did, as opposed to…. I've got lots of friends who I have to say things like that to, but they do it to me, too. They let me know if I've done something offensive, because it has never been my intention to be offensive. *If I'm offensive, it's because I'm ignorant that I'm offensive.*

Craig: People that know you, trust you, they accept that. What we're coming back to is to be able to be brave enough to trust somebody.

Sparky: Yes, that's true.

Craig: Sparky, you're awesome.

Sparky: Like I say, I want to leave this world better than I found it. Yeah.

14

Clare Milliner

AVONDALE, PENNSYLVANIA, 2015

Clare Milliner majored in music performance and later became a lawyer.

"I look at old-time music as a way to have fun. I don't look at it as a way to get fame or fortune. It really saved my life in a very dark time. I found people that played old-time music, and they took me in and accepted me for who I was. I found that I was entering a community of people that are very caring."

What touches you most about the music?

"It's how it makes me feel when I hear it, then I want to play it. Then it's the fun of trying to work it out on the instrument. That's like problem-solving. Then it's like turning somebody else on to it, 'Hey, listen to this!' and you play it for them, and you share it. Then the fun of getting other people to play it, and then every time you hear it, you're in that place again. What do I love about it? Gosh, there's so much! I mean, what's not to like?"

"I can't imagine what my life would be like if I hadn't found it [the music]."

Old-Time Community Role: The *Wunderkind*. One of the strongest, smartest people I think I've ever met. Maybe life didn't exactly go her way early on, but it certainly didn't cramp her style. Clare is a fiddle-playing, tune-collecting, festival-hosting force of nature! Just lifting the book of tunes she wrote with Walt Koken requires strength (not for the faint of heart). But the challenge of learning and playing *all* of them, just for fun, in one sitting? Unbelievable!

Clare Milliner: I am the youngest of five kids. Mom loved music. In fact, she taught music in the public schools in Philadelphia in the '30s. She made sure we all learned an instrument, and mine was the violin. I'll tell you, she had to make me practice. It was not easy, but now I'm so thankful that she did that.

Craig: Clare, I had the good fortune of sitting down with Walt Koken earlier this morning, and as I told him, I consider the two of you—you are the first family of old-time music.

Clare: He might be. I don't know that I would characterize myself like that, but I'm more of a documenter.

Craig: In your performances with Walt, you inspired existing audiences in the present. And thanks to your documentary work, you have captured all these wonderful fiddle tunes to guarantee that this genre of music is going to be around for many years to come.

Clare: Well, it's true, but, you know, I look at old-time music as a way to have fun. I don't look at it as a way to get fame or fortune. It really saved my life in a very dark time. I found people that played old-time music, and they took me in and accepted me for who I was. I found that I was entering a community of people who are very caring.

Clare Milliner. Found herself in the music. Now saves music for others.

It's interesting because people that play old-time music seem to be mostly either professional or very, very skilled artisans. The carpenters that play old-time are the best. Then, in addition, there are a lot of professional people, doctors, a lot of doctors, and a fair number of lawyers, too.

I found myself in a community of really fascinating people. It almost felt like I was in a meditative state when playing with the people. A non-verbal communication goes on while you're playing, and it takes you out of the present moment, and it takes you someplace else. I found myself in places that I hadn't thought about in a long time and places that I had never been before. I still find that happens, but in the beginning, it was really intense. I was hooked on it.

Craig: I want to pick up on that.

Clare: I'm better after I've had a drink.

Craig: That was so amazing. Very few people talk about the community. You can talk about the music, you can talk about the history, but what you mentioned here is that the music found you at a low point in your life. It brought you back to places you hadn't been to for a while, and the community surrounded you and hugged you.

Clare: Well, I had actually never felt that kind of acceptance before. I'm not going to say.... I didn't have a terrible life. I had a great life growing up. I played music. I majored in music in college, but I got married very young. When we separated and divorced, I found myself alone as a single mom. It wasn't easy. I had no money whatsoever. I was in debt. It was a mess. I was living on the family farm, when this other lady with a baby about my baby's age says, "Why don't you go over and visit my husband because while I'm bartending at night. He's sitting home playing the fiddle." Very generous of her.

When I went over there, he started teaching me old-time tunes, and in order to remember them—I don't have a good aural memory—I took manuscript paper, and I would write them down. I started compiling a body of tunes but what I found was, wow, he took the time to show me these tunes. I felt like it doesn't matter what I've ever done in my past or how depressed I am now or anything else—we're sitting here playing the fiddle. After a while, a group was started, and we'd get together every Friday night and play tunes. This was my introduction into old-time music.

Craig: Are you a classically trained violinist?

Clare: Yes. My mother loved music, and she had me sit on a couple of phone books on the piano stool when I was four and showed me how to play piano. Then when I was about seven or eight, she had me start to learn violin. I did that. I have a cousin who also plays violin. She went on to be a professional classical violinist. We would take lessons together. It was a good discipline. I would practice as soon as I got home from school. I guess I was about 11, 12, or 13 years old.

I started taking lessons from a piano teacher who said, "Look, why don't you skip your senior year of high school and come and enroll in the college here and take lessons from me, and then your mother won't have to pay for every lesson. It'll simply be part of the tuition." I was 14 when I started at college. I always thought I would leave and become a writer or something, but once you jump in the river, it takes you. I stayed and I majored in music and got a degree in performance. Now what do you do with that? I taught in a private Quaker school here in Westchester for a couple of years, which is how I got into music.

Craig: Did Granny play any music?

Clare: She sang. She loved to sing.

Craig: You were around a lot of music as a kid.

Clare: Yes, I was. Constantly. Here's something interesting. My mom was always very musical and everything, and I never thought that Dad was musical at all. Well, lo and behold, he tells me that when he was about five years old, he remembers standing in back of his dad holding a harmonica for him to play while his dad played the guitar, before the days of the harmonica stand. I have his guitar—a little Washburn guitar from around the turn of the century.

Craig: Nice.

Clare: Lo and behold, he tells me his mom played banjo and fiddle. I asked him one time, "Well, what tunes did they play?" He said they got together every Saturday and sat around and ate and played tunes. Again I asked, "What tunes did they play?" The only one he could remember was "Little Brown Jug."

When I was about 11, in the summer of 1970, I experienced a magical night. I was in love with Jimmy, my brother's best friend, who was five years older than me. My brother had learned how to make wine out of dandelions. Of course, his friend came over to test it out. On this summer evening, we all sat around in the kitchen—and what did Jimmy bring over with him but a banjo. He sat there at the kitchen table, and I sat on the floor, and they drank dandelion wine, and the only tunes he could play were "Over the Waterfall" and "June Apple." To me, that was the most magical—well, all of the circumstances together were magical, and so the music was part of it, but I think that's what old-time music is. He was playing this music, it was part of an expression of what was going on that night, and you play the music to convey your feelings. That hooked me on old-time music.

Craig: When you went through the depth of despair you started to talk about earlier, it brought back memories.

Clare: Yes. Well, what happened was after I met my husband and he said, "Well, why don't you go to law school?" I thought, "Really? Oh, yes." It was the last thing I ever wanted to do, but I said to him, "Oh, I've always wanted to go to law school," so I did. Again, it was like jumping into a river and you can't get out, and so I went through law school. I did all right, I passed the bar and everything, and during that whole time, I didn't really play any music at all. I didn't play any classical; I hadn't even started to play old-time music yet.

When I met the guy who taught me some tunes in the beginning, and then we all started playing music, what it brought back to me wasn't really specific memories, but feelings, being in a certain place or having a certain feeling. That's how I think about the tunes. Every tune puts you in a certain frame of mind. It's like a magic spell. It puts you in a certain place.

Craig: When you first find a tune, do you listen to the tune first to interpret it or do you look at the title first?

Clare: Oh, I listen to the tune, always listen to the tune. Some tunes have fantastic titles, and they're not that good. A lot of the very, very best tunes are like "Boating Up Sandy." There's a lot of "Boating Up Sandys," and a lot of "Sugar in the Gourds," and they're all very different, but some of them are really fantastic tunes, so it's the tune itself.

Craig: What touches you most about the music?

Clare: Oh, there's so much. It's how it makes me feel when I hear it, then I want to play it. Then it's the fun of trying to work it out on the instrument. That's like problem-solving. Then it's like turning somebody else on to it, "Hey, listen to this!" and you play it for them, and you share it. Then the fun of getting other people to play it, and then every time you hear it, you're in that place again. What do I love about it? Gosh, there's so much. I mean, what's not to like?

Craig: Had you not gone through your path of darkness, do you think you would have discovered or found this music?

Clare: I can't imagine what my life would be like if I hadn't found it; it would certainly be completely different. This music is a big part of my life now.

Craig: Well, you're a wonderful emissary for it, in addition to performing, and as articulate as you are with your day job as an attorney. If you run across somebody who never heard of it before, how would you describe old-time music?

Clare: It's hard to describe because they all immediately say, "Oh, bluegrass? I like bluegrass," and I have to say, "Well, it precedes bluegrass. It's where bluegrass came from," and their eyes glaze over, you know, and all you can do is simply show it to them. Both Walt Koken and I have found is that anybody who hears it loves it, and they don't have to know what it's called. It's music of the people, it's music, really, that anybody can sit down and learn to play. It doesn't matter how old you are, of course, it's better when you're younger, but anybody can sit down and play it.

Craig: It's a form of language.

Clare: Yes.

Craig: It's a concurrent form of language. You're talking, I'm talking at the same time, and if you say something, I'll say, "Yes, I understand what that's like."

Clare: Right.

Craig: Sometimes I play along with you because I've been there and done that with you, too. It's also this community builder we've talked about. Now, Walt had mentioned this Brandywine Festival. Can you talk a little bit about that?

Clare: Oh, absolutely. That's one of my favorite things in the whole world right now. The first festival I ever went to was the old Brandywine Festival, which was put on by the Brandywine Friends of Old Time Music. I went there in the middle of the night. I arrived about two in the morning and the place was going strong. Everybody was playing music, and it was such a wild time, I had never seen anything like that in my life. This festival ended because they weren't making enough money. They were making money off the bluegrass festival, but not the old-time festival, so we lost a nice festival in our area.

I grew up on an old family farm out here in Pocopson Township. It's a beautiful piece of land, and my dream was always, wouldn't this be great for a fiddle festival? It was always sort of a pipe dream. Well, last year I had to lie flat on my back for a while, and what came to me but these visions of the fiddle festival, and I could see the gate where people came in, I could see them camping there. I talked to Walt and to my son Paul about it, and Paul said to me, "Yes, Mom, imagine this, you're standing here."

We were standing outside on the farmland at the time. Paul said, "It's dusk, there's people over there, and over there, and they're all playing music." Little twinkling lights are all over the place. Last June, we made that a reality—it happened. Not only that, Walt came up with this wonderful idea about the contest. You know how contests are, you get up on stage, your fingers turn into bananas, you don't play nearly as well as you did a minute ago in the campsite. We decided, the heck with all that stuff. Let's have a contest where the judges drive around in golf carts, and they visit everybody at their campsite—and you're judged there.

Of course, that's what we did, and we encouraged bribes, and by the time the contest was over, we decided we would give everybody the blue ribbon, and they were thrilled. It was a beautiful time of year. I picked it because it was my father's birthday weekend, June 20, and the weekend closest to that because he bought the place. He passed away in 2010, and it was sort of my way of thanking him and remembering him, but also, it's a fantastic time of year, and the light there at that time is so magical.

Craig: Tell me how you met Walt.

Clare: We met at a music festival, of course. He had recently started back playing banjo after a hiatus of some time, and I think he had started playing the violin again. We sat down and played together. I knew tunes that he didn't know, and I showed them to him, and I think he may have thought, 'Oh, this is great, I like these tunes.' Both of us were there with other people, so nothing happened for a while. Walt was very brave, and he made the decision to move here to Ithaca from Trumansburg, New York, and we have had a wonderful time ever since then.

Craig: [Facing Walt seated on the couch.] I'm tempted to swing the camera around so I could show your grin. It's beautiful.

Clare: My law practice

Walt Koken. Part of the Koken-Milliner music saving team.

interferes with playing old-time music, but it's necessary. I actually enjoy practicing law, and it does keep lobster on the table and champagne in the fridge.

Craig: You don't get those things in old-time music.

Clare: We started going to this little island in the Bahamas—the island of Exuma, one of the most beautiful places in the entire world. We had our bass player with us one year. We couldn't ship the bass down to be with her, so we were looking around on the island for a bass. Not only were there no basses on the island, there were no stringed instruments on the entire island. Now it's a given. But back then, it's just a small island and the little kids had no violins, no guitars, no nothing.

I felt like, "Wow, we ought to give something back. We come here, we take in all this beauty, they love us, all this stuff. Let's give something back." It was obvious. We wanted to give stringed music to the little kids on the island. We started a nonprofit organization called the Orpheus Foundation. It's on Facebook, and we have a website. Two years ago, we sent down 21 violins.

Craig: Fabulous!

Clare: ...and a cello. A bass is now on its way. One of the kids who started to play one of those violins is now teaching the other kids on the island. There's still a lot more to do, but it has taken off, so we're thrilled.

Craig: Are you planning on going down there to continue the teaching?

Clare: What I would like to see is funding to encourage teachers who are on the island, people there who can teach, or at least train them to teach. If that's not possible, really one of my dreams is to send old-time musicians down there, fund their trip for a week at a time. Wouldn't that be a wonderful vacation?

Craig: Where can I sign up?

Clare: Okay, you're in.

15

Mac Benford

St. Augustine, Florida, 2015

Mac Benford majored in American history and English. He ended up a teacher.

"I wanted to play baseball, but I also realized that fateful fall into music had been set up. When I came up through grammar school, the stuff you learned in music class was often American traditional music. We sang 'Down in the Valley' and 'She'll Be Coming Around the Mountain.' We watched these black-and-white cartoons of Farmer Al Falfa and millions of little mice dancing. I realized the background music for that was 'Arkansas Traveler' and 'Chicken Reel.'

"We started out playing a lot on the street corners on the Berkeley campus, the San Francisco State campus, as well as tourist places like Fisherman's Wharf and Golden Gate Park. This was invaluable preparation for performing on a stage. We were able to actually make a living. I think it was in the spring of 1968. Then I had a pretty good run for 15 years after that. Of course, we learned back in those days how to live quite elegantly on very little money."

"People still talk about how we [the Highwoods String Band] seemed to almost levitate on stage!"

"I certainly made more teaching than I ever did performing. We were very lucky. We were at the right place at the right time. I think it all worked out just fine."

Old-Time Community Role: The *Clever Opportunist*. Mac is really smart. He's good with music, with people and with capitalizing on opportunity. His story is one of timing, luck and endurance. But he reached levels seen by few old-time bands, especially the levitating kind. No group will ever match the energy and sheer joy of the Highwoods.

Craig Evans: You're 75?

Mac Benford: I'm a month and a half short of 75.

Craig: Yes, but I still don't know how you look so good.

Mac: Sex, drugs, and old-time music.

Craig: Mac Benford, I am so delighted to sit down and talk to you. When people think of the great names of banjo players, they think of Wade Ward, they think of Kyle Creed, they think of Tom Ashley. They also think of Mac Benford. When I was first thinking about putting together this series, you were at the top of the list. Thank you for sitting down today to talk about old-time music.

Mac: My pleasure, I'm glad to talk about old-time music.

Mac Benford. The heart of the Highwood String Band.

Craig: Let's actually talk about when you first got hooked on this music. How old were you, and where were you?

Mac: When I first really got hooked, I was in college.

Craig: Wow.

Mac: My parents had felt that any well-educated young person should have music lessons, so I was forced to learn the piano ... and hated it. I never had the slightest interest in making music a big part of my life. I wanted to play baseball, but I also realized that fateful fall into music had been set up.

When I came up through grammar school, the stuff you learned in music class was often American traditional music. We sang "Down in the Valley" and "She'll Be Coming Around the Mountain." We watched these black-and-white cartoons of Farmer Al Falfa and millions of little mice dancing. I realized the background music for that was "Arkansas Traveler" and "Chicken Reel."

My dad's people lived in southwestern Pennsylvania. His dad, my grandfather, was a foreman of a big logging operation there. I can remember him singing around the house "The Wreck of the Old 97" and classic early country music like that. I went off to college in 1958, right at the time of the big folk-music boom. Traditional music was the big music of the time. The Weavers, the Kingston Trio, the Rooftop Singers all had huge hits on the radio and on jukebox play, which was how you determined what people were listening and paying attention to. It was set up so I would be exposed to that music, and when I was exposed to it, it felt "Oh yes, this is the real stuff."

In high school, I was pretty severely nerdish, but I learned if I could play the guitar, it seemed to be a ticket to popularity. At that time, Folkways Records was starting to put out some real traditional music, and some reissues of Uncle Dave Macon. The Carter Family music was available on LPs, and, of course, the New Lost City Ramblers. I started listening to that stuff. Over the course of the summer, I became totally *hooked on the real version of traditional music played in the traditional styles by the traditional people.* It was the sound of the banjo that really, really grabbed me.

Craig: Who taught you? Then how did you start to evolve?

Mac: Well, nobody really taught me. I never had lessons from anybody, but I listened a lot. I read Pete Seeger's book, and I learned "up pick, brush down," so I worked on that. Of course, very early on I figured out that fortunately, you could see some of these great players. They were still alive, and they would still come out and play at these southern fiddlers' conventions. I think 1964 was the first year I went down to Galax and Union Grove and got to meet and watch and hang out.

Craig: Did any one of those guys in particular really strike your fancy?

Mac: Two in particular. Wade Ward and Kyle Creed. I got to spend a fair amount of time with both of them. I could listen to and see those people at the fiddlers' conventions and at the folk festivals, and listening to the old '78 records. There were so many styles of banjo playing—finger styles, frailing styles, and clawhammer. Somehow, we had the idea that to be an accomplished banjo player, you had to learn all of them. We wanted to play like Pete Steele, we wanted to play like Doc Boggs. We wanted to play like Wade Ward. We wanted to play like Earl Scruggs and Ralph Stanley.

Craig: Where did you attend college?

Mac: I went to Williams College in Massachusetts.

Craig: What did you major in?

Mac: I switched around a lot. I started out majoring in American history and ended up majoring in English.

Craig: Wow. You finished with a degree in English?

Mac: Yes.

Craig: Okay. What happened next? Where does the music weave into this? I know there's a trip to the West Coast, and I'm curious how that happened.

Mac: Okay. Well, I graduated from Williams with the idea that I wanted to be a teacher. A bunch of us read this book called *Summerhill*, which had some radical ideas. I don't know if you ever ran into this book by A.S. Neill. Out of college, I got a job at a very, very progressive co-ed boarding school in the Berkshires called the Windsor Mountain School. I taught there for three years. My wife and I were having problems, and we realized that being house parents at a co-ed boarding school was not really the ideal place to work out our marital problems. We decided to take a year off. Where should we go? This was 1967.

Everybody was heading out to California … it was the "Summer of Love." So off we went. I don't know if that was the smartest place either to work out our marital difficulties. We couldn't and split up. I was living in San Francisco and I ran into an old friend from college. He said, "You ought to come over, as a bunch of people over in the East Bay get together fairly frequently and play old-time music. It'll make you feel better." Out of that grew Dr. Humbead's New Tranquility String Band and Medicine Show. At this time, your band names had to be elaborate, like Big Brother and the Holding Company and the Strawberry Alarm Clock and…

Craig: Jefferson Airplane.

Mac: Yes. It was a very exciting time. Tune in, turn on, and drop out. We were there for all three of those things. It was quite a scene with people who started to take their art to the streets, which is fairly common now, but then it was a fairly radical thing. Through the '50s and early '60s this activity was begging or panhandling, and, of course, that's really what it was. We started out playing a lot on the street corners on the Berkeley campus, the San Francisco State campus, as well as tourist places like Fisherman's Wharf and Golden Gate Park. This was invaluable preparation for performing on a stage. You didn't have a captive audience. If you didn't hold them, you lost them. We were able to actually make a living. I think it was in the spring of 1968. Then I had a pretty good run for 15 years after that. Of course, we learned back in those days how to live quite elegantly on very little money.

Craig: You went through a number of bands that have all become, I don't want to say household names for everybody, but for those of us that follow the music. What was the progression? How did you get in? How did Fat City go? Then, finally, Highwoods. Then how did the Highwoods head back to the other coast?

Mac: You know, bands do two things: play music and break up. It happened that that band broke up at the same time that Walt Koken's band, the Busted Toe Mud Thumpers, did. They had been based in Ithaca and had traveled across the country. They were originally intending to go up and make a fortune playing for the people working on the Alaskan pipeline, but they got sidetracked and ended up in Berkeley. Bob Potts had grown up in San Francisco and had a wonderful band that played on stilts. The three of us were all at loose ends, and we started playing together—which became the Fat City String Band.

Craig: What's the derivation of the name?

Mac: Fat City is a slang term for high cotton; it means the same thing.

Craig: I wondered because the way you set that up, you said, "We were living good, and it felt good, and so we're in Fat City now."

Mac: Exactly. That's what it was. In the summer of 1971, we decided to make a cross-country pilgrimage. We were footloose and fancy-free, so let's go play some of those fiddlers' conventions. We did very, very well. Won a lot of blue ribbons and prizes as a trio. We also stopped by the Smithsonian Folklife Festival in Washington,

D.C. We managed to catch the attention of the traditional music establishment—that, of course, was at the Folklife Festival. Ralph Rinzler and Mike Seeger set the stages for the success that the Highwoods later cashed in on. At the end of that, we had a blast.

But, of course, it was hard. Three wild characters—Bob, Walt, and I—were all trying to live together in an old 1953 Ford panel truck. For some reason, we all decided that we'd stop smoking altogether that summer. By the end of the summer, we were sick and tired of each other, and we went in different directions. But I guess we began to miss each other. Walt had started playing with Doug and Jenny, who were attending Cornell in Ithaca. In those days, old-time bands often had two guitars but very, very rarely had a bass fiddle. We thought, why not add a bass and have that big rhythm section drive what Walt, Bob, and I had been able to get with banjos and fiddles? It would be a powerful sound.

The plan originally was, and again, this is back in the days when we were footloose and fancy-free, we thought we'll have a great time in the summer if we can convince Bob to come out from San Francisco. The five of us, now including Jenn and Doug, will travel around to those fiddlers' conventions, and have a great time, and maybe win some prizes and earn some money that way. We had no real thought of having a career as a performing band. We went to Union Grove and had a great time, and the five-piece band sounded great. When Mike Seeger and Ralph Rinzler heard that the three of us had gotten back together and had added two more pieces, we got hired to play the Smithsonian Folklife Festival. What luck! We were a big hit at the Smithsonian festival and gained a lot of very prestigious jobs. As a result of our exposure there, we became the Highwood String Band.

Craig: What's the derivation of the Highwood String Band?

Mac: That's funny because there was a Charlie Poole song that we liked. If you've listened to some of Charlie's old '78 recordings, he didn't have the clearest diction in the world. In one of his songs called the "Coon from Tennessee," we thought the chorus went, "I'm going to live in the high woods till I die." It sounded like he was using high wood very much like we used Fat City. It turns out what he was singing was, "I'm gonna live anyhow until I die." This was back in the day. We threw the I Ching to try and get some guidance for what we should call ourselves. I remember one was Fire Hexagram representing Fire over the Hexagram representing Mountain, and we thought, "Oh, Fire on the Mountain." That's what we called our first record, and, of course, it had that tune which was one of our favorites.

Craig: Yes. There was such energy in the way you guys played. How could you keep that energy going?

Mac: We all shared a sense of where the beat should be. When everybody is hitting those marks right on, and it's right up on the forward edge of the beat altogether, it has this energy that is irresistible. Physically, people still talk about how we seemed to almost levitate on stage. Now, Walt was pretty much the musical leader,

The Highwoods String Band, a 1970s, Grammy-nominated folk sensation. From left: Doug Dorschug, Jenny Cleland, Mac Benford, Bob Potts, and Walt Koken (courtesy Mac Benford).

and we all were very good listeners as the music was going on and knew exactly how to support that. Jenny, with those solid bass notes. Doug, with his excellent guitar playing. Bob, he had a style that was perfect. It wasn't exactly the same notes that Walt was playing, pretty close, but it was exactly the time that Walt was playing. That's what made those two fiddles work brilliantly together. Most of our shows went really well, which is why we were so successful.

When the Highwoods band broke up, the splash that I made as part of the Highwoods has served me for the next 30, 40 years. My next band was called the Backwoods Band. I wanted to focus on much more arranged material when that band broke up. Then my income from music started to go down, and I'd started a new family and my expenses started to go up, at that point I took a straight job. Maybe I should say a little bit about what I'm doing right now.

Craig: Please do.

Mac: When it started to hurt to play clawhammer style, I started playing more and more fingerstyle, which I'm doing a lot of these days. Lo and behold, I find that I'm playing back to the old Pete Seeger "up pick, brush down" that I started at the very beginning.

Craig: I know you're teaching a lot these days, too.

Mac: Yes, I am. Walt and I once had a conversation. We visited Tommy Jarrell early on and had some great times. After one of these visits, Walt and I were talking that maybe someday, if we made a name for ourselves, young kids would come to our house like we came to Tommy's to learn. Lately, I started to think, no, that's not happening. Then I thought, but it's really good that it's not happening because we get hired to teach at banjo camps so the lessons are passed along. And we don't have to figure out where people are going to sleep or what we're going to feed them like poor Tommy did.

Craig: Unlike Tommy and Fred, you get paid, too.

Mac: Yes, we get paid very well. I certainly make more teaching than I ever did performing.

Mac: We were very lucky. We were at the right place at the right time.

Craig: If you could do anything different, would you?

Mac: No, I think it all worked out fine.

16

Sheila Kay Adams

MARSHALL, NORTH CAROLINA, 2023

"The ballads are—I consider a gift from generations ago, because the people that taught me were into their 60s, 70s, and 80s."

"This country is in a pretty big mess right now. Unless we start to fall back on some of these old traditions, like storytelling, community singing—it's hard to argue and fight with somebody when you're laughing over a story or you're sharing a sacred song that you'd like to sing, as a community, or even one of the old love songs that tell such great stories."

Sheila Kay Adams was named a National Heritage Fellow by the National Endowment for the Arts.

Old-Time Community Role: The *Flamekeeper* ... and *Flamekeeper's Keeper*. Musically gifted, Sheila brings her storytelling and musical skills to stage with little effort and maximum impact. As a teacher, she demonstrates excellent skills in understanding and articulating difficult concepts. It carries over into her life. She herself had some excellent teachers in her family and community. She paid attention ... and cared for them, deeply. That love, selflessly shared with audiences across the globe, is woven into her soul.

Craig Evans: Sheila Kay Adams, of Marshall, North Carolina. Thank you for sitting down with me today to talk about traditional music and more. Most of the people that will be watching this today are already fans of yours, but for those that aren't, you are a seventh-generation ballad singer, and it doesn't get much more traditional than that, an internationally recognized storyteller, an author, a musician—specifically, you play clawhammer banjo.

In addition to appearing at countless festivals, like this one, in Lanesboro, Minnesota, music camps, and teaching workshops, both here and abroad, you have been featured on NPR. You've also appeared twice at the Smithsonian Folklife Festival, and your contributions to North Carolina folklife have resulted in them honoring you with a Brown-Hudson Award. On top of all that, you have been named a National Heritage Fellow by the National Endowment for the Arts. Congratulations.

Sheila: Thank you very much.

Craig: You've certainly contributed enormously to traditional music, and as such, I would like to know your story. I figure a storyteller is probably best at telling their story. Let's start where life started for you.

Sheila: I was born in Madison County, in North Carolina. My family have been there since 1732.

Craig: Oh my goodness.

Sheila: They've been there a long time. Of course, I'm not that old. My mother was born and raised in the same little community that I went home to, when she brought me home from the hospital. It was a little community that's called Sodom, and it's spelled just like the one in the Bible, and that's the only similarity with the one in the Bible, it's spelled the same. My father was working a public job at the time and was gone.

As a result of that, I spent a lot of time with my great aunt, Dellie Chandler Norton, who is a great ballad singer and also a banjo player. I had a first cousin, Jerry Adams, who was probably the best banjo player I've ever heard. He played a two-finger style. It's called Madison County two-finger style, because it had its own distinctive sound to it. I started out that way, and then heard Dwight Diller, when I was a teenager, play a clawhammer banjo, fell in love with Dwight, and fell in love with the banjo, too, his style.

Sheila Kay Adams. Sharing stories of humor and love from her past channeled through her soul.

Started playing banjo and been singing ballads and playing banjo since I was about five years old. That would make it about 65 years ago now.

Craig: You carry the ballads, you carry the stories of North

Carolina. Do you feel like it's in your bones, or how did you come about deciding, "This is what I want to do as a career"?

Sheila: When I was—I guess 17 years old was the first time that I ever went out on stage. Granny (Dellie Chandler Norton) made a very big impression because it was a round robin, on stage, of traditional ballad singers. There were probably, gosh, 15 or 20 chairs, in a semicircle, out on this stage. One of the ballad singers had passed away, and as a result, that left a chair open. They had a flower in the seat, and Granny just reached over and plucked the flower out of it and said, "I'm going to give this—" now, I'm going to get emotional—"I'm going to give this to my great niece, Sheila, because she's going to come out here and take the place of this person, who has passed on." That was when I got started. I was 17.

Craig: The torch was passed, as a flower.

Sheila: Literally. What better symbol than a rose?

Craig: Tell me about the root of the stories that you generally tell. Are they part of the mountains?

Sheila: They're not Jack Tales, grandfather tales, or any of those. They're real, true-life stories, that came about, growing up over in this little community called Sodom, because a place called Sodom is going to have bunches of characters. Boy, it sure did. There were nine traditional ballad singers that were still singing, and every single one of them was a character, especially Inez Chandler Chandler, with a double barrel Chandler, as she called it, at the end. She's bound to be a character. She was a Chandler that married a Chandler.

Craig: All right. We won't take it any further than that, no need—

Sheila: No, well, I don't have a family tree. I have a family wreath, that just goes around, around, and around. [Laughs.] I learned a bunch of the family stories from Daddy, and then I also was just a part of a lot of them.

Craig: These stories are really close to your heart, they're close to your home. They are family.

Sheila: Yes.

Craig: All right. How about the ballads?

Sheila: Oh, now you're speaking to my heart. The ballads are—I consider a gift from generations ago, because the people that taught me were into their 60s, 70s, and 80s. Granny lived to be almost 95, taught me a love song a couple of weeks before she passed away. Those were gifts that were given to me by my closest family members.

Craig: What do we learn from ballads? Why are they worth saving after seven generations?

Sheila: Oh, Granny said they had moral messages in all of them, and the consequences that comes with bad behavior, because in lots of these ballads, you—somebody winds up getting their head cut off, especially the big ballads, as she called them, the big, long ballads. She actually referred to them as long-winded ballads, because it took a long time to sing them. They're the ones that have all the blood and gore, cutting off of heads, kicking the head against the wall, and all of that stuff in them. They're just near and dear to my heart. I just love them because, like most children, I was attracted to that violence that was going on in the great story that was unfolding in these songs.

Craig: Now, these are English or Irish?

Sheila: They're English and Scottish.

Craig: How far back do the roots of some of these ballads go? Are these something a bard would take from town to town in the 14th or 15th century?

Sheila: Oh, absolutely. As a matter of fact, the oldest ones that I know go all the way back to when the Normans invaded the Saxons in 1066, songs like "Little Margaret," "Fine Sally." All of those are about the lovely blonde, blue-eyed girl who loses out to a darker-complected French, the Normans.

Craig: I'm assuming there's also messages in there about "Don't go down to the river with Willie."

Sheila: Oh, that's exactly right. Just don't have anything to do with Willie, to start with, unless you're Barbara Allen. [Laughs.]

Craig: I wonder how many versions of those songs are out there?

Sheila: Oh, there's hundreds of them.

Craig: Was it like this was a common theme, so the creative people back in the 16th and 17th centuries would take the characters that people knew and then write another virtuous story about how things should be presented a certain way?

Sheila: I think so. I think that's exactly right. For myself, riding in the car is the best place for me to think about banjo tunes, to get them into my head, listen to them over and over on the CD player. It's a way to learn traditional ballads, because you have the time. As a bard was going from place to place, they would probably make up the songs from the place they had just left, and by the time they got to the next place, they would have a whole crop of new songs.

Craig: Interesting.

Sheila: And they had patrons. They would entertain a patron's family for parties and gatherings. The bard was the main entertainer there.

Craig: Musicians of that era. Today, we can flick a switch and we've got music on demand. Back then, if you didn't have somebody in the family or the community, you had to wait for it to come to you.

Sheila: That's exactly right.

Craig: Do you perceive these people as being superstars?

Sheila: I think so. They would've been the superstars of their generation, for sure. Especially in Scotland and Ireland, they sing a lot about a bard sitting under the tree, listening to the birds that sing, and thinking up the stories to take to the next little village or whatever. Now, the English, not so much, but in Scotland and Ireland, you hear songs written about bards.

Craig: Today, if you're a representation of a bard, what do you consider a good story?

Sheila: The first thing you have to do is to start out with what's called the bare bones of a story. They're like a joke. You have to have your punchline. You have to have the bare bones of the story, which is what, basically, a joke is. It's just a quick story. What I do is, I just literally go back into my memory, and I will remember, like the time Amos Lundy, he passed away, his wife sent him off to Marshall, and they fixed him up, brought him back to the house.

Then Little Betty, his wife, and her sister wrestled him out of the coffin to change his clothes because they didn't like what Little Betty had sent off with him to the undertaker to get fixed up for the funeral. They downed him right in the floor and changed his clothes and then couldn't pick him up to put him back over in the coffin. It was a whole community event that took place around getting Amos back into his coffin in time for the setting up. Now, that's the bare bones of the story.

What I did was see—I was not there for the conversation that took place between Little Betty and her sister Vine, but I had heard them talk enough to where I knew what they said. "Looking at him a-laying there in that coffin, I believe I'd like him better in that blue suit." They changed his clothes. Then, at the end of the story, which takes about 25 minutes to tell, Little Betty is standing there, looking at him in this blue suit, and she says, "Now that I look at him a-laying there, I believe I did like him better in that other suit." That's a true story. Basically, what I do is, I just take these memories from my childhood and turn them into stories.

Craig: All right, let's bring us up to today, because we're deluged with noise. We have stories, we have music, we have animosity, we have things that interrupt us in our daily routine. Where do storytellers fit today?

Sheila: This country is in a pretty big mess right now. Unless we start to fall back on some of these old traditions, like storytelling, community singing—it's hard to argue and fight with somebody when you're laughing over a story or you're sharing a sacred song that you'd like to sing, as a community, or even one of the old love songs that tell such great stories. If we didn't have those blessed people right now, I think we'd all be in even more serious trouble.

I think they're our way out. Storytellers and the bearers of these traditions, ancient traditions, are the way out of this mess. I have got about 14 young men and women who are willing to learn the traditional ballads. I have literally groomed these people from when they were small. A lot of them are related to me. Some of them I met when they were in school and I was a schoolteacher.

My daughter and I got the North Carolina Award for Mentoring Apprenticeship so that she could learn more of the ballads than she had learned up to this point.

Craig: Have you updated how you tell stories? Our attention spans are so short today. Have you found that keeping them long is better, or do you shorten them?

Sheila: What I have found is that if you engage with your audience—you've got about seven seconds in order to catch the attention of your audience now, but if you engage with them in that first seven seconds, then you've got them through the whole story. They won't wander off.

Craig: That sounds like that's one of the most important parts of a story.

Sheila: Oh, it is. What I normally do is—since I started out with Amos and Little Betty, I just say, "Well, when you grow up in a place called Sodom," and I've got them right there, that's all it takes.

Craig: [Laughs.] You got me!

Sheila: That's what I'm saying. That is all you have to say. I've got a great lead-in, and in this little community of Sodom, there was a little church house on the side of the mountain called the Low Gap Church, and they had a snake handler in there one night, and all of Sodom went. Don't tell me you don't want to know the rest of that story.

Craig: [Laughs.] I don't have enough time, film, or battery.

Sheila: I know, but it's a great story. You have to have that hook. Same deal when I was writing my book. "We're all born with a row to hoe, and Larkin Stanton had one of the roughest rows I've ever seen." When I'm playing banjo, I do the same thing, because you've still got seven seconds. You have to get their attention. I think storytelling, and I think music, in general—I mean, listen to the sound here [festival music playing in the distance] that we're hearing. How can you argue or fuss with somebody when you've got this in the background? It's just heavenly.

Craig: Between your drawl and the speed at which you speak, I have found this tremendously relaxing. Then we have the music behind us, on top of all that.

Sheila: That's right.

Craig: I walked in late to a class that you were having on ballad singing and meeting house songs. What's the differentiation between the two?

Sheila: Ballad singing, those are the love songs, and the meeting house songs are the sacred songs. A lot of religious folks there, around home, stopped singing the love songs because the religion told them that it was a sin to sing about non-secular things. Now, for the ballads, you've got to stay in the story while you're singing, but in the meeting house songs—I've got so many memories of them that it's difficult to do that, but I have to think of something else.

Craig: Now, I noticed your style was that you closed your eyes.

Sheila: I do.

Craig: What do you focus on behind your eyelids?

Sheila: On that one, what I focus on is just—I think about—I'm over home, and

I'm standing on Mama's and Daddy's porch, I'm probably 20 years old, and I'm singing that song for Dwight Diller.

Craig: Let's segue into that. Dwight is an irascible character. You either loved him or you avoided him. I was one of those firmly in the love camp. What did you learn from Dwight?

Sheila: Everything about the banjo. Dwight was the first person that actually sat me down and said, "Sheila, this is what you have here." He said, "I don't think you realize." Dwight was the one that sat down with me and said, "You have got these people who are dying, literally dying, to teach you these songs, to teach you how to play music, to teach you how to be a good person, and you need to pay attention because you're going to regret this if you don't." I took him at his word. I was about 17 when he told me that.

Craig: Wow.
Sheila: Right about the same time I got on stage with Granny, with that rose.

Craig: Did you consider that a divine nod, or a wink, that this is your path?
Sheila: At the time, I didn't, but, boy, looking back on it—It didn't take me long to look back on what he had said. When I told Granny, she just cried, because she said, "He's exactly right." Dwight was one of the biggest influences in my life.

Craig: Have you prepared a story about him?
Sheila: Not yet.

Craig: You're working on it?
Sheila: Yes. Yes, I am.

Craig: I want to be in the audience when that appears.
Sheila: Yes. Well, part of it is that—he just passed away in February. The Dwight that I remember was so gentle with me, and understanding. The idea that he's no longer here—knowing Dwight, he is somewhere, doing a boot camp with angels, or something, because underneath all of that stuff that made Dwight who he was, was a good soul.

Craig: He had a beautiful heart.
Sheila: Yes, he did.

Craig: He responded to kindness. In fact, kindness saved him. Let's segue over to music. You're a banjo player.
Sheila: I am a banjo player.

Craig: Tell me how you got into the banjo.
Sheila: When I was eight years old, Jerry Adams, my cousin, gave me a little Kay banjo. He said, "I want you to learn how to play this well." I had watched Jerry play, and I had watched my cousin Linda play. Of course, I came from a family of music-makers, Byard Ray was my uncle and Obie Ramsey, a cousin. I messed around

playing two-finger style until Dwight came into my life, when I was a teenager, and then I switched over to playing clawhammer style. I've been messing around with a banjo ever since.

Craig: What banjo do you play now?

Sheila: I have got what I call a war horse. It's just a banjo that an old boyfriend of mine made for me, a fella by the name of Steven Roberts. It's just the best sound in a banjo I have ever heard in my life.

Craig: What do you look for in the voice of a banjo?

Sheila: It's got to have a really deep sound. I don't like a high, tinny-sounding banjo. I like for it to have a real solid sound to it.

Craig: One thing I want to ask, now that we've established that both of us are 70, we are now the age of the people that taught us what we know. Given the legacy of what you present in stories and songs, what advice would you give to somebody just beginning as a performer or a storyteller?

Sheila: Be curious about everything, because that's the best material. It's life that gives you your material for your stories. It gives you your music, it gives you the tunes. Get involved in life, grab a hold of it with both hands, and hang on. That's exactly what I'd say. Learn everything you can.

Craig: A hundred years from now, somebody finds this tape, what story would you like to pass along to them?

Sheila: It was in 2013, and it was almost exactly five years from the day that my husband committed suicide. I had more or less just given up. I was outside, mowing the yard. I remember saying, "Well, I guess it's just time for me to stop all this stuff," because it was just too hard. It was hard, because Jim and I played on stage together. We were partners in every way you can imagine. I loved him very much. Still do.

I happened to glance down as I was mowing the yard and I saw that I was getting a call from Washington, D.C., 212 area code. I thought, "Well, that's weird." I didn't answer the phone, and then, about five minutes later, I felt my phone vibrate in my pocket, I pulled it out, and it was a message from George Holt that said, "Urgent." I thought, "Oh no." Well, George, at that point, was the head of entertainment at the North Carolina Museum of Art.

I thought, "Oh, I bet George's going to offer me a job," or whatever. I opened up the email and was looking at it, and he said, you are getting a call from Washington, D.C., that you need to accept. You need to take the call. When I answered the phone, it was Barry Bergey, he's head of the National Endowment for the Arts. I said, "Hey, Barry, are you wanting me to come up and be the emcee this year?" He had asked me to do that before.

He said, "Nope, I want you to come up and get your awards." You have absolutely no idea, Craig, how that lifted. It was like it happened at the exact moment it should have, because I was on the verge of giving up.

Craig: Perfect timing.

Sheila: It's made a huge difference. The other thing is, and I'm not sure how this one's going to turn out, but I think it's going to turn out really well, is, this time next week, I'll be performing with Yo-Yo Ma.

Craig: What story will you be telling with Yo-Yo?

Sheila: The one about—it's a sign, it's about butterflies, that my grandmother and I—we had been out in the woods digging ginseng and had gone down to this little branch. We're sitting there with our feet in the water, because it was so cool. We heard a strong breeze, the sound of a strong breeze, but there wasn't any wind. I looked up, and about that time, this big yellow and black butterfly came and settled on the bank beside me, because it was all mossy, down where this little hole was, this little pool. Then they just came falling down out of the sky, one after another, after another, until they covered up all of the moss banks of the stream. Then they started landing on me and Granny. That was the day that she said, "It's a sign. I know it's a sign of some kind." She said, "It's a sign that you're supposed to learn them old love songs." That was when she taught me my first one.

Sheila Kay Adams' National Endowment for the Arts award.

Craig: Is Yo-Yo going to play in response to your story?

Sheila: He is going to actually accompany me as I sing "Black Is the Color of My True Love's Hair."

Craig: My gosh. That'll be beautiful.

Sheila: Yes. I'm really looking forward to it.

Craig: When is it, again?

Sheila: Going to happen next week, the 26th of May.

Craig: 2023.

17

Paul Brown

Winston-Salem, North Carolina, 2015

"The sound of the banjo, for reasons inexplicable, just knocked me over. I don't know how else to describe it. It was just absolutely thrilling to me."

"Mom used to sing these songs all the time and no doubt she was singing while I was in the womb. She reported to me too that when she put on good music with a beat that I would start to kick."

"In the early '70s, after I left school, I did start to make some trips [to North Carolina] because I was really interested in learning more about how to play my banjo and I wanted to play the fiddle as well because I just enjoyed the sound of it. I just loved hearing a square dance fiddle played. My first real visit to one of the old-timers of the South was to Fields Ward who was living in Bel Air, Maryland. I sought Fields out after having heard some of his early recordings from the Library of Congress. He sounded so much like my mom, so I became curious."

Paul saw radio and traditional music as a means to strengthen communities and help people understand. That understanding guided the rest of his career.

Old-Time Community Role: The *Individualist*. At the high point of his NPR career, people would easily recognize Paul's pleasant, melodic broadcast voice. As with his banjo playing style, it is pleasing and distinct. Akin to his journalistic style, Paul's early pursuit of his interest in traditional music has rewarded us with stories and deep knowledge of those playing and contributing to earlier music communities. Paul also loves cool, old French cars.

Craig Evans: My visit down here would not be complete if I didn't ask about your cars.

Paul: Here they are. Here are my two fun cars. They're both works of art. They're both transportation. At least one of them gets me there every time. That's the Mazda Miata. Now, back here we have a little more problematic of a proposition in terms of actually getting from point A to point B. It's a 1960 Panhard PL17 with the two-cylinder, flat-opposed aluminum engine and front-wheel drive. It'll go 80 miles to 85 miles an hour, on a good day, if everything is working right. Cruises right down the highway. It's very aerodynamic. It weighs in at just 1,760 pounds for a big four-door car and it's fun to drive.

Craig: It's a French car.

Paul: Yes, sir. Panhard is actually the oldest make of car marketed in the world and no one knows it. The first Panhard was commercially sold as a line of cars in 1891. That's before Mercedes-Benz and well before Ford. This car was the product of the social and political conditions of post-war Europe and France in particular. It's just a grand piece of artwork on wheels, which is why I have it. I love it. It's art.

Paul Brown. Articulating the joy of traditional music through understanding words and artful fingering.

Craig: You're having a love affair with this car.

Paul: It's great. The only problem is it frustrates the heck out me.

Craig: [Laughs.]

Craig: Paul Brown, you are not only an exceptional performer, you are a collector. You collect stories, you collect tunes, you collect styles of which people play both fiddle and banjo. With your career as a broadcaster, 14 years at NPR, I know you have been saving these precious stories for posterity and I want to thank you for that.

Paul: You're most welcome.

Craig: Today, I would really like to hear your story as to how you first got into the music.

Paul: I think I got into the music before I was born because my mom knew songs from Central Virginia, from the Piedmont near Bedford and Lynchburg from when she was a kid. Mom used to sing these songs all the time and no doubt she was singing while I was in the womb. She reported to me too that when she put on good music with a beat that I would start to kick.

I grew up in New York State and I was born in New York Hospital. The family moved north in the '20s. As soon as they moved, my grandmother started sending my mom and my aunt back to Virginia every summer. From the time my mom was seven years old until she was out of high school, really, and into college. She was down at this old former plantation house called Bellevue in Goud, Virginia. It was there that she learned songs from two African American brothers, John and Harry Calloway, and also from the white people. There was Jane Henderson, another was Emily Abbott, Francis Huff. My original core repertoire and my original understanding of traditional old-time music starts before memory.

Craig: Your grandparents on your mother's side, how long had they been in the South? Were they actually plantation owners and were they musical?

Paul: My grandpa was from a German family out in Wisconsin and he was an early naval aviator who actually gave his life for his country in 1924 as a naval aviation pioneer. He crashed out in California on takeoff. My grandmother's family were old-line Virginians. I know my grandmother used to sing a lot and I remember hearing her sing ragtime and stuff like that. It was music of her generation.

Craig: You mentioned singing. Were there also fiddles and banjos?

Paul: My mom did not play. She only sang but she would take me around to square dances, even in New York State. She liked to hear this music. She loved it and she remembered it from her childhood, I think. Then she would take me to hear people. One time she took me to hear Sonny Terry and Brownie McGhee because there was a record of George Pegram and Harry and Jeanie West and some other folks that I got for Christmas at one point. Mom was aware of Peter Seeger and Woody Guthrie because she'd gone to Highlander Folk School after she got out of college at 39.

Craig: Was your father musical?

Paul: Dad was from an immigrant family of Poles and English and he appreciated classical music. He understood that I loved the banjo as well as to play the piano. He didn't quite relate to it as well as my mom did. Mom was more into indigenous music, music with the sort of blues and grit and struggle that she'd heard when she was a kid. What they both really appreciated was music well played and they could be pretty hard on me. Neither one of them played an instrument, but if things were unclear or the timing was bad, they would let me know right away.

Dad would say, "Don't just grind through your oatmeal, son. Play this. Play the tune so it's exciting." I did an interview with Earl Scruggs one time at his home for the radio. Earl talked about getting too fancy for his mom and his mom calling out to him, "Earl, if you're going to play something, play it." Earl Scruggs and his brother used to practice timing very carefully by walking around the house playing a tune. They'd be supposed to meet up on the front of the house and still be in time. I recognized that a parent with high standards can be very helpful to a kid learning to play music.

Craig: You mentioned you had a love of the banjo. When did the banjo come into play?

Paul: Now, I'm not exactly sure. I don't know who the first banjo picker I heard actually was. The sound of the banjo, for reasons inexplicable, just knocked me over. I don't know how else to describe it. It was just absolutely thrilling to me.

Craig: You were what? Eight, nine, 10 at this point?

Paul: Less. I started asking for a banjo by the time I was about five and my mom wouldn't let me have one. Dad stayed out of that one but Mom wouldn't let me have one.

Craig: Why?

Paul: This went on for years and I'd listened to the records and I'd want the banjo and I'd ask her if I could have a banjo. "No, you can't have a banjo yet." Then, when I was 10 years old, we were out in South Dakota on a vacation trip. We were in a car wreck and my little brother was killed in the car wreck. My sister and I and all the rest of the family survived. Eventually, we got home back East. That summer, I asked my mom again in the depths of all of our despair and grayness if I could have a banjo. This time she said, "Yes, you can have a banjo, but you have to pay for it yourself."

I did pay for it. We went to Sears Roebuck, the catalog store. We did the usual thing. I remember sitting down at the kitchen table with Mom and she said, "All right, let's see if they have banjos." They were two, as I recall. One of them I decided I wanted; it was a $39 standard neck with a resonator and it was one of the last years of the Sears Roebuck banjos when they were all wood. I saved up for it, did yard work, and cut grass for people and all that stuff. Eventually, I had the $39 and we ordered the banjo and it came in. It was the biggest day of my life.

Now, years later and I was sitting with my mom. She was very old. I said, "Why didn't you let me have that banjo all those years? What was it? I kept asking you and you would keep saying no and then one day you said yes." She said, "I could tell that you wanted it, but I thought you were too small to play it when you were five and six. I was afraid it would be too big for you and you'd give it up. Then the other thing was that I wanted you to really want it. One way to know that you really wanted it was to wait for it and then to pay for it yourself."

Craig: It was good parenting.

Paul: Yes, an act of love.

Craig: [Laughs.] What a great story. You have a banjo and you're a young man. You had been listening to it. Did you have any skills that you could play at that point? How did you learn?

Paul: One of the things that appealed to me about this music is that I could follow the melodies and I could pretty much remember the words. I grew up when rock and roll was coming on big and all this stuff. I will be honest: I never really learned the titles of the rock songs and I never learned the words. I never focused on it, but I could understand and listen to the words and remember the words to the old traditional songs for some reason. I always had a pretty decent ear, good enough, in fact, that I never really learned how to read music as well as I should have.

I took piano lessons for 10 years and I never became proficient at reading because my ear would take over and I had the ability to hear timing. I was good on rhythm. I had the ability to transfer a melody that was in my head and in my ear to an instrument. I could figure out whatever key I was in some way of playing the tune to get the major melody notes that I needed. I got that banjo book that Peter Seeger put out for Christmas after I got the banjo and I took one lesson. I basically had to figure it out myself.

What I did was I just started to do some finger picking with my thumb and my index finger. Then I went back to the book later. I found some other tunings in it so I started to tune the banjo around. Then I would listen to recordings and hear that they couldn't be in the tuning that I was in. I had a good enough ear to do stuff like that. I could tell if something—the interval between the first string and the fifth string was not what I was getting.

I picked a lot of this stuff up by ear for years. In fact, it would've been in college when I met some other folks who played a little banjo before I actually really was able to pay attention to another banjo picker and learn by sight as well as by ear.

Craig: Where did you go to school?
Paul: I went to Oberlin.

Craig: I know you met a number of people there that were instrumental in your learning. Do you want to talk about a few of them?
Paul: I went to Oberlin because I wanted a liberal education with a big, huge dose of music. When I got there, Rodney Miller, the New England fiddle player, was already there. He's a little bit older than I was. A guy by the name of Tom Hammond played the clawhammer banjo and he was a good friend of Rodney. They had a radio show that they would do on Friday nights called *The Country Hour* at the campus radio station. David Molk was there. Then a little later, David Winston and Brad Leftwich showed up. Then I dropped out at the end of the second year, but we were all there at once. It was combustible. It was really fun.

Craig: I was going to say, were you just hanging out with each other all the time?
Paul: Not all the time, but whenever we could. Brad was starting to learn to play the fiddle. Rodney was pretty well along with his fiddle playing.

Craig: A number of your peers at that time were taking an interest in the greats that were down in North Carolina. Did you start participating in the sojourn south at that point?
Paul: In the early '70s, after I left school, I did start to make some trips because I was really interested in learning more about how to play my banjo and I wanted

to play the fiddle as well because I just enjoyed the sound of it. I just loved hearing a square dance fiddle played. My first real visit to one of the old-timers of the South was to Fields Ward who was living in Bel Air, Maryland. I sought Fields out after having heard some of his early recordings from Library of Congress. He sounded so much like my moms so I became curious.

I also went down to North Carolina and into Southwestern Virginia and started to visit with Tommy Jarrell, Fred Cockerham, a little bit with Kyle Creed. I had been aware of Benton Flippen and I was totally thrilled by the way he played the fiddle. Didn't even know at the time that he was a banjo player as well.

Craig: Clearly, you're consumed by the music at this point.
Paul: At that point, I was.

Craig: Had you just moved down there? Did you find work down there?
Paul: I had been a furniture upholsterer in New York State. I went to trade school and I was working there. Then I worked in a school for developmentally disabled young adults and teenagers. Then I decided I'd go back to the upholstery. Then I decided I wanted to go back down South and stay because I wanted to learn more about the banjo and fiddle while the older folks were still alive. I would say there were a few things. I didn't want the economic rat race of living up North. I wanted to learn more of the banjo and fiddle and how the music should sound and where it came from.

I wanted to understand more about where my mom and her folks came from. That was where I belonged. It was where my heart was so I moved. I just picked up and left. I got an NEA Folk Arts Apprenticeship grant to study the banjo. I was going to study with Fred Cockerham at first, and he passed away, and I transferred it over to Tommy Jarrell at the NEA's suggestion. So began a wonderful story for me of learning from Tommy and from a number of other folks around him and around those communities.

Craig: There's one thing that you just introduced that really doesn't align with everything. You got an NEA grant.
Paul: It was an apprenticeship grant, which paid the senior musician, not the younger musicians. We were responsible for our own support and that sort of thing. This provided a small stipend for the older person to spend time with a younger musician. I found out about it by chance when I was out at the Festival of American Fiddle Tunes. I think probably Alice Gerrard and Mike Seeger were talking up these grants, and then I thought, "That sounds like a good idea."

Craig: How long did you actually spend with the greats?
Paul: From 1980 until the present. That's how it's been. The rest of my life has centered, to a certain extent, on that quest of understanding.

Craig: When did you discover how important these messages were and aspire to save these messages?

Paul: When I first met Fields Ward and heard him sing up close and watched him play his guitar. I went to hear Fred Cockerham play music in New York City one time in the early '70s and went with my mom, as a matter of fact, and another friend. I was very profoundly affected by that as I watched him play the fiddle and listened to the notes that he was getting and tried to figure out how he was doing that and why. I heard the blues in it and I heard some jazz in there and some old-time stuff, but he was bending things all over the place.

I just thought, "Music doesn't sound like this anymore and I just have to understand it." I never had a career until quite late. I don't know how I survived that. Same thing when Terri McMurray and I got married. She was around the area for similar reasons. We just didn't have anything but what we had was music. We had these wonderful friendships and the opportunity to be around Luther Davis, the old fiddle player, and Robert Sykes and Tommy and Ardina, Tommy's daughter, and Essie Sykes, the wonderful flatfoot dancer, and all sorts of people. Now, I would not take $1 million for those times.

Craig: Understandable.
  Paul: Not anything.

Craig: I know after a period of time, call it providence, but you discovered radio.
  Paul: Yes.

Craig: How did that happen?
  Paul: The quick story is that if I go all the way back, I loved hearing stories. Then my dad had a 78 album of Edward R. Murrow. I can hear it now. His early recordings as a radio journalist as he created the field. I used to listen to those 78s over and over and over again. I thought very dimly, "Wouldn't that be a cool thing to do, to be able to find out about things and tell people that was my childhood consciousness of it?" My adult consciousness is, "Wouldn't it be a great thing to be able to find out about people and their stories and to share them with other folks so that they can understand the world a little better?"

Then, I forgot all about it until I got to college. I was with the college radio station for a while. Someone there said, "You'd be really good at this. You should go into this field." I completely forgot about it for 12 years. I was working overnight at a truck stop outside of Mount Airy, North Carolina, and we were playing on a fairly regular basis at WPAQ in Mount Airy. I would go over there with Robert Sykes and other musicians and we played. Verlen Clifton, who was one of my musician friends and a former member of the Camp Creek Boys, said, "You ought to go over and see Mr. Epperson and think about getting a job. He'd love to have you."

I did go see him and wound up working there for a couple of years. That changed my life. Here's a radio station founded and constructed on the premise of what was going on in 1948 and they're still doing it. Their 1948 model really goes back to the 1930s with the live studio music and all that. I have got to do this. Once I got there, I started to realize and understand a lot better the positive power of these new media to strengthen communities and, once again, to help people understand. That understanding guided the rest of my career.

Craig: Now, I know there was a series of programs you did back in the '80s and '90s called *Across the Blue Ridge* and the Blue Ridge CD. Can you talk a bit about what you did at that period of time? What were those shows?

Paul: I did a radio documentary for NPR called *Breaking Up Christmas—A Blue Ridge Mountain Holiday*. I wanted to explain to people and help them understand at holiday time a Christmas tradition that they might not have been aware of. What was happening in the mountains? That was the reporter in me. Here's this great tune that everybody around here plays, "Breaking Up Christmas," and it would be a great story, so I did that.

That won a prize, the National Federation of Community Broadcasters' Silver Reel, second place. I was very happy about it. People loved it. Did a lot of field work out in the mountains here, went to some events, recorded a square dance, you name it, and it worked out very well.

Across the Blue Ridge happened when I wanted to share with the public radio NPR audience some of the wonderful music that we had been broadcasting on WPAQ and also explain it in a way that was suitable to a public radio audience. There's one small set of elements that is important to public radio listeners. They want something they haven't heard. They want to be made aware of something new.

They want intelligence. They want super-high quality. They want great storytelling. If you understand those things, you can understand every successful public radio program from *Car Talk* to *A Prairie Home Companion* to *Morning Edition* to *All Things Considered* to *Marketplace*. They all have these elements in common. I felt that there was a good shot at producing a music-based program that would tell these wonderful stories of history and the musicians themselves. It was very successful. Basically, it was *All Things Considered* but music.

Craig: Let's change gears a little bit. I want to talk about you as a performer and a player. When you play fiddle and when you play banjo, are you thinking, do you have goals in mind? What are you experiencing?

Paul: When I'm just playing for myself, I just want it to sound good. I want it to feel good for me. I know that I'm doing well when I can feel, I don't know whether you would call them chemical or physiological changes in my body. They're almost similar to doing some athletic activity and feeling really fit and really relaxed and really full of air and oxygen.

Music has a profound, relaxing effect on me. Now, when I'm in jam sessions, you're interacting with other people all the time if you're a good musician. You really want to be listening and figuring out how you can contribute and the figuring out that's often subconscious.

You don't necessarily think about it rationally, but you may be feeling "What's going to work best here? Where's my place? What can I contribute?" Then translate that in the language of the instrument that you're playing so that you're not interfering but you're supporting and you're leading when you need to and helping people along and all that.

When I'm performing a show, you've got, whether it's solo or not, it's an interaction, obviously. Just as I used to do on radio, even as a newscaster of world news to millions of people, when I go out to perform somewhere, whether it's for one person, two people, or a large crowd somewhere, I just try to offer something up to that person that they'll find valuable, that they'll enjoy, and I try to perform to just to one person. There may be a crowd out there, but I want everybody to feel that it's one to one, that we're there together. I do try to pick music that will be interesting to people.

For me, a typical set of music will be a combination of the familiar and then some things to take them on an adventure and then give people a sense I'm going to bring them back home safely. It's very exciting to me and it's really, really rewarding when it goes well. My mom used to tell me about songs and sometimes we'd sing one and she'd say, "Do you know what that's about?" I'd say, "No." That she'd have me think about it.

Then, maybe if I wasn't too close, she'd help me till I understood. There's an old lullaby that she used to sing and she asked me about it one time.

> Cow and the sheep go into the pasture
> Cow said, sheep, can't you run a little faster?
> My poor lamb, safe from harm, go to sleep, little baby
> Sheep says, cow, have a sore toe
> Cow says, sorry, I did not know
> My poor lamb, safe from harm, go to sleep, little baby
> Little black lamb on the hillside
> The buzzards and the flies just pecking out its eyes
> My poor lamb, safe from harm, go to sleep, little baby

One night she asked me, "What does that mean? What do you think that is?" I didn't know. She said, "That's an African American slave woman or house employee taking care of a white child and singing it to sleep while her little baby is without anyone to care for it and nowhere near as secure." Mom used to share things like that with me from my very early age. I have kept the interest because I found it fascinating, all the stories of the songs.

I want to help continue that tradition of understanding the story of the song and maybe the people behind it and the lives they lived and why that song reflects the happiness or the struggles or the disappointments or the tragedies or the triumphs or whatever of people's lives and help other folks understand that.

18

John McCutcheon

ATLANTA, GEORGIA, 2019

"I think there's something about human beings playing music together that is so joyful and fulfilling even when you're not very good. You're going through this act of communion. It's the jam session. It's the circle at Clifftop. It's the all-night session at Musicalia when you're just playing and you're not speaking, but there's something that's happening there."

"I'm standing on the side of the road hitchhiking, and I got a banjo. It's like having a free bus pass in Appalachia. I never had to stand very long."

"I was not prepared for the generosity and openness that I encountered. I was never, ever, ever turned away or treated with suspicion. People were, 'Here, let me give you some food. Where are you staying tonight? Do you know where you're going next? Do you need a ride? You want to come to church with us? What are you doing for Thanksgiving? Gosh, you got to be someplace.' That was beyond the music. Sure, let's play."

"People will go a lot further on what they feel than on what they know, and that's what art can do so powerfully."

Old-Time Community Role: The *Musical Storyteller*. Whether he's telling them, creating them or making them live, John is the consummate performer. Everything he does, he gives it his all. His fiddle, banjo, guitar and dulcimer playing are peerless. And his songwriting is equally as formidable. John is a force of nature … for good!

Craig Evans: All right. You had started to tell me the story about your grandson asking to learn to play a traditional instrument.

John McCutcheon: Oh, yes! My job in our family, a job I absolutely loved doing, is singing the grandkids into submission, whether it be singing them to sleep as infants or into their third and fourth year when it was time for a nap. We would have this set repertoire of songs that we would follow. When they come over, they love coming into this room and having complete access to everything. There's a little hammered dulcimer somewhere over there that I put at their level. And I have little ukuleles and eighth-size violins.

My grandson, Sam, the one who happens to be turning five today, said, "Poppy, will you teach me to play the violin?" Of course, as a musician I learned from elders, and I never took lessons in any instrument. I sought out people who had been playing their entire lives and apprenticed myself to them. This was the next step in the circle.

I happened to be at the Kate Wolf Festival in California, and I scoured the grounds and found a little eighth-size fiddle and brought it home and set it up for him. Right now, he's getting used to this very unusual way of playing a musical instrument, of sticking it under your chin. He'll

John McCutcheon. Master performer and storyteller.

sit and just saw away, and I'll play something. Get him on the G and the D string, and we're playing together.

I think there's something about human beings playing music together that is so joyful and fulfilling even when you're not very good. You're going through this act of communion. I think it's why those of us who play old-time music, we don't care if we get up on stage. It's the jam session. It's the circle at Clifftop. It's the all-night session at Musicalia when you're just playing and you're not speaking, but there's something that's happening there.

I didn't start off playing fiddle and banjo music. I started playing a guitar when I was a teenager, age 14. I think it was the first time I ever heard a Pete Seeger album, and I realized it was a live concert recording. I'd never been to a concert before, but I knew, essentially, that it was one guy showing off for everybody else, and everybody's paying him or her to show off for them. This was something entirely different. Some people think there's a great divide between folk music and old-time music. I live in so many different worlds musically, and I love them all, and none of them exclude the other. They're all extensions, and they all have some commonality. One of them is the sense that whether I'm on a concert stage or in a jam session someplace, the sense that we are doing something in concert with one another—and this is old. You're fulfilling your role in this right now. That's all that matters.

I was going to St. John's University up in Minnesota. A program started, and I signed up right away. It allowed you to set up a little committee of people—it was almost a graduate program— and design a curricula. I had just started to play the banjo, which was a really lonely thing in Minnesota in 1970. I convinced my advisor to let me take a three-month independent study of hitchhiking around the Appalachian South and visiting banjo players. That's a three-month independent study that I'm still on 47 years later. I never went back. When I arrived, *I realized that I couldn't excise the banjo from the community in which it lived.*

That's the thing about academia that is so artificial. You go into a little room, and you study one very focused subject to the exclusion of everything else—17th-century French literature, for instance, theology of Thomas Aquinas. When I moved to the South, and found myself in Roscoe Holcomb's living room, it wasn't like "Could you slow down and repeat that?" That wasn't the way he learned, and it wasn't the way he was going to teach. I had to learn to listen and remember and mimic and then take it someplace else.

These people were not interested in being a subject. I was a musician. They were a musician. They wanted to play. I did not realize, as a 20-year-old, how audacious it was to knock on somebody's door and say, "Hi, I'm from a thousand miles away, and I like your music" or "I've heard of it" or "I've heard about you." Some of the people, like Roscoe, I'd heard his recordings. John Cohen, who did Roscoe's recordings, would very fastidiously document all this stuff. There were maps to his house and I thought, "My God, these people are alive." That was my and other people's road map. I'm standing on the side of the road hitchhiking, and I got a banjo. It's like having a free bus pass in Appalachia. I never had to stand very long.

People would say, "You play that thing?" I'd learned to say, "Oh, I play at it," which is the proper response. They'd say, "Well, let's hear it." They'd pull over, or not. I'd get my banjo out, and they'd say, "Oh, you play that old-fashioned way," meaning frailing, clawhammer, knockdown, whatever you want to call it, like So-and-So. Then I would say, "Really, where does So-and-So live?" Then the prospect of eavesdropping on a musical encounter more often than not intrigued my drivers who had just picked me up because I had a banjo. Then I would go see So-and-So who would introduce me to a dozen other people.

I was not prepared for the generosity and openness that I encountered. I was never, ever, ever turned away or treated with suspicion. People were, "Here, let me give you some food. Where are you staying tonight? Do you know where you're going next? Do you need a ride? You want to come to church with us? What are you doing for Thanksgiving? Gosh, you got to be someplace." That was beyond the music. Sure, let's play.

One of the reasons I'm surrounded with this orchestra of instruments is, again, because you couldn't excise a banjo player from his or her communion with a fiddle player. Then as a fiddle player, once you started messing around on the fiddle, you realized, "Oh, this is the same fingering as a mandolin, and I know how to do this from the guitar." Eventually, I realized all these sonic elements were connected.

At 20 years old, "No" wasn't in my vocabulary. It was like "You want to learn to play the hammered dulcimer?" "Sure." "How about the mountain dulcimer?" "Sure. Why not?" "Oh, there's shape-note singing at the Weirs Cove Baptist Church this Sunday." "Yes, absolutely. Let's go." Then I would get involved in that, or I'd go to the dances at Carcassonne, Kentucky, because that's where the musicians I knew were playing. Then I became interested in traditional dance.

It was the kinetic version of sitting in that circle playing the tunes. This was the natural human response to hearing this music. Let's dance, this stuff seemed so hands-on, whether it be growing your own food or making your own entertainment, writing your own songs, or telling your own stories—it was all part of the whole. No wall existed for me between all these things. I remember being at a party after the American Folklore Society meeting in Washington, D.C. We were at all Alan Jabbour's house, and the Balfa Brothers were there, and I had brought up Roscoe. Mike Seeger was there, who rode a really interesting line. He could work in the world of folklore quite legitimately, but yet, he also understood that Tommy Jarrell just wanted to play. He didn't want to be your monkey show.

A group of academicians were stewing over in the corner because we were muddying the waters here, by playing music, and laughing, and telling jokes and drinking whiskey, and whatever we were doing with the subjects. Like I said, I totally get that. It's really loosened up in the last 30, 40 years. Yes, I ran afoul of it a lot.

Craig: Almost 50 years later, you'll be playing with your grandson, accompanying him on a one-eighth-size violin at his school today. What is your role as the senior?

John: I was the beneficiary of my peers and contemporaries. Roscoe learned to play from someone by observing, standing on the side, imitating, eventually joining in. That's how the music happened. Someone younger than them was going to benefit from their experience and their knowledge and expertise. Today, it'll be really sweet because I will be accompanying him. I'll take the banjo out and he'll take the fiddle out. He'll saw away at the strings, and the kids will go, "Sam, Sam."

Craig: At some point, you decided, "I'm going to make a career out of this."

John: Oh, no, I had no designs. Making a living as a professional musician is so unlikely. Like the mainstream music business, which I knew was done with folk music. I came into it in the backwater of the folk music revival of the '50s and '60s, which was great because everything was a gift. There was no gold ring. There was no standard by which I could judge success or failure in terms of ... did I get a major label record recording contract? Am I playing at Carnegie Hall? Am I on television? No.

No. It was, "Wow, I'm figuring out a way to do this that allows me time," at the time when I was in my early 20s, "when I could play the odd gig here and there, and then spend the rest of the time learning, going out and visiting people and going home and woodshedding." It quickly became not only about music. I came into this thinking I was on this three-month independent study. I have a goal. I have to meet banjo players. I have to become a better musician.

Like I said earlier, *I couldn't excise the banjo from the community life of which it was a part.* I might play with a banjo player in church on Sunday, and he might say, "Well, come on, I got to go play on the picket line over in Harlan County for the Brookside strike," or whatever, or "There's a pie supper tonight" or "There's a square dance" or "We're having a house party," any of these things.

Then I became interested in the function of music in the community, and it was as though this was what I was supposed to be doing academically—and I thought, *this* presented it. This then occupied my life from that point on—*how music is relevant, how it is instrumental rather than ornamental.*

In the best of these times, whether we are singing gospel music at a church service or in a concert hall or singing a baby to sleep, there is a communal, dare I say, spiritual, function to all this, and it's sacred. The day I met my buddy Si Kahn, showing up on a Harlan County picket line on Thanksgiving Day, and thinking, "I've got something that can be useful, that can be helpful." It doesn't matter whether you're a carpenter or a musician, a teacher, or someone who delivers the mail, *you want to be useful.*

I remember calling Pete Seeger's house and talking to his wife, Toshi. She told me Pete is 89 years old, pacing around the house, worried that he's not being useful anymore. I thought, "That's what it's about, isn't it? It's about, you have this skill, and no matter what the skill is, you want to feel like you're being useful to your community."

Craig: Your role in life, to some degree, is to use metaphors or stories that are commonly found in traditional music and song and bring them to events, times, people, places where it provides some form of elixir that either moves things forward or helps create an emotional environment. That scene is more than something superficial. It's actually felt deeper.

John: Well, it's what I want to happen for me in an event like that. I remember telling a group of young performers with whom I was doing a workshop, "Listen, anyone who doesn't know how to get a standing ovation shouldn't be in the trade, and anyone who needs a standing ovation shouldn't be in the trade. You can't. It's artificial. You got to come to terms with that. You got to admit that and figure out what are you out there for."

Again, now, I'm talking about performance. It's an entirely different ethos when you're in a circle. I had learned this music I loved from people I loved in situations that were wonderful and beautiful and had great value to me. I wanted my audiences to enter into that and have it be more than only "I'm singing you a song for the next three minutes. It's going to be a nice little diversion." I wanted to communicate everything that had made me love this.

I would create this environment. I knew I didn't want to be academic or pedantic. "I learned this song from So-and-So in Such-and Such. He learned it from…." I'd heard that, and I wasn't giving a lecture, I wasn't conducting a class. This was entertainment. I saw how entertainment worked in community situations in the communities that I was in. That's what I wanted. I wanted people to feel like "I'm participating, I'm here, I'm risking all this."

I would create these things that had touches of familiarity for the people but would hopefully bring them into this. It seemed to work. What was really illuminating to me was when I would go back to some of these places where I had employed that technique, and they would say, "Well, what happened to the story?" because I figured I'd done this before, so let's get right down to the music. They would say, "We like this story as much as the song."

Early on, I thought, "Oh, I guess I'm onto something here." Then I married the best storyteller I know and started being invited to storytelling festivals. I'm a reader. Every good writer I know is a reader. That's how that strange combination of story and song came to be. I like going down this path that has something to do with the song. It creates an environment for it without explaining. It's like when someone explains a ballad, and then sings it. "Didn't you just do it twice?"

Craig: One of the things I really like that I'm hearing is you became a performer to share the love and the communion and the community you felt when you were experiencing those as a 20-year-old. You feel that's an important role to play—whether it's at something like a local function or it's a politically-motivated gathering. You're bringing in experiences that are about humanity. The beauty of it is when music comes in, it seems to lower the bar to acceptance. In other words, you're here as a musician, and you can sail in some of these messages of humanity that actually help calm people.

John: It's also a transmitter of information, inspiration, and connection. I was introduced to folk music when my mother sat me down at age 11 and made me watch the March on Washington. That was the first time I ever saw or heard folk music because it was Bob Dylan and Joan Baez, Peter, Paul and Mary, in addition to Mahalia Jackson and Marian Anderson. Music was a very big part of that day because of my mother's interest in the Civil Rights movement.

She had been a social worker before she became my mother. She would see this stuff, and music was connected with it—music I recognized as coming out of the church. I was raised a devout Catholic, groomed for the priesthood; in fact, I went to seminary for a while. I recognized this as music that was a part of people's lives, and it had been changed slightly, usually by changing the singular pronouns to plural, like, "*I* will not be moved" to "*We* will not be moved." "*We* will overcome." Think about the brilliance as the Civil Rights movement began, of a clergy-led social movement that employed completely unexpected tactics in the whole preaching of non-violence. It used music because people already had a spiritual and deep cultural connection that kept them buoyed and connected and inspired—it was like everything fell into place right there.

Folk music was also connected with this movement, and it was firmly put in the world of purpose. I was telling an audience this weekend when Pete Seeger died, he had written "If I Had a Hammer" and "Where Have All the Flowers Gone?" I thought those songs had always been around. The greatest compliment a songwriter can have is that *the song is judged on its own terms*. It's not a Bruce Springsteen song. It's not a Bruno Mars song. That's the beautiful thing about traditional music—it has to be a good song and it has to be listened to, remembered, and repeated, and the whole process happens over and over again.

Somehow, hundreds of years later, people are hearing about "The Rose and the Briar" intertwining up the church tower from two lovers' hearts. It made it. The story was powerful enough and well told enough and well sung enough that it survived. When I have my songwriting camps, the very first lesson is about traditional music. This is the basis of everything I do and how I write. Get to know this. This is the most important thing I can tell you. Get to know traditional music, and you'll learn how to write.

Craig: One of the things I've been searching for, but I have not found the answer for in 160 interviews, is how can we define traditional music in the light of what it actually is? Because it is history, it's emotion, and it's humanity that travels down the river of time. We can pick it up, we can play it. We can't break it, but eventually we put it back and it goes on to educate others.

When you write your songs, it's been noted you write beautiful stories that have meaning, but the meanings are about humanity, "Christmas in the Trenches," even something simple about a birthday celebration, but they become part of this lexicon that we call traditional music. It's so powerful.

John: Your question about what is traditional music—people get in fistfights about it. To me, it's more about function than definition. That was the thing about seeing the March on Washington. The most powerful moment for me was when the cameras scanned the audience while Peter, Paul, and Mary were singing "If I Had a Hammer." Everybody was singing, my mother was singing, watching it on television sitting next to me on the sofa. What was this? This was amazing. I grew up Catholic, so people didn't sing very well in church.

It was a powerful moment—this whole participation thing. I keep coming back to that, very cinematic, and it's how I write. I see the picture in front of me, which is why I use story. I watch this play out and then I simply write it down. I learned to play the guitar by checking out a book from the library, *Woody Guthrie Folk Songs*. I remember one of the first songs was "The 1913 Massacre," which is the story from Calumet, Michigan, about a New Year's Eve tragedy. Woody Guthrie takes us back to 1913 near Calumet, Michigan. A Christmas ball is being held for some copper miners in a place called Italian Hall.

John: I'll take you in a door and up a tall stair. You are immediately there. Everybody who listens to it sees their own version of this door and this stairway. They immediately have this picture of the Italian Hall. That's what conscious songwriting can do. It can create this picture in which everybody has their own vision, but they all have a vision. They're seeing this play out in front of them. That's what traditional music taught me. I look for that in my own writing.

What is it that can employ these techniques and bring everybody into this, and what can happen because of that? I do a workshop with organizers trying to encourage them to use more music in rallies and demonstrations, saying, "Okay, name three speeches from the Civil Rights movement." Nobody can do it. Now, let's start talking. Let's name all the songs you remember from the Civil Rights movement. When you're trying to influence a group of people, you can't only pour ideas into their head. People will go a lot further *on what they feel than on what they know, and that's what art can do so powerfully.*

Someone like Nimrod Workman, who sang traditional songs, but he also fought in the Battle of Blair Mountain. He had a whole robust political life that was not separate from his life as a musician. He ended up singing songs about these other events he had been a part of, and it's why I wrote "Christmas in the Trenches" because when I wrote it, most people in the United States hadn't heard that story. This was more than about this historical event, but I'm going to let you draw that conclusion. I'm not going to lead you by the nose and say, "This is what you should think about this." I'm going to tell you the story.

Craig: What is your role? What is your purpose? What is your legacy?

John: It's not an intentional thing, it's a result of what you have done.

Craig: What gives you the most satisfaction?

John: A job well done. Every musician, no matter who they are, through all of time, has taken everything that he or she has at their disposal to become the best they can be. The fiddle player, for instance, in my experience, who elicited the most from people was this guy Bechard Smith from Scott County, Virginia. He was scratchy and he didn't always play in tune, but boy, I've especially never heard more women say, "Oh, when he plays…"

He was a funny-looking guy. Didn't have many teeth left, had a big, ulcerated sore on his neck. He wasn't a hound dog or anything like that, but something about his music really moved people. It didn't have to do with ear candy. It had to do with how it made them feel. I would much rather hear sighs than claps, because that's when you've connected.

My grandson Sam doesn't know what I do. He only knows I'm his Poppy, and I play music for him, and yes, my voice comes out of the roof of the minivan, singing what he and his sister call Poppy music. He doesn't know that I stand up on stage and sing for people. I sing for only him.

HISTORIANS AND AUTHORS

Dwight Diller (left) and me in 2015.

19

Dwight Diller

Marlinton, West Virginia, 2011

"I was trying to figure out how in the world to pick up pieces, but when you're mentally ill, people don't want anything to do with you. Who were the people that accepted me? The old mountain people. Who took me in? It was the Lee Hammonds."

"Because they embraced me, it wasn't the music so much. It was accepting me. My mental illness was, I'm bipolar. The music was rescuing me from suicide, and the Hammonds rescued me from suicide. I'm sure they sensed it."

"Don't ever forget that everybody you meet is standing in a pool of tears. Well, what do people who stand in a pool of tears need? They need music. It's fragile, but it's powerful."

"I don't have to really like you one way or the other, but my boss says, 'I got to love you.' One of the ways I can show you that I love you is to let you know that I will give you every single thing that I can possibly give you, try to teach you to be better musician than I am."

Old-Time Community Role: The *Suffering Prophet*. There's only been one Dwight Diller. He lived a challenging life, but he profoundly affected those he reached. I was one of the blessed. Dwight had a mission, and that mission was to help others learn to play old-time music. He could give you a sermon on kindness with multiple examples of how those that could least afford it gave it to him. It saved him. But he figured if he could teach you the banjo, it might open doors for you to be one of the kind ones. At the end of his teaching, he'd shake a bony finger at me and said, "Now, remember, go teach someone else how to play and don't charge 'em."

Craig: Dwight Diller, of Marlinton, West Virginia, thank you for sitting down to talk about not only banjos but about banjo history. I've got to say, if it wasn't for you, I wouldn't be here. You not only taught me how to play banjo, but you also taught me a reverence for the music, and you started to teach me about community. For all of that, I thank you. As a matter of fact, I would like to dedicate this entire series to you.

Dwight Diller: Well, all right.

19. Dwight Diller

Craig: Let's start off. How did you first get into the banjo?

Dwight: My mother is from down here in Pocahontas County, and she married my dad. He'd come in from Pennsylvania in the '30s. I was born in '46 after both of them came back from the war. When I was about four or five years old, I was walking down the streets of Charleston. I saw an old man sitting on the sidewalk. My parents didn't really want anything to do with him, but he was sitting there playing with the banjo, had pencils in a cup, and that stuck in my mind all those years. January '66, I had been in Morgantown at West Virginia University [WVU] for three semesters of summer school, and I dropped out and went into the navy. My cousin and I were carrying water to make syrup out of, and I remember tellin' him, "I want to play the banjo."

Dwight Diller. Mentor and hero to many old-time students.

Craig: Right out of the blue?

Dwight: Yes. Lee Hammonds, an old man who I've spent so much time with, was born in 1883. He said often, "Don't never spoil a good notion." I've had some notions in my life, and some of them have been pretty good. One of them was to record the Hammonds. Nobody here wanted anything to do with that, and so I went out on my own and did it—and a lot of stigma was attached to me for doing that.

Craig: I'm not sure I understand why.

Dwight: West Virginians are being taught to be ashamed of themselves, ashamed of who they are, ashamed of their culture, and ashamed of their history. This place is just et' up with shame. Permeates the whole culture. This place is full of despair and depression. I grew up in a beer joint down in Hillsboro. In the '50s and early '60s, my aunt and uncle ran it—and I lived with relatives all over the county, anything to keep from living at home. What was I hearing? I was hearing the music on the jukebox, and I was internalizing Little Richard, Johnny Cash, and Jerry Lee Lewis.

I finally figured out a few years ago that they were the ones who influenced my music. I've been teaching my students here this week, and I've been showing them where the music comes from—not where it's going, but where it'd come from. I've been playing these old Black blues musicians. Their rhythms are just as much the source of this music. People say, "Well, Diller studied with the Hammonds." No, Diller didn't study with the Hammonds. They were my neighbors. What the Hammonds did was they accepted me because I'd been booted out of the navy.

When I came back here, I was trying to figure out how in the world to pick up pieces, but when you're mentally ill, people don't want anything to do with you. Who were the people that accepted me? The old mountain people. Who took me in? It was Lee Hammonds, one Hammonds family. Another Hammonds family became famous because of the Library of Congress.

Craig: I know that when they took you in, they started bringing out instruments, and you started to listen.

Dwight: No, no, no, no.

Craig: How did that start?

Dwight: No. I asked them to bring out instruments.

Craig: You were still wanting to play the banjo at this point, right?

Dwight: Yes. I asked Sherman something about playing the banjo and he said, "Well, sir, boys, I think I got my brother down here at Stillwell, and I'll believe I'll take you down there." We got in my car and drove down there. Burl was living with his sister Maggie, another sister, Ruie, and another sister, Emmy. They were up against it. They'd moved off of Williams River, off that cold mountain up there, and were living with Burl where it's a little warmer, but there was, of course, no running water or no…

Craig: Electricity?

Dwight: They had electricity, but it was like these old houses, one bulb in the center of the room.

Craig: Sure.

Dwight: I believe I had a banjo with me. They played on it for me, and then Burl got the fiddle out. I wasn't interested in the fiddle at all, but I listened. I had the $100-a-month GI bill to go to college on. I also saved up and bought a reel-to-reel tape recorder and started recording. Of course, the Library of Congress found out about it, and so they came in. They went through all of my tapes and picked out what they wanted and then came back and rerecorded it.

Craig: What inspired you to record it in the first place?

Dwight: A notion.

Craig: Were you afraid that it would be lost?

Dwight: Yes. I cared about the old stories. That's what was down deep because I grew up with the old stories—with the Hammonds, and at that time, I was wanting the banjo. Then the fiddle came, and Maggie started singing some, and nobody had paid any attention. The last time they were really, really playing the music was around 1930, when the timber boom was over, and the land had been raped, plundered, and pillaged. The culture and the interpersonal relationships were gone. The community was gone, and so I came back in and started visiting them, and I was showing a lot of interest in their music and who they were and what did they do.

They were being themselves. There was no "I'm going to try to prove something or anything." They were musicians, most of them in West Virginia. Because they embraced me, it wasn't the music so much. It was accepting me being I'm bipolar. The music was rescuing me from suicide, and the Hammonds rescued me from suicide. I'm sure they sensed it.

Craig: You're learning about the music and the community?

Dwight: I'm not really learning about it as I was "studying" it. The main thing was I'm around people who accept me. I started hearing some stories and, well, I was really sucking them up because I'd been doing that since I was a little boy—but I wasn't learning about the music as such. I was hearing the music because I don't really know about music. I don't really know about the banjo, but I grew up in these mountains, so I can feel it.

Here we are, we got the mouth of this hollow, and there's a long hollow here, and right across Knave's Run, there's another long hollow. A mountainside's over there, and creeks that go like this, and the roads go like this, and this music goes with the lay of the land.

This stuff is so powerful, so extremely powerful, but it's also fragile. *You've got to really be careful because the spirit of the music will walk away, and you won't know it.* If you start using it for your own glory—the spirit of this music, the spirit of these mountains—I operate in another world, the spirit of the Lord—it'll walk out. You start using that to manipulate other people and to get yourself ahead, it won't stand it. That's what I'm talking about: money and power. If you start using it for your own glory, it won't work.

Craig: That spirit wants you to look within and develop what's within.

Dwight: To Diller [points to his head], this can never, ever, ever play music. It can look at dots on a page, but I'm operating in a world where there's spirit and there's heart. *What's happened, something takes place, a brokenness. I quoted my seminary professor because my instructor said, "Don't ever forget that everybody you meet is standing in a pool of tears." Well, what do people who stand in a pool of tears need? They need music.*

It's fragile, but it's powerful. You all got a brokenness in there, and I want you to play your music from that brokenness because this music is a celebration of life, and these modal tunes from Central West Virginia, what they insist on if they're played properly is that you face your own death. Until you face your own death, you ain't ready to live.

Craig: Because in the face of death, all irrelevance falls away. That's your point.

Dwight: Yes. There's nothing like knowing that you're going to get hung tomorrow morning to start getting your priorities straight. Life has beat on me so much, but I have to count it as a blessing because I've been called to the ministry a long time ago. How in the world can you minister if you ain't been broke? All you got is fluff. You can't tell anything. This is what the music's about. Until I absorb part of your pain, which is empathy, that's what teaching you is about.

Craig: Let me play student for a minute. If I come here, and I've got the pain, and I've stripped away the irrelevance, and I'm open and I'm vulnerable now, how is the music going to administer to me?

Dwight: Well, first of all, I have to let you know—that I love you.

Craig: I get that.

Dwight: I don't have to really like you one way or the other, but my boss says, "I got to love you." One of the ways I can show you that I love you is to let you know I will give you every single thing that I can possibly give you, try to teach you to be better musician than I am. That means I got to do stuff to call you out of you because I have to do stuff to bring you to the point where you start letting down those walls to protect yourself. Well, the only way you can open up is if I open up first.

Craig: That's what you do.

Dwight: Be vulnerable. I have to be vulnerable. That's what the music's about—being vulnerable. Don't come in here and tell me you know 50 tunes. If you tell me you know 50 tunes, I wonder, "How in the world can you say that?" He really know tunes—it's like how many friends can you really have, close friends, over a lifetime? Maybe this one's there for a while. That's the way it is with tunes.

Craig: You were my teacher, and everything you've told me happened. You sat with me, you understood where I was, and you wanted to make sure I learned it right.

Dwight: No. Well, be careful with the word "right." Show me your hand. See, if we looked at it closely, those are different fingerprints. You've got your pulse inside of you. I've got my pulse. I don't want any Diller clones. I don't work towards that. I want to sit beside you, yes, I have to show you some stuff, but you can do it. That's the thing I want my students to know. *You're good enough. As long as you respect the music, you let this come out.*

I want to give you as much of my heritage as I can because this is my heritage, but I want you to take it back, say, to New York City. You go walk the sidewalks in New York City, with your pulse, but then I want you to start paying attention. "Look at these mountains." You have a mountain over there in New York City that's maybe as high as that mountain over there. They have all kinds of valleys going in and out.

Well, I want you to play the ambience, these mountains in New York City with the wind blowing, and all that kind of stuff, and all these different people groups. Here, here, here, here. I want you to play that. Say, "I'm playing Manhattan-mountain banjo." I hadn't thought about it like that. I'm playing Manhattan-mountain banjo.

Craig: I want to tell a story on you. When I sat at the jam on a Saturday night in Lansing, Michigan, with a room full of people that probably hung out at Elderly

Instruments, forty or fifty fabulous musicians were sitting around us. You came down the stairs, and there was one place next to me and you said, "Is anybody sitting there?" I said, "No." You sat down and said, "Now remember, no notes. You can't play any notes." I said, "Yes, Dwight." Then a guy came in and stood across from us. We'd played a tune. He was playing banjo. He'd been one of your students. He was really good. He was not making a show of himself. He was playing the way you instructed.

At one point you stopped and said, "Now, I want you to watch him. He's the best musician in here." I said, "Yes, I've heard him play. He's pretty good." You said, "No, no, no." You watch him. He played a couple more numbers, and at that point, he looked around. He'd been the best banjo player in the room. Then he put his banjo down and picked up a guitar and came back.

For the next three or four songs, he started playing guitar, and you said, "Did you see that?" I said, "Yes, I saw that." He said, "That's why he's the best musician in the room. The tune was so important to him. He listened to it carefully, and he heard banjos and he heard fiddles, and what was missing was the instrument that he could bring, a guitar. Because it was about the tune, to make the tune the best it could be. There was this reverence."

Dwight: Yes.

Craig: Now, that story was probably the most profound story that stuck with me from my experience with you. I want to say something else to you. It's about showing compassion and love and loving on each individual person. You pay attention to the one. You've always paid attention to the one. I was one of the ones. You have touched hundreds if not thousands of ones like me. You've demonstrated compassion, and you came alongside them and given them everything you have, and said, "Trust this. Reach deep into this. Look around yourself and continue to grow and minister yourself through this."

Dwight: I help you.

Craig: Yes.

Dwight: You're gone. If I can help you again, great, but I want you to do it on your own. I want you to fight your own way through.

Craig: I want to say thank you for that.

Dwight: Well, I appreciate it, but it's what I'm about. It's what I do. I'm driven. I have to do that. I have to do it that way no matter what it costs. There's hardly been any money.

Craig: Well, that's a part of it.

Dwight: Last thing I want to say, then … it's not about me. It's not about me. It's not about me.

20

Bill Malone

Madison, Wisconsin, 2017

"My daddy was a cotton farmer. We didn't own the land. He was a tenant farmer, so it was a pretty bleak life, particularly for my mother. She never enjoyed being out there on the farm, and she longed to escape, and her way of escaping was through music. That's how I got introduced to music and found out the kind of power that it could exert in people's lives."

"Country is a latecomer to the American music scene. When I was growing up, the term that we used, and I think it was pretty widely used, was 'hillbilly.' Outsiders, of course, came up with the term, but we embraced it, saying, 'Okay, you want to call us hillbilly? That's what we are. We're proud to be farmers or children of farmers.' The record labels didn't quite know what to do with this music when they first began to exploit it in the 1920s. I think the Brunswick Label used 'songs from Dixie.' The Columbia label used 'old familiar tunes' to describe its first catalog of old-time music."

"One revelation was finding exactly how interrelated country music has been with other forms of music. From the very beginning, it drew heavily upon other styles, both of antiquity and more recent. I got thinking about every form of American music from jazz to blues to gospel to rhythm and blues to country, even protest music had some sort of Southern connection."

Old-Time Community Role: The *Historian*. If it wasn't for people like Bill, we'd have no history or records to teach us how we got here. A wizard at remembering and placing people, stories and facts, Bill has written the seminal books that will provide answers to students of traditional music for years to come. He's also a fervent fan of those that paved the way.

Dr. Bill Malone: I had the reputation of being a singer but, above all, of knowing many, many songs. One weekend I went with my supervising professor, Dr. Joe B. Frantz, and some graduate students to Houston to attend the Blue Bonnet Bowl. We sang one song after another, and over dinner that night out of the blue, Dr. Frantz said, "Since you like that music so much, why don't you write a history of Nashville publishing?" That's the way he phrased it. He was a business historian. I said, "You can do that? You can actually write on something you like?" He said, "Yes," so I got into the topic with no preparation for it academically.

The only preparation I had was growing up in the country music culture and hearing and singing the music all my life. What started out as a history of Nashville publishing became a general history of American country music.

Craig: Dr. Bill Malone, author, historian, teacher, radio DJ, and professor emeritus from Tulane. Thank you for sitting down to talk to me today about traditional American music.

Bill: I'm glad to be able to do it.

Dr. Bill Malone. Author of books about his passion and love of traditional music.

Craig: We're sitting in your home in Madison, Wisconsin. How long have you been here?

Bill: Around 21, 22 years.

Craig: Are you still affiliated with Tulane, even though you're up here?

Bill: No, I'm officially an emeritus now.

Craig: Initially, you're from Texas. In fact, if I remember correctly, you were born in 1936.

Bill: August 25, 1934.

Craig: Tell me a little bit about how music first came into your life—because it created this theme that traveled with you throughout your entire life.

Bill: I was born at home on a farm in East Texas about 80 miles east of Dallas and 20 miles west of Tyler. My daddy was a cotton farmer. We didn't own the land. He was a tenant farmer, so it was a pretty bleak life, particularly for my mother. She never enjoyed being out there on the farm, and she longed to escape, and her way of escaping was through music. That's how I got introduced to music and found out the kind of power that it could exert in people's lives.

What I would call the revolutionary event in our life was when Daddy bought the Philco battery radio in 1939. Before that time, of course, I was introduced to music through my mother. She sang all the time, particularly when she was working or when she was nursing some sort of grievance. She would sing the old gospel songs—sentimental parlor songs. I grew up hearing them and knowing them and seeing how much they meant to her. The coming of the radio in our home in 1939 was so important because it introduced us to the world outside to let us know things were happening at other places. I began to hear the radio hillbilly singers, as I called them, coming out of Dallas and Fort Worth and Shreveport, Tulsa, and to me those people became part of the family.

Craig: Who were some of those names?

Bill: Out of Dallas, they were the Callahan Brothers and the Shelton Brothers, and the old ballad singer named "Peg" Moreland who sang what he called "diddies from the past." From Fort Worth, the Chuck Wagon Gang, a gospel group that still exists today. Obviously, they're not the same people, but a Chuck Wagon Gang still exists. The Stamps Quartet out of Dallas also was doing gospel music. Then about the same time we got the radio, we began listening to the Grand Ole Opry from Nashville. That's when the Opry went national, formally broadcast over WSM, which was a powerful 50,000-watt clear-channel station.

It could be heard all over the South at various times, but in 1939, the Grand Ole Opry gained network status over NBC, and so we began hearing Roy Acuff and Bill Monroe and all those other people who were on the Opry. On one hand, we thought that we could do what they were doing. We could also sing songs if we wanted to. If we tried hard enough, we could be radio performers. On the other hand, they were exotic to us. My brother tuned in the Carter Family about every weekday night. They were performing at that time out of XERF in Ciudad Acuña, Mexico.

The Carter family sang about cowboys out on the western plains, and mountaineers way back in the remote recesses of the Blue Ridge Mountains, that sort of thing. It was wonderful. They brought fantasy to us, for one thing, which was very important during those Depression years. It was a way of escaping through those songs about cowboys and mountaineers and hobos and railroad people. Fantasy on one hand, reality on the other because they sang about things that we knew, the everyday details of life and of people's struggles to cope with adversity and to make something worthwhile out of their lives.

Craig: Your mother's side. She was the one with the music?

Bill: Mom grew up in a musical family. I don't know if anybody played any instruments except maybe a piano, but they all sang. Her parents and grandparents knew shape-note music. My mother grew up hearing those old religious songs. Her father was a railroad man who worked for the Cotton Belt railroad. He was an engineer, and I think he eventually may have become a conductor too. Mom was always fascinated with railroad life, and she loved the sound of a railroad whistle. She loved railroad life, and so I could always sing a railroad song to her, and she was very happy about it.

Craig: One of the things you mentioned are songs of despair, I think were your words. Did she use traditional music as a form of emotional outlet?

Bill: Very much so. Generally gospel songs. "Farther Along" was one of her favorites, as were "Drifting Too Far from the Shore," "We'll Understand It, All By and By," "Leave It There." Some people call that "Take Your Burdens to the Lord and Leave It There," but that was a special favorite of hers. You could always tell when she was worried about something—or maybe when she had a grievance against my father.

She would burst out of the song, but beyond that, aside from the fact that she used music to accompany her everyday labors, sometime we'd get together and sing. I did that well up until adulthood. When I would come home from my teaching job, I'd get out my guitar, and we'd sing every song that came to mind.

Craig: You leave your hometown of Tyler and you go to school at some point.

Bill: I first go to college in Tyler. I attended Tyler Junior College from 1952 to 1954, and then on the strength of a $35-a-semester tuition and a little bit of money that my daddy had managed to accumulate selling a few stocks and things like that, I went off to Austin in 1954—and stayed there. I earned the BA in '56, MA in the '58, and my PhD, 1965.

Craig: This is all in history?

Bill: All in history.

Craig: Why history?

Bill: I love stories. I love to hear my parents and the old timers around home tell stories. Then I guess the same thing that drove me into history is what drove me into country music. I love the stories found in both of them. All the while I was there in Austin, I was always singing around the departments. If I wasn't singing, I was humming, and I'm sure it's a pretty irritating habit for a lot of people to be around someone humming. I still do it. I can't keep from humming. I began singing for parties.

Craig: When did you first become a musician yourself? When did you first start playing?

Bill: Early or mid-1940s. My older brother, Wiley, worked for a neighbor and got a cheap guitar and began learning chords on it. Then the other brother, Kelly, began picking up the chords too. I didn't learn at the time. I always sang with somebody else as accompaniment, but I remember the one song that we all played, and the song, it still means a lot to me today. It's Rex Griffin's "The Last Letter." I think he wrote that in about 1938. He was actually in Dallas for a while singing over local stations where he introduced it, and that's the song my brothers learned to play on the guitar. Later on, I made it a point to learn that same song—one of the great songs of unrequited love, "The Last Letter."

Craig: I'm jumping ahead here, but I can't help it at this point. What you've demonstrated through members of your family is how traditional music has been used to convey something you're feeling. What was it about country music that you delved into and dedicated your life? Was that the draw—or was there more?

Bill: It was accessible. For one thing, it was usually melodies that told stories you could easily hum or sing and words that could be understood. I've always been impressed by that story. It might be apocryphal, but it's told as if it was the truth. This comes from Nat Hentoff, the jazz critic and writer. He said that Charlie Parker, the great progressive blues musician, often went into a little cafe or bar in New York and put his nickels in the jukebox—and he played country songs. Charlie's friends couldn't understand it. "Charlie, how can you be playing that stuff?" and Charlie said, "Listen to the stories, man. Listen to the stories."

Now, the next year, the country music told stories that people could identified with. When you heard Hank Williams sing, it sounded like he was singing directly to you. He understood your problems. You believe that he was coming from the same place you came from. Although he was from Alabama, we from East Texas, but he sang those true-to-life stories, and with great conviction. That's a wonderful thing about Hank Williams. I think his singing could insinuate itself into the hearts of anybody, if they would just listen.

Craig: What are some other standards or tunes that you think are the best examples of country music today? Let's maybe take one of those and break it down and talk about it.

Bill: Songs from the past?

Craig: Yes.

Bill: I've always loved a song like "Pictures from Life's Other Side" a lot, with its little vignettes about the tragic side of life. The gambler who gambles away his mother's ring and then falls over dead. The two brothers that meet in the night, one of them is a good boy, the other is bad, but they have a fight and the bad boy takes his brother's life. There's a woman. She has a child, I guess, maybe out of wedlock, but she jumps in the river and dies. Morbid stories, but still true stories that if we have an experience, we know about them, and I think they tell something that's real.

Craig: Grimm's fairy tales, do you think the—
Bill: I think they're cathartic.

Craig: Yes, but are the vignettes to show values?
Bill: Yes. Sometimes you have to learn not to do what the protagonist has done. If you want to escape Willie's fate, you don't knock up your girlfriend and kill her. Or there are songs about the sacrifices of mothers and the hard work of fathers, and about the desire for the open road, the loneliness of life on the farm—and you hit the road and follow that lonesome railroad whistle you've heard or maybe jump on a freight train and go someplace. Rambling songs are one of the major parts of the

country music repertoire—but the songs extolling home and its contentment and treasures, that's another side. I think there two sides of the same coin.

Craig: What are some of the other categories? Clearly, we've touched on the things about despair. What about joy? What about freedom?

Bill: Fiddle tunes are probably the oldest category of songs in country music. Some of those made the transit across the Atlantic. Many of them came from African American sources, in fact, a surprisingly large number. Some were made in this environment.

It's tunes people could listen to for enjoyment or dance to them. What people used to call "frolics" were a very common part of both Southern and Midwestern rural heritage. I didn't learn how important country dances were in the Midwest until we moved up here and I learned that they were still going on. What I thought was strictly a Southern phenomenon was Midwestern, maybe New England too.

The Saturday night tradition of inviting the neighbors in, moving furniture out of the front room, and getting a local fiddler, whoever you could find who could play tunes until midnight or early in the morning and have a house party. That's another very common term. That's where Bob Wills and a lot of Western swing musicians and others first learned. They learned how to play music in the dance environment. They learned to play for their customers. They wanted to keep people on the dance floor. They wanted people to listen to what they were playing, and so they learned to improvise and come up with new tunes and new ways of playing them.

Craig: We've touched on lots of different sources for this music. When did the term "country" start to be used to categorize all these different sources?

Bill: Actually, country is a latecomer to the American music scene. When I was growing up, the term that we used, and I think it was pretty widely used, was "hillbilly." Outsiders, of course, came up with the term, but we embraced it, saying, "Okay, you want to call us hillbilly? That's what we are. We're proud to be farmers or children of farmers." The record labels didn't quite know what to do with this music when they first began to exploit it in the 1920s. I think the Brunswick Label used "songs from Dixie." The Columbia label used "old familiar tunes" to describe its first catalog of old-time music.

I think that's a good term too because these were songs and tunes that were floating around in the community and were familiar to people. People didn't necessarily know them in their entirety, but they knew them in fragments. After the music began to be commercialized, then they began to lengthen the songs and come up with their own. I should say that "hillbilly" began to be used around 1925. Although the term itself is older, it was first applied to a country dance band in 1925, and then other people began to use it, and the record labels began to exploit the term, but it wasn't until after World War II.

Mainly as a result, I think, of the music's expansion, it's commercial strength, that people began to say, "Hillbilly, that's not a good term. We ought to come up with something better than that. Something more respectable." People like Ernest Tubb and Red Foley and others began to use the word "country" to describe the music, and it gradually caught on. Actually, as far as human history goes, it's a pretty late development.

Craig: I know you've written the preeminent book about country music, but I know you've written a lot of other books. Walk me through some of the things that you've written.

Bill: *Country Music, USA* was the first book, and it's unusual in that on the cover, they tried to make it an old-time placard—the kind of placard you would find pasted on a wall or on a post. That was 1968.

You asked about revelations earlier. One revelation was finding how country music has been interrelated with other forms of music. From the very beginning, it drew heavily upon other styles, both of antiquity and more recent. I got thinking about every form of American music from jazz to blues to gospel to rhythm and blues to country, even protest music had some sort of Southern connection.

I may have been one of the first persons to use the term "Southern" music. In around 1979 I wrote a book called *Southern Music, American Music*. Also growing increasingly aware of how strong myth figured into the shaping of the music and its perception. Three of the most important myths are:

1. The idea that the music developed untouched way back in the remotest recesses of the Southern Appalachians.

Bill Malone's book *Country Music, USA*, first published in 1968, is now celebrating an updated, 50th anniversary edition.

It's a very romantic concept but not true. Appalachians have been important, and many, many great musicians have come out of the Appalachians, but the music is far broader than that. The music came from a thousand different sources.

    2. Of course, another very controlling myth, and one's very appealing to people, is the myth of the cowboy and the idea that he'd have to shape American music, which is another overblown idea.

    3. Another myth, but I think a strong reality, is that the music has drawn heavily on the themes and styles of the city. A lot of the oldest country songs were born on Tin Pan Alley in New York City. People like Gussie Davis, an African American composer; Charles K. Harris, the man who wrote "After the Ball," a huge pop hit of the 1890s. They didn't know they were writing country songs.

In fact, they weren't—they were just writing pop songs, but those songs endured. They moved out into the hinterlands. They were embraced by people and, eventually, they showed up on hillbilly records, and they're still performed today. A lot of these songs can be heard today in bluegrass music, for example, which has long been a receptacle of old music.

My book, *Country Music, USA* has been, in many ways, an encyclopedic work, and a lot of people read it for that reason because they want to find out something about their favorite performer, their favorite song, but I always wanted to have a chance to do something more interpretative, too.

I finally did that with the book *Don't Get Above Your Raisin': Country Music and the Southern Working Class*. In it, I treat different topics that have been central to country music's history: home, rambling, religion, politics, the dance tradition, humor. I devote a chapter to each of those and treat them chronologically to try to explain how they've been treated in the music over the years.

Craig: I know you've written some biographies.

Bill: Yes. Three are related with each other. I've always been impressed with Mike Seeger's versatility. The fact that he could play any instruments there was, and not only play them, but play about every style associated with them. The first time I got to know him was at a conference in London on the Carter Family. Then I asked him, "Has anybody written your biography? If not, I'd like to write it." He embraced the idea, and the result was this book called *Music from the True Vine*, with the subtitle *Mike Seeger—Life and Musical Journey*.

"True vine" is the term he used to describe the cluster of Southern styles which interrelated with each other and which helped to shape American music as we know it. In fact, with his longtime associate, they had a mutual discovery. When he went down to Baltimore in the late '50s as a conscientious objector and began working in a TB hospital, he met members of the Dickens family. I think at least one of the Dickens brothers was a patient at the hospital. He began playing music with him, and then one day the brother said, "Oh, you ought to meet my sister, Hazel. She knows a lot of songs."

Hazel was living in Baltimore as part of that great throng of Appalachian migrants who had moved on to Baltimore during World War II. And then years later, he got to know Hazel very well. They began playing bluegrass music with each other at local house parties. Both of them gave each other credit. Hazel said that Mike validated her life and music, making her realize that it was respectable and worthwhile. Of course, Mike gave her all the credit for introducing him to this great body of old-time music and to the people who played it.

This book is a collection of about 40 of Hazel's songs, along with her commentary as to why she wrote them. I wrote the lengthy introductory biography which appears in the book.

Bill Clifton had been one of my favorite singers in the 1950s. He left the United States in 1963 and lived many years of his life in England after he had to inspire an interest in the music there and on the European continent. I heard his music in Washington, D.C., when he came back to the United States and played there. I tell that whole story in the introduction of this book, *Bill Clifton: America's Bluegrass Ambassador to the World*.

My most recent book, *Sing Me Back Home: Southern Roots and Country Music*, came out in 2014. It is a collection of various articles, essays, and liner notes that I've written over the years.

Country Music, USA first came out in 1968 and has been republished for its 50th anniversary.

Craig: Do you have any idea how many copies have been sold?

Bill: I think it did very well for a while and was the biggest seller University of Texas had for a long time. I still get a little bit of a royalty check each year. For a while, it was used in classrooms when the great discovery of country music came. And when music departments began accepting country music as a legitimate discipline, people began to use it as a textbook. I never had any idea that the book would do that well. In fact, I didn't have any idea that country music would do as well as it has since then.

I often despaired of country music's future since it was becoming so pop-oriented, and I thought it was losing its identity. I hope I have something to do with telling people about its origins—and encouraging people to study it and then go back and listen to the pioneers of the music.

Craig: I do know that through the years, Smithsonian Folkways has contacted you.

Bill: I should have mentioned that. I believe it was in 1981, I put together a collection of classic country songs for the Smithsonian, called *The Smithsonian Collection of Classic Country Music*. I chose all the songs and wrote the commentary for each song and wrote the overall large-size paperback book which commented on it. I was glad to do that. I think the book introduced country music to a lot of folks who wouldn't have paid attention to it otherwise.

Then, in October of this year, I'll be going to Walpole, New Hampshire, to be part of Ken Burns' documentary on country music, which is coming out either next year or the year after. I've read scripts for them. I was on camera for two or three hours.

Craig: Congratulations on such an acknowledgment.

Bill: Thank you. This brings me up to today, I think.

21

Dom Flemons

Washington, D.C., 2018

Dom Flemons studied English, history and literature in college. He received a degree in English.

"*The Black Banjo Gathering was a revelation because I found that string band music is African American music.*"

"*As you get deeper into the music, you find that the beauty of the music is the cultural interchange that happens between the whole culture, Black and white, and then of course you get Native American, and you get all these other types of music that end up showing up because it's America. It's a mixing and a melting pot of everything.*"

"*Once I started studying in North Carolina, I found that there was a discrepancy between rural Black culture and urban Black culture. It's still a fairly new idea to be able to talk about both as separate things that can be brought together into a single room. In popular culture, African American culture is urban; it is never country. Either you start in the country and you go to the city or you just stay in the city.*"

"*String band music is always based in a rural atmosphere or a root that is rural. That's something I found that hadn't really been written in the books. Again, to bring it back to the Black Banjo Gathering, when I met Joe Thompson, all of a sudden I realized, 'Wait a second, Lead Belly is not the exception to the rule like the books would have him described, but he is the rule, and the blues is the exception. Blues was the commercialized form of Black music.'*"

Old-Time Community Role: The *Researcher*. Dom was born with many, many gifts. Most of us recognize his performance skills and banjo-playing acumen. But it's his mind that's the most amazing. He's deep into Black music history, uncovering stories that will demonstrate just how much Black input has shaped and defined our traditional music. And there's much more beyond that. Dom will prove to be one of our time's most proficient historians. But one cannot overlook his music. It's stellar.

Dom Flemons: We [the Carolina Chocolate Drops] kept a really heavy schedule, doing 250 to 260 days a year, all the way through the entire time we worked. It went all the way from schoolhouses in North Carolina to school programs during Black History Month, all the way up to the Grand Ole Opry, and then touring different parts of the world. After we had done so much stuff, covering so many goals, we looked at the yellow pad and realized we had covered every single goal on it, maybe four or five times in our nine years together.

Craig: Right up to the Grammy.

Dom: I was glad we did the Grammy the first time and won it the first time—because we were nominated a second time and didn't get it. People wait all their lives to get a Grammy. It wasn't lost on any of us that we got it the first time. Now, it's a part of all of our careers, no matter what any of us decide to do.

Dom Flemons. Co-founder of the Carolina Chocolate Drops. A peerless musician and historian for our time.

Craig: Dom Flemons, Grammy award winner, co-founder of The Carolina Chocolate Drops, host of *The American Songster*, and Black music historian, thank you for taking the time to sit down today to talk about traditional music.

Dom: It's my pleasure, Craig. Thank you so much for having me.

Craig: I'd really like to start with the story of you.

Dom: Life began for me in Phoenix, Arizona. I was born on August 30, 1982. I had a pretty straight-ahead upbringing, I guess. My father is African American from Flagstaff, Arizona. His parents were from east Texas, where his father came from. Then his mother came from right outside of Little Rock, Arkansas. After World War II, they moved out to the West Coast. My grandfather became a Church of God in Christ preacher, and then he moved to Flagstaff to follow the sawmill work. My grandmother was a domestic; she worked at the college for a while.

They were the main two church people in the Black community of Flagstaff. My mom's family is Hispanic. My nana was married to my mom's biological father, and they ended up divorcing. Then she remarried a fella named Bill Dickey, who was a very light-skinned Black man from Darby, Pennsylvania. He was an insurance man

Grammy awarded to the Carolina Chocolate Drops in 2018.

as well as a golfer. There was a middle-upper-middle-class Black culture, and then there was a country-upper-middle-class. African American culture was multifaceted from the get-go with me. Also, Phoenix is a place where a lot of refugees come.

In high school, I knew a lot of Serbo-Croatians and Native American, Dene, Sioux, and Papago cultures. When I was in fifth grade, I started playing the drums—rhythm has been a lifelong passion for me.

About junior year in high school, a documentary, *The History of Rock 'n' Roll*, was on PBS. One of the episodes was called "Plugging In," and it talked about the '60s folk music revival—Bob Dylan, Ramblin' Jack, Phil Ochs, Judy Collins, and Peter, Paul, and Mary were in it—the transition from the New England folk music scene over to the California music scene. The episode ends in Monterey with Hendrix and Janis Joplin and all these folks.

The whole documentary is great because it had Louis Jordan and Muddy

Waters and it had all the Sun Records folks like Elvis and Jerry Lee and Carl Perkins. Then also '70s and '60s music from The Beatles and The Beach Boys. I got a nice cross-section of how the music fit in a timeline because I was always interested in history. I was also interested in literature, and what music meant as literature, and what it meant culturally for people. I'd hear a song on the radio that meant something to so many people at one time, [it] was always of interest to me.

From there, I found a bootleg copy of the movie *Festival*, Murray Lerner's documentary on the Newport Folk Festival from '63 to '66, which opened me up to a bigger idea of what folk music was. At first, it was only singer-songwriters and traditional players like Koerner, Ray and Glover and people like that. Then when I saw the Newport film, it opened it up to people like Doc Watson and Mississippi John Hurt and Dock Boggs, Brownie McGhee, Sonny Terry, as well as Bascom Lamar Lunsford, whose clogging group is in this movie, and Ed and Lonnie Young with the fife and drum.

Again, since I was into drums, fife and drum music was on my radar forever after that point, which is how I ended up starting. I decided to start playing guitar. I went to the coffeehouse like any other kids, 16–17 years old, learning songs, playing them, and experimenting. I would learn people's whole repertoires because it was available. It was a time right before the internet was super-prevalent. I still had to go out and buy records and search them out and do research.

I had to sit and sit with that because I had only so much time and money to be able to focus on the music. I was still going to college at Northern Arizona University. For a time, I had a stint where I stopped playing music, and then I started doing slam poetry. I started writing satirical pieces. I was interested in people like Lord Buckley and David Steinberg, and Bill Cosby's early records, and Richard Pryor.

I started taking all those ideas of this early stand-up comedy, because at the time, it was still before people who weren't DJs but were interested in vinyl. I was able to go to any shop, and for $2 to $3, I could get the entire collection of any artist. These faraway labels with all these musicians from long ago was slightly romantic for me. Like, wow, I wonder what these musicians were like. They have such intellectual ideas.

Craig: I want to go back for a moment and talk about you as a kid.
   Dom: Oh, yes.

Craig: Because what I just heard was how interested you got in things. It's like if you discover something, you have to discover everything about it.
   Dom: Oh, absolutely.

Craig: You were always that way?
   Dom: Absolutely.

Craig: What was the first musical experience? I know you got into drums, but were your mom and dad musical, were your grandparents?

Dom: They weren't musical in the sense that they played instruments, but they had a great appreciation for listening to music and buying records. My dad, for example, used to go visit his family in Las Vegas, where he got to see James Brown in 1963—and he could see any of the show acts that were in the Black section of town. Being from a small town, they had only one radio station. He was also exposed to the pop music of the day and the country music of the day. He was a big fan of Buck Owens, Hank Williams, and Charlie Daniels.

Craig: I took you off track there, now I want to take you back to college. Music is a passion with you at this point. What are you studying?

Dom: Oh, I'm studying English. I was interested in history and literature, which evolved into a love of Shakespeare, a love of Chaucer, a love of William Wordsworth, Edwin Arlington Robinson, and a lot of the classic poets including T.S. Eliot and Ezra Pound. Again, I was able to supplement this as I also started listening to folk music, because people like Eric Anderson or Bob Dylan constantly reference these guys. I was also interested in voices. I started doing a thing that I now called vocal contortionism, where I mimic different voices.

T.S. Eliot would be like, "And then the women, they come and go, speaking of Michelangelo, and shall I eat a peach." I got into the nuances of doing that. Bob Dylan had a particular sound to him when he said, "Go away from my window. Leave at your own chosen speed." He had a reedy voice like that. Records were also a way to be able to bring literature and culture together for me in a way that I could hear it in a unique voice.

Craig: Are you performing at this point?

Dom: Absolutely. At first, it was such a personal thing that I loved, and I learned the songs on my own, but I found that nobody knew any of this music. Britney Spears is really popular at this time. The Spice Girls and the Backstreet Boys were very popular. I was also watching *The History of Rock 'n' Roll* and seeing the emergence of something like The Beatles. I felt like I was in a very similar period, when pop musicians were all you'd hear … schlocky pop music. I had more interest in the depth found in this more intellectually-based music because I was reading a lot at the same time.

Then I tried to busk; I took my guitar out into the street. My father was more interested in me getting my education. When I told him that I wanted to be a musician, he said, "Just go to college. Then let's talk." I'm glad he did that because later on as I became more of an academically-based musician, then I could turn around and say, yes, I got a degree in English, I got a BA. I've at least paid my dues as an academic on a basic level.

Craig: What happened when you were out of college?

Dom: The funny thing happened. I met a fellow at the local coffeehouse, Sule Greg Wilson. He was one of the few Black people I had seen at this particular scene. At that time, fiddle and banjo music wasn't really of interest to me. I was always interested in the songs and the songsters and people that were presenting multiple types of songs. Singing and playing at the same time was always of more interest to me than instrumental music. When I met Sule, he told me about this event that was formulating called the Black Banjo Gathering.

I said, "Man, I don't have any money to do this. I'm a college student." They worked it out so that they took care of my accommodations if I could get there. Tony Thomas picked me up from the airport in Charlotte. Then I went out to Boone, North Carolina, for the first time, and became part of the Black Banjo Gathering. Here's the first time I met Mike Seeger, who had changed my life profoundly. I was into his album *Solo: Old-Time Country Music*, which was a revelation for me, to be able to mix and match different traditional types of music in a way that fit musically.

I met Cece Conway and Joe Thompson, who was working with Bob Carlin. Also met Cheick Hamala Diabate from Mali and Daniel Jatta from The Gambia—and Rhiannon for the first time. I met Don Vappie, the great four-string banjo player from New Orleans, and Algia Mae Hinton. It was fantastic to go to North Carolina and see a vibrant scene of musicians who were interested and also that they might be willing to pay—which was important. In Phoenix, I couldn't find gigs. Rock bands, DJs, and reggae bands were what paid.

So for me, it was also a way to say, "Let me try to do this music thing." I was done with my obligations to my parents, and I'd finished college two months after that, and so I said, "Alright, I'm going to pack everything up and go." I sold everything I owned—well, maybe about 75 percent of everything I owned—packed up the rest, jumped in the car, and drove to North Carolina with no notion except that I knew Rhiannon and the two of us had talked about doing music together. It felt like I was on an open highway heading out to a new adventure.

The Black Banjo Gathering was a revelation because I found that all the books I had read, it was not prominent that string band music is African American music. Alan Lomax put together an album called *Roots of the Blues* for New World Records, and it features a Black string band, Miles and Bob Pratcher. I found myself interested in this string band music. As you get deeper into the music, you find that the beauty of the music is the cultural interchange that happens between the whole culture, Black and white, and then of course you get Native American, and you get all these other types of music that end up showing up because it's America.

It's a mixing and a melting pot of everything. The perception of the music, which has been this way since the early 20th century, is that it's Black and white music. It comes from the idea that, if you break it down with someone like Ralph Peer, they started out recording ethnic music in New York—Greek music, Italian music, German music, and, at the time, there was a Southern Black audience that had been untapped. When Mamie Smith's "Crazy Blues" ended up being released through the songwriter Perry Bradford on Okeh Records, that showed there was a Southern Black audience.

It became race records, because if you think back on people like Booker T.

Washington, *uplifting the race* was the key phrase of the day. Of course, there's a working-class white population that follows right behind that. Then they made hillbilly records, which, again, hillbilly is not necessarily the most positive term to say for poor white people. Nevertheless, race and hillbilly ended up being the two ethnic categories for Black and white music.

Now, whether the music itself was that separate on the ground level is completely arbitrary. When it comes to old-time music, a lot of where people come from are the field recordings that were made outside of the commercial industry. When you get into the non-commercial world, you start finding a lot more cultural interaction was happening. Then you start understanding people like John and Alan Lomax and how they wanted to go out there and say, "Wait a second, these people are not telling the full story, so we need to go out with the Library of Congress and tell the true story."

At first, when you read something by Alan Lomax, you might think, "Oh, he's a little bit ambitious," but if he's coming from an idea that there's a mass media world that is completely expanding and taking everything over, and you have the notion to document it, all of a sudden, you see that this guy had done a righteous deed and how he decided to document it.

I got into an album of Library of Congress stuff that Electro Records put out, and they had a section on square dances.

Also, being interested in the type of music, the songs—I've never been a big fan of hip hop in a general sense—string band music had this link that was so close to what makes hip hop so important, being a dance music, being heavy on the beat, and the particular way that you phrase the words. I found this needed to be discussed.

I took a class in college called Ethnic Notions. It talked about stereotypes in literature. We talked about African American stereotypes, we talked about Native American stereotypes, and then gender stereotypes. For the African American section, we read *Autobiography of an Ex-Colored Man* by James Weldon Johnson, Nella Larsen's *Passing*, and *Pudd'nhead Wilson* by Mark Twain.

We talked about minstrelsy and blackface minstrelsy as being a thing that was completely horrible and was awful. Then also we watched the movie *Bamboozled* during the course. Knowing that I listened to people like Gus Cannon and the Memphis Jug Band, Jim Jackson, and Papa Charlie, and it dawned on me that elements of the minstrel show showed within these guys' particular style, but they didn't seem like they were putting themselves down. They seemed to take pride in the music they were doing. I was searching to figure out how does this fit?

Because the Black intelligentsia is saying never talk about minstrelsy, but I'm seeing a folk tradition that carries elements of this. Why aren't these two things in a single room? Once I started studying in North Carolina, I found a discrepancy between rural Black culture and urban Black culture. It's still a fairly new idea to be able to talk about both as separate things that can be brought together into a single room. In popular culture, African American culture is urban; it is never country.

Either you start in the country and you go to the city or you simply stay in the city.

You have exceptions like the movies *Sounder*, or *The Autobiography of Jane Pittman*, or *Roots*, but even those are still pushing away from the country, moving into the city. String band music is always based in a rural atmosphere or had a root that is rural. That's something I found that hadn't really been written in the books. Again, to bring it back to the Black Banjo Gathering, when I met Joe Thompson, all of a sudden I realized, "Wait a second, Lead Belly is not the exception to the rule like the books would have him described, but he is the rule, and the blues is the exception."

Blues was the commercialized form of Black music. Now we think of blues, jazz, and spirituals and then gospel as being the main Black folk music. But there's a bigger section of reels and jigs, and square dance music, and also folk songs, or they call it blues ballads, but kind of a Frankie and Johnny, and that type of folk music. That's a big section of the puzzle. I found when people study the roots of the blues, they talked about field hollers, spiritual music, and work songs, but there's no guitar in any of that music. When you add string band music into it, that element is missing.

All of a sudden you get guitars, banjos, and when you have banjos in it, a whole vocabulary of rhythm is brought up that once translated to the guitar becomes blues as we know it.

When I met Joe Thompson and saw him playing his music, it changed me and made me understand Lead Belly, Charlie Patton, Mississippi Sheiks, and all that stuff. It's what connects the blues and all those types of music and even early jazz. Because when you think of the structure of a jazz band, think of a string band, banjo, fiddle, guitar, add horns, take the fiddle away, and add a drummer.

I came across the Library of Congress recordings of Jelly Roll Morton, which gave me a different notion of jazz's folk music. String band music and brass band music start becoming this very odd nucleus of folk music that, again, you can translate it on the fiddle—and banjo—very easily. All of a sudden ragtime starts becoming a part of this nucleus. The Black Banjo Gathering, to say the least, put into focus a lot of ideas I had been structuring. Okay, people don't know about this. We have to put this in context so people can write the books that will include this particular section of the history.

Once you add that, it's like a tapestry that wasn't all there—it's like 75 percent painted in. Then when you add the string band music, now you've got a full tapestry. That was my drive. So, Sule and Rhiannon, we started a group called Sankofa Strings—our first step into it. Sankofa is a West African proverb that Sule had taught me that actually means "go back and fetch it"—go back to the past and bring the stuff that's going to fit into the present to bring you into the future. It's depicted by a bird touching its beak on its back wing to represent what it's taking with it.

This has been the foundation of my work ever since I first heard that proverb. We were Sankofa Strings first, and our idea was to be the blues, jazz, open-string band idea.

I didn't meet Justin Robinson at the Black Banjo Gathering. Rhiannon and Justin met at the Gathering because Justin had wanted to meet Joe Thompson. Joe Thompson needed a banjo player to hold the structure of the songs together to play fiddle with him. Rhiannon started becoming the regular banjo player. When I joined them, I started adding all of the different elements that I had known from folk music.

I brought jug band music and fife-and-drum music. I started thinking to myself, "I've read that Charlie Patton played with the Mississippi Sheiks casually as a family band in their own community. How would Charlie Patton have approached string band music?" Same thing with Lead Belly. He has a string band background; he also worked with Blind Lemon Jefferson. What does that sound like? I got into that. I was also into modern jazz. When I played jug band stuff, I started thinking to myself about one of my favorite basses, Charles Mingus, who has a lot of songs that have blues forms where he uses single-chord riffs.

I started bringing a little bit of bebop jazz into the jug band idea. When you do that, it starts getting into these really interesting rhythms, and it made the music sound different than other string bands. We brought something that had a slightly different beat to it. It was supposed to be raw, it was supposed to be exciting—and it turned out that it was.

When we started the Carolina Chocolate Drops, it was such a new idea that we brought the excitement of the Black Banjo Gathering with us in every show, and that rubbed off on the audience. People were taking something bigger away from the shows than even what we were producing on stage, and that was powerful. By that point, I'd been playing six or seven years, and I knew that standing ovations don't happen out of nowhere, and this group got standing ovations from the very first gig we ever did. It was a really big idea. Of course, as I went along, I was always also interested in being a solo musician. As we did the band stuff, I made sure to produce other works as I went along and put out two records of *Dance Tunes, Ballads and Blues* and where I first came up with the title *American Songster*.

I had read the term "songster" in a book from Paul Oliver—the term talks about musicians who sing and play a variety of music for the community. For me, that was very empowering to have a term that was also easy for people to understand because, again, we had to become the Carolina Chocolate Drops over Sankofa Strings because it was easier to say Carolina Chocolate Drops. I have always focused on music of the United States, so I thought that that was a really nice term—*American Songster*. I kept that term going and then really fully embraced it as I decided to leave the group in 2014.

I needed to reestablish myself as a soloist. I put an album out called *Prospect Hill* where I wanted to do an overview of all the stuff I had picked up along the way. I did that with both original music and with traditional music. I also took all the ideas I'd learned in the studio to create different soundscapes so that it would also be an instant creative endeavor outside of writing the songs and trying to do a one microphone type of thing. *Prospect Hill* turned out pretty good, never meant to be a big seller, but it was meant to be a business card because I saw that was the way the industry was going.

After I finished *Prospect Hill*, I knew the next album had to be a Black cowboys record. I was traveling back to Phoenix to visit family, and I found a copy of a book, *The Negro Cowboys*, by Phillip Dunham, in a gift shop, which talks about how 5,000 Black cowboys moved out west. After Reconstruction, it was one of the first ways that ex-slaves could make their own independent wages out west, outside of the plantation, and find a new life—this notion really drew me in.

I thought, "There needs to be a folk Black cowboy record," because the only other real Black cowboy was a singing cowboy by the name of Herb Jeffries, who worked with Duke Ellington and Billy Eckstine, and he made several films as a singing cowboy. He saw the popularity of Gene Autry, and as the story goes, he saw a group of kids in Harlem playing cowboys, and they left a little Black boy out because they said there are no Black cowboys out on the range. Herb Jeffries, knowing the history was different, decided to correct that.

For me, I wanted to try to correct that in terms of a CD and an album that would cover the basic idea of Black cowboys. It would bring together the Black songsters of Texas, bring a little bit of the Buffalo Soldiers, bring in Bass Reeves, who was the first deputy U.S. Marshal of the United States who was African American and is said to be the inspiration for the *Lone Ranger*. I put a little Tex-Mex feel on the string band music on the album, and it would be part of the *African American Legacy* series. I've followed the *African American Legacy* series on Smithsonian Folkways for quite a while.

The series was created to let people know there was going to be a National Museum of African American History and Culture, so they had about five or six releases before the museum opened. I thought to myself, "If I'm gonna do a Black cowboys record, it needs to be on Smithsonian Folkways, and it needs to be a part of the *African American Legacy* series." I started talking with Dan Sheehy over at Smithsonian Folkways and he liked the idea.

Craig: I've had a chance to see it. I picked it up today from my contact at Smithsonian Folkways, Atesh Sonneborn. First off, the liner notes are to die for. Did you write these stories about the cowboys? Did you write the stories about the songs and the tunes?

Dom: Yes, it was my wife and me. With so much information, it took two years to come up with the final product on the notes. At the same time, I was contacted by the National Cowboy Poetry Gathering in Elko. Andy Hedges, a good friend, is quoted in the liner notes. He knew that I was working on Black cowboy stuff, so he had them reach out to me. I went out to Elko, Nevada, and I was a part of the National Cowboy Poetry Gathering.

After I did my first show, a fellow grabbed me by the sleeve and said, "My name is Willie Matthews. I'm a Western artist. I do paintings, and I want to do the cover to your record." He pulled me to the side, and we talked a couple of hours. He called

Don Flemons' *Black Cowboys* recording from 2018.

before I ever had an album. This one is beyond just me putting an album out—this one's meant to be the foundational scholarly work for this particular subject.

Craig: Is this your future? Is this what you hope to do from this point on?

Dom: I think so in some ways. Smithsonian Folkways says they want to do more albums with me. I have a good friend named Laurent Dubois, who Is a Duke professor. Yes, he works on Caribbean music. I met him at the Black Banjo Gathering. The Afro-Caribbean transition of banjo from Haiti and different parts of the Caribbean into the United States—that album hasn't been done yet. It would be great to do an album based around that idea. As I tell a lot of people, I'm so glad that I can feed the music that's fed me for so long. That's powerful enough in and of itself.

Craig: Your passion is contagious.

Dom: That's the idea!

22

Tim Brooks

Greenwich Village, Connecticut, 2019

"During the 1820s, Americans were beginning to have a sense of themselves as a big expansionist country. A country that has boundless opportunities. A country where you can say anything you want. A country that doesn't have the rigid social structure. We're a very different kind of country. We need our own culture too."

"They kind of cast around. They had characters, Mike Fink, the river boatman, and frontiersman Davy Crockett. He was a real person, of course, but he became a cultural touchpoint too. One of them was Jump Jim Crow, who was the lower-class Black man from the South. We were looking around for something that would express ourselves as Americans, optimistic and upbeat. No kings and queens and none of that oppression of the individual. What came out of that was the minstrel show. It came from the lower and the middle classes, largely mocking the upper classes, and the wealthy, and the barons of various industries."

"The composer Dvorak said in the 1890s: 'Americans, look to this field. Your African American influences are your folk music.'"

Old-Time Community Role: The *Professor*. Tim has a pet peeve. When it comes to music history (think recording artists), he doesn't like confusion or incorrect reporting. He wants to find the facts to set the record straight, present them fairly and let the reader or listener make up their own mind as to what's true. He's written 10 books (so far) about mostly forgotten (or avoided) subjects in music history. He is the most competent and persistent researcher I know. And hopefully his most recent book on minstrelsy will both enlighten and help heal.

Craig: Tim Brooks, television and recording historian, folklorist and author. Today we're going to go where few people dare to tread, and that's into minstrelsy. I've just completed a 12-volume, 165-interview documentary series on our traditional music community, of which the music of minstrelsy plays an integral role. Within our community, this music that we play is largely regarded as having both Black and white roots.

In fact, many thought leaders from within say that one cannot separate the instruments or the culture from the community of participants. Beyond anecdotal stories of Blacks and whites and that history, facts seem elusive. This year you finished reviewing and documenting the difficult subject of minstrelsy.

Today, I'm looking forward to a candid discussion that will help us all appreciate and celebrate the good that's within minstrelsy while addressing and acknowledging the social and cultural damage that this era actually represents. This really is a minefield of a subject. It's a difficult subject. Why did you decide to get in and write about this?

Tim Brooks: I guess I must like minefields. I don't know. I did not intend to write a book about minstrelsy. I intended long ago, at least 20 years ago, to write an article. It was going to be an article specifically about recordings. The reason I wanted to write the article is because I had been working on an earlier book called *Lost Sounds*, which was about the earliest Black recording artists prior to the Blues Revolution. That was an eye-opener for me.

Tim Brooks. Music history truth-finder. Incredible storyteller … in print and in person.

As I was doing that and going through newspapers of the period, African American as well as general circulation papers, I kept seeing references to the minstrel shows going on. I thought, "That's curious," because the books I've seen say it was all dead by then. Obviously, it wasn't. Moreover, I kept running across records that were reproductions of the opening of a minstrel show, which is called the minstrel first part, "Gentleman be seated," and then there's some jokes and there's a format that I'll get into.

I've seen this stuff around me. Nobody was writing about it. Nobody was even acknowledging it. I thought, "This is a good subject. It's an offshoot of what I'm doing. Maybe I'll do something on that." It was meant to be an academic look at this, complete with footnotes and so forth. There had been a number of books written in the 1990s, very influential books still used, about minstrelsy and its origins. None of them dealt with this era, this later era of recordings and so forth. Nobody had a collection of these records, even the Library of Congress. It's very hard to find them. You just find scattered examples.

Nobody wanted them, particularly. They weren't expensive in the main. I assembled my own ever-growing collection of these records, the different types, listening to them and what they told me about the sound of a minstrel show, not just how somebody described it many years ago. That grew into television because I had also written about television and I knew there were some minstrel shows there that nobody ever seemed to have acknowledged. What were they like?

Then radio, I did a book on radio; the shows were very prominent on radio as well. And movies, which is the first time I've been in the field of movies. There are already a lot of good scholars in that field, but that rounded out the four major mediums of the 20th century. What I hope I've shown in this book is that in fact it was of our era, if our era is radio, and television, and movies, things that we still experience and that are rerun all the time, for that matter. It was very much a part of that too. It was not just in local grange halls, and it was not just on some low level; it was big, professional, Busby Berkeley productions.

Craig: With big names.

Tim: Big names and famous stars and so forth. Elvis Presley was in a minstrel show—who knew?—in his high school days. That's what the book was about. That took me to a much broader canvas than had traditionally been shown.

To do that, I had to get into where it came from because I didn't think a book that started in 1900, a lot of people wouldn't know what it was building off of. So I had to use the previous research to put together an introductory chapter.

[Cylinder record plays: "Gentlemen be seated."]

Craig: The key elements that you gave me when we talked about *Lost Sounds* were the concepts of presentism and historicism. Because if you bring something back from the past, those values aren't relevant today, and they really cause issues.

Tim: Presentism says you take today's values and you judge the past actions of people in the past according to our values. Historicism says that you look at the past in terms of its own values. Were these people and actions progressive in moving forward racial justice, for example, or were they regressive in pushing back, according to their values?

Because they had different values, they had different realities, they had to face different things that were possible in their time. I think we have shifted a good deal toward presentism. I would not want to be purely historicist—that's ignoring everything that's happened, and, hopefully, advances that we've made in thinking and in justice.

On the other hand, if you ignore that, you are condemning people that, in fact, were as smart as you are—maybe smarter—who were really trying to improve the situation that they were given when they were born and when they grew up and move justice forward.

Craig: Can we set the stage for the minstrel show? Where did it come from? What years did it start? Describe America at the time it happened.

Tim: In the 1820s, there were individual stage performers, white performers who put on blackface and do dances and sing songs. They were largely in the Northeast. Many of them were Irish immigrants. There were middle- or lower-class people who were pursuing a career on the stage, and this is the way they could do it. Why did they use blackface? The best we can figure out is that it's a mask. It's called a minstrel mask. It's like a clown's mask. It separates the person from the character or could be some other mask too. It was a mask to allow them to act as a cartoon on stage. You're not looking at a real person. You're looking at this cartoon up there.

It was liberating for the performer too. Because he—it's almost always he—could say things and do things that he might not be comfortable doing in his natural state. Bert Williams, a Black man, actually wrote about this, how he was a conservative proper man but this allowed him to be more outrageous.

They picked, unfortunately, one of the most vulnerable parts of our population, African Americans, many of whom were in slavery at that time, about whom the mass public knew very, very, very little. There was hardly any interaction, particularly in the North between the white population, the majority population, and African Americans.

They certainly didn't know what was going on in the South. There was limited communications then. You could take a parody of an uneducated Black man and make that your clown figure. That's essentially what they did. None of this is excusing it. It's very racist, as a matter of fact. However, at the time, that's what they were doing for representation.

I do believe the attraction of this minstrel performance was that it was almost always upbeat. It was funny in the humor of the time at least. It was clean, which was important.

There was a lot of innuendo and parents didn't want the kids to see certain things [chuckles] that could be found on the vaudeville stage or on the variety stage as it was then. The minstrel shows never had any of that. I've never found a minstrel recording, film or anything where they're telling dirty jokes. They just didn't do that.

Craig: You had mentioned previously, and specifically, in this book that lampooning historically was the humor of the day. You could lampoon an enslaved Black African. You could lampoon an Irish person. You could lampoon a Chinese person. But lampoonery, in fact, you went on to describe the minstrel show as the *Saturday Night Live* of the day.

Tim: Making fun of the extremes of all kinds of cultures. It's important to remember that minstrel shows were not just about African Americans. They lampooned everybody. The rich, the politicians. They did travesties on *Hamlet*, you name it. It was mockery of the extreme characteristics of various immigrant groups, Chinese and Irish, and this and that. These were Irishmen, obviously, who were putting on the blackface but they were lampooning themselves too.

Especially at the beginning. What happened is in 1843, after a decade or so of these individual performers, four of them got together and said, "Why don't we form a group and put it on the stage?" They call themselves the Virginia Minstrels. Boy, it was one of those moments in cultural history where it just took off.

Craig: You called that Big Bang. It happened at the Bowery in New York on February 6 of 1843. Tell me about the format of this show. Was this original to America? Did they steal from something?

Tim: The environment in which this took place—you have to put yourself back then—was one that was very much dominated by British culture. We had won our independence from Britain in the Revolutionary War. We fought another war with them in 1812, of course, where they burned our capital down. After that, the two countries were surprisingly cooperative in trade and in commerce and also in culture.

The plays that you would see if they were high culture, there'd be *Hamlet*, there'd be British plays. If it's low culture, it would be British actors and comedians touring the U.S. Often it would be literature, it'd be songs, drinking songs from England. It was all England all the time.

During the 1820s, Americans were beginning to have a sense of themselves as a big expansionist country. A country that has boundless opportunities. A country where you can say anything you want. A country that doesn't have the rigid social structure. We're a very different kind of country. We need our own culture too.

They kind of cast around. They had characters, Mike Fink, the river boatman, and frontiersman Davy Crockett. He was a real person, of course, but he became a cultural touchpoint too. One of them was Jump Jim Crow, who was the lower-class Black man from the South. We were looking around for something that would express ourselves as Americans, optimistic and upbeat. No kings and queens and none of that oppression of the individual. What came out of that was the minstrel show. It came from the lower and the middle classes, largely mocking the upper classes, and the wealthy, and the barons of various industries.

It really touched a nerve, just like *Saturday Night Live* did in 1975. It was something fresh. It was fun. It was fast-paced and so forth. The fact that the principal comedians were these two white men in blackface was almost incidental at the beginning. That changed somewhat in the 1850s as we came up to the Civil War era. Slavery became an enormously divisive issue in the United States and during the Civil War. At the beginning, it was really quite broad that way. The other thing about it, and several books have pointed this out, is that the participants in this, the actors who are doing this, white men in blackface, burnt cork, were in effect early ethnomusicologists.

Many of them went to the Black quarter, which whites never did at that time. They listened, they overheard, and they brought back some of the sensibility—not all of which was mockery, by the way, but some of the sensibility of Black culture, and Black music, and Black instruments like the banjo and that sort of thing. They were watching where others weren't watching because there was very little to find in the white press or anything about what's going on with the African Americans culturally. But these were people that were out there watching and absorbing some of it.

They brought some of that, often distorted, but they brought some of that to the bigger public. That was the first thing that happened. The second thing that happened, of course, was that African Americans themselves began to appear in minstrel shows as the real thing. That gave them a chance to present their own musical sensibilities, which, of course, wound up having an enormous effect on our culture.

Craig: In reading through your book, I know that the minstrel show usually was composed of different segments.

Tim: Well, before the Big Bang, before February 1843, there were individual performances, which would be 10 minutes or 15, a short act. They didn't have a set format. A couple of the most popular of those actors had a particular character they would do. Zip Coon, which was Washington Dixon, was about a free Black in the North who was dandified and talked in language he didn't understand. He had built a song around it with a very catchy chorus to it, and that was his act. It was quite popular during the 1830s.

Some of them had songs or dances. Dances were important to this, dances that they specialized in and that they were known for. Regarding content, there really weren't any minstrel songs. The songs that were sung and the music that was part of a *minstrel show was the current popular music of its day, whatever that happened to be*. If it was Stephen Foster, then it was Stephen Foster songs. They didn't come out of the minstrel show. In the 1940s, they were doing, "I Don't Want to Walk Without You, Baby." Big band songs in minstrel shows. Whatever was popular at that time. It would change over time.

The most insulting and demeaning songs, the ones that really mock African Americans—and I have written another article with a Black scholar about this—were songs of the period from the 1880s to mid–1910s. It was a period called Coon song era. These were songs that really mocked and demeaned African Americans and really Jim Crow songs. Those are songs that were introduced on Broadway. They were introduced in sheet music. They were on the vaudeville stage and, of course, they were in the minstrel show. They didn't start there by and large; they weren't in the minstrel show before that era. When those songs, thankfully, finally, phased away in the World War I era, they left the minstrel show too, and other songs came in. The music was really a reflection of whatever current popular culture was doing. That was kind of a surprise to me, because I thought it's all what we think of as "minstrel songs."

Craig: I wanted to touch base on a few of these tunes because I know some of the people that will be watching this will be heavily representative of the traditional music community.

Tim: Sure.

Craig: You did an analysis of 150 playbills from the first 10 years of the minstrel stage, and many of the songs that were performed, hits of the day, as you'd mentioned, were things like "Miss Lucy Long," "Old Dan Tucker," "Stop Dat Knocking." Other tunes that were popular in that era were like "Arkansas Traveler" and "Turkey in the Straw," which was renamed after Zip Coon because it's such a slanderous label, and "Golden Slippers."

Tim: That's right.

Craig: This is from 1848, from Frederick Douglass. "Minstrelsy is the filthy scum of white society who have stolen from us a complexion that was denied to them by nature, in which to make money, and pander to the corrupt taste of their fellow white citizens."

Tim: At the time there was very, very little pushback even from Black Americans. Now that quote from Douglass, it is reproduced many times in several of the books I have read. I think it's reproduced because the authors agree with it, frankly. What they don't ever mention was that six months *after* that quote, Frederick Douglass *actually saw* a minstrel show for the first time. That quote was written in the context to review a group called the Hutchinson Family Singers who were a group of abolitionists, and he was writing about their cause, and he denounced the minstrel show as part of that. Six months later, he saw a minstrel show put on by Blacks, and he was very equivocal about it.

He was a very farsighted man, and he said, I still don't like some of the jokes and what they're doing, but there's potential here. This is putting our people, meaning African Americans, on the stage, allowing whites to see, and there's a great deal of talent up there among these Blacks. This could be a good thing for us.

Craig: I think it's worth reading that quote into this record.

> It is not, however, of their pecuniary success that we would speak, but of the real good done to their hearers. When we entered Minerva Hall, there was evidently some ill feeling towards the colored part of the audience, but as the glorious harmony proceeded, caste stood abashed—the iron heart of prejudice, pride, and scorn, seemed to melt away, and the general expression of the audience, among white and black, confessed the truth of a common origin and a common brotherhood. We all looked and felt alike. Our hearts were touched and saddened by the "Slave Mother's Lament"—cheered and delighted with the "Good time coming"—wrapped in admiration of "Excelsior"—filled with indefinable associations by the "Old Church Bell"—softened to tears by the "Bridge of Sighs"—inspired with a dauntless courage by the "Psalm of life," and terror stricken at the "Ship on Fire" [*North Star*, Rochester, 27 October 1848].

Tim: That mirrors a line of thought that emerged later in the century, too, that this is an opportunity for African Americans to get out there, to be heard, and to have their own impact and present themselves as "the real thing." There was a lot of appeal to that, and whites went to those shows and wound up creating big stars, Black stars for the first time. Even in the 1840s, unlike most, he could see that. The objection to the minstrel show was almost entirely that it was low-class, not that it was racist. This was true among white academics and elites as well as the few Black elite that there were at that time, like Douglass.

They said, "It's just low-class stuff." It's gutter snipe stuff and so forth. I found very, very little, except perhaps for that one quote, that was actually on a racial basis. The other big surprise I had of this research journey was, when there were controversies—and later, too, in radio and television—every time there was attack on a minstrel show or doing a minstrel show, for some reason, there would be a counter to it from members of the Black community. They would say, "*Amos and Andy* is not a bad show, and this is why, and you're destroying our history" or something like that.

The Black community itself was quite split on this, all the way up to the 1950s actually, another century. That was a surprise to me because I had absorbed what many of these scholars say that Frederick Douglass, in that one quote, speaks for all African Americans. No, he didn't even speak for himself because he changed his mind, obviously, or modified his views. Often in history, we tend to look at things in extremes, almost caricature … such as, this was all this and this was all that. When you get close to it, there are nuances there, and there may be good along with the bad. In this case, the entrée of African Americans into American culture. What could be more beneficial to American culture? That's what Dvorak was talking about in the 1890s when he said, "Americans, look to this field. Your African American influences are your folk music."

Craig: When America wanted to show who America is, we're different from Britain.
Tim: Right.

Craig: We were in our teenage years, we were being rebellious to come out and show a culture and a music represented by enslaved African Americans. It's holding it up, something that's original and unique. And as you mentioned in *Lost Sounds*, it was also the first time Blacks were put on stage. It was their entrée into entertainment in America.
Tim: It was also the entrée for instruments like the banjo.

Craig: Okay. Back to the format of the show again.
Tim: Sure. In 1843, these four dudes put on a show. They need work. They put on a show [laughs] and it's a big hit. And, naturally, big hits spawn many imitators.

Craig: Why were they a hit? Why were the Virginia Minstrels such a hit?
Tim: Taking what had been an individual thing and taking four of them together, going back and forth, created a kind of party atmosphere. I argue that the minstrel show, in a sense, was a party. Think about it. Usually, a play or a symphony or something, the audience is here and the performers are there. It's like you are in your place, and there's a wall in between. You can look through the wall or the window, and there they are on the other side in their place. In a minstrel show, particularly as it opens, there's this whole cast on stage at once, and it almost melds with the audience.

Everybody's laughing at the jokes. The cast is as well as the audience. Everybody's singing along, everybody's part of it. It's like going to a party. That breakdown of the traditional wall between performer and audience is a very interesting aspect which has not been explored very much. It's one of the reasons that I think it took off so much as local productions. Grange halls and local organizations were forever putting on minstrel shows all the way up to the 1950s or later. Because it was a great kind of bonding thing. They got together, and the audience all felt they were part of it.

You had the four coming together creating something. Now the four quickly became six or 12 or larger groups. This idea of a group of people, all of whom know each other, all of whom are bantering back and forth in a very easy kind of way. Telling jokes to each other, putting each other down humorously. One will get up and sing a song, that kind of thing. It was very inclusive.

Craig: When did it take the form of the intro, the olio, and then finally the grand production, be it something formal or informal?

Tim: That brings us to Christy, Edwin Christy, who was an entrepreneur.

Craig: That's approximately 1850?

Tim: No, this is in the 1840s. In fact, he argued that he invented the minstrel show. He said, yes, I was before those four guys. But he was a big promoter, so I don't know about that. In any event, at roughly the same time he saw what was going on. He formed his own minstrel troupe, the Christy Minstrels. It took a few years but they got to New York in 1846, I think '47 era. They established themselves in a theater and stayed in New York.

Craig: Christy brought in Stephen Foster.

Tim: Yes, as a house composer.

Craig: Wow! Yes. Some of the tunes and songs that are being played now in the 1850s, "Old Folks at Home," "Oh! Susanna," "Camptown Races," "Ring de Banjo," "Masses in the Cold, Cold Ground," "My Old Kentucky Home," "Hard Times Come Again No More" and "Old Black Joe." Again, so many of these tunes are played in our traditional music community. It's nice to put them in perspective here.

Tim: Foster was always short of money and Christy, seeing his talent, offered him a contract to write for his shows. Many of the famous songs. Steve Foster is acknowledged as one of the greatest composers this country has ever produced, certainly in the popular genre. After being introduced in Christy's shows, they, of course, grew beyond that.

Christy, who was like the Barnum of his time—he's a great promoter—developed this format of three acts.

The first act was called the minstrel first part. That was everybody on stage, as I was describing, gentlemen be seated and blast from the orchestra. They all rattle their tambourines and sit down, and then they go into the jokes and the back and forth and individual songs. Then there's a second act, which is called the olio under his model. That's a series of individual acts like vaudeville, very separated acts. They might be in whiteface too. They're not necessarily blackface. Then there's a third act, which is called the afterpiece and that is an extended skit of some sort. Maybe a parody on an opera or something like that which might have or might not have been Black. There was this three-act format.

The group in the minstrel first part at the beginning would consist of these originally four but later six or eight men sitting in a semi-circle at the front of the stage using very simple instruments. The banjo was a foundational instrument for the minstrel show but also tambourine, bones, castanets for the rhythmic clicking sound. Typically, the tambourine player would be on one end and the bones player on the other, so they became known as Tambo and Bones, the two end men of the minstrel show. The banjo, often a fiddle, would be in the middle.

Later on, they had a separate orchestra so they'd just have tambourines and bones and things and then the orchestra would be more music. Later still, the interlocutor was introduced, and he was usually a physically larger person who sat in the middle of this semi-circle and acted as an MC essentially. It's interesting. He's often portrayed in academic literature as the White boss. He's the master and these are his slaves, that kind of thing. But in many of the minstrel shows that I've seen, he's one of the crowd. He's very much part of that. He might be in Blackface himself or maybe not. That was the structure. Quickly it grew bigger and bigger and more and more troupes formed during the 1850s, leading up to the Civil War. It got enmeshed in the whole national debate about slavery.

During that period, the minstrel show really took on a darker tone and became anti-war and pro-slavery, often giving rosy pictures of how good the masters were to their slaves. This was during the 1850s, so less of the usual general mocking of all culture. During the Civil War itself, it reflected men in the music of that period which started out to be very martial and turned into very sorrowful, this cruel war and the slaughter that was going on as part of the war.

Coming out of the Civil War in 1865 and the late 1860s was interesting. At that point, other parts of American theater and culture were changing dramatically to bigger, more spectacular events. There was a lot more stage machinery and big effects. The minstrel show was beginning to look old hat by that time. So the minstrel shows also expanded. You got troupes not of eight to 10 men but of 20, 40, 60, 100 people on stage in ranks behind each other. A show might start out with a rank of just a few people in front, then the curtain would rise and there'd be another rank of 20 more. Another curtain would rise, and there'd be another rank behind that. It would impress you with its size. They'd call themselves gigantians and megatherians and all these elaborate names. They became very big, spectacular productions.

Craig: You had mentioned in the book how it started with people on stage in almost garish, outlandish rags for costumes. By the time now that you're discussing this, they had graduated to tuxedos and classier things because it's a classier show. Did the price go up?

Tim: No, it was inexpensive entertainment all throughout. Remember it tracked primarily middle- and lower-class people that didn't have a lot of money. You didn't have box seats in a minstrel show. This is for the masses. They were for the people, so the prices were kept low. The costuming changes started in the 1840s, not long after that original troupe which was dressed in rough clothing. Christy introduced actual tuxedos in some, and a modified tuxedo evolved from that which was a minstrel outfit. It had widened lapels and huge bow ties. It was a parody of a tuxedo, almost.

This outfit became minstrel garb, but then in the late 1800s, in order to seem different and fresh, and not your grandfather's minstrel show, you got things like 17th-century court outfits. There are movies of this. They're dressed in the frills that might have been in King James days or something like that. Usually, the end men, the two comics, or sometimes four comics, two on each side, would have the big lapels and the bow ties … the tux minstrel outfit. The others could have been all kinds of different things. There were actual whiteface circus clowns in some of these shows too. They varied it a lot later on. But it was rags and tatters only at the very beginning.

Craig: Okay. We've got blackface. We have whites representing Blacks with their shows, and we also have Black minstrel shows. When did that happen? Are they paralleling at this point?

Tim: It surprised me, but the Frederick Douglass quote from 1848 is of a Black minstrel troupe. Even as early as that there were Blacks who were putting on minstrel shows. There's a fascinating picture taken apparently at a Union camp during the Civil War of five Black minstrels. There's Tambo, there's Bones entertaining the Union troops. African Americans entertaining the Union troops. But it was after the war that Black minstrelsy really took off. There were big Black minstrel shows too. Most of them were run by white entrepreneurs who would hire the Blacks. Not all of them; there were some Black managers as well that had their own troupes.

There was a generic term for them. The white minstrel generically were called Christy minstrels for a long time, no matter who was running the show. And the Black minstrels were called Georgia minstrels because one of those early Black-run troupes was from Georgia and called themselves that. They had major stars of their own, and they went on a parallel track. There were some integrated shows, too, that had both Blacks and whites, usually not interacting with each other. They would have two first parts, one for the Blacks and one for the whites in front of the audience.

Craig: The audience—is it a completely segregated audience?

Tim: No. We don't know a lot about this, but apparently, the early shows were almost all white audiences, which is not surprising because Blacks were excluded from theaters at that time. You would not have a theater that would integrate its audience. You'd be burned down if you did that in the 1840s or 1850s, and there wasn't much attraction for Blacks watching whites imitating Blacks. However, when the Black show started, of course, Blacks flocked to those. "These are our people on stage." Later on, whites did too, especially after the Civil War. They were fascinated by the real thing, as it were, not the counterfeit. There's a whole theory of thought that maybe whites didn't realize these weren't real African Americans. Yes, they did. There's lots in print about that. They knew that this was imitation. So when the real thing came along, there was interest in that.

Craig: What else is notable between 1870 and 1890?

Tim: That's a period, 1870 to 1890, when there was a body of minstrel songs that were written specifically for the minstrel shows and became frequently heard in minstrel shows. Many of them were parodies of spirituals. Songs like "Putting on the Golden Buckle" or "Climbing Up the Golden Stairs," that sort of thing. In a sense, minstrelsy was at its peak as a professional entertainment because you had very, very big troupes. Haverly's Minstrels and Primrose and West were probably the best known. They would tour the country in special trains to accommodate all their stage machinery. Colonel Jack Haverly was one of the principal minstrel moguls of the 1870s, '80s, '90s, and, of course, he put out his own songbooks and joke books.

Craig: Were those sold at shows?

Tim: All the time and they can be found today too. They were put out as books that help you make your own minstrel show.

Craig: Oh, goodness.

Tim: It's full of routines and jokes and so forth, and a lot of them survive, and you can find them on eBay. Huge audiences would come to this. In the late 1800s, minstrelsy was extremely prominent. It was not only in the Northeast, which is where it started, now it was across the country partially by these touring troupes. And there were cities that had their own resident troupes like Carncross in Philadelphia, for example. That was in residence there for 30 years. Then in the Southern cities, you would have it too. Minstrelsy was very popular.

The 1870s and '80s is when vaudeville started to really emerge, arguably out of the olio of the minstrel show. Tony Pastor was a key figure. He was an entrepreneur who did for vaudeville what Christy had done for the minstrel show. He followed the format of clean family entertainment. And this idea of successive acts, unconnected to each other, took hold. That really started to put the pressure on minstrelsy, and minstrelsy became, as I put it in the book, not dead, but it was sharing the stage, essentially. It didn't go away.

Craig: Somewhere between 1890, according to your book, *Lost Sounds*, and 1909, the recording industry started to take an interest in minstrel music, and not just minstrel music, but Black performers as well as white performers. Let's pick up on your book at this point.

Tim: *Lost Sounds*, which was tracing the earliest Black recording artists, is all of them, whether they're minstrels or whatever they are. The recording industry starts in 1890, give or take a year because that's the year in which Edison finally came out with a usable home phonograph that an ordinary person, not an engineer, could make run. And it spread widely. He had to sell the software. He had to have something that would play on them, of course. Both for records and for radio, there was a person that made a difference.

In the case of records was a man named Leonard G. Spencer. He was from a very prominent Washington family. His middle name was Garfield. Leonard Garfield Spencer. President Garfield was his godfather. His mother was a big women's rights advocate. His father ran a business college that introduced Spencerian penmanship. He was a very modern guy for his time. He produced records as well as sang and played the banjo. In 1894, he came up with the idea of an audio recreation of a minstrel first part, the opening of a minstrel show, which was very familiar to almost everybody in those days.

It would start with a blast from the orchestra and "Gentlemen be seated" and then the jokes and the interlocutor would ask, "How you doing today, Mr. Bones?" and so forth. He worked out a format that fit within three minutes; that's all the cylinder record could take. He introduced these in 1894 on a company that ran out of New Jersey that made cylinders, wax cylinders. They caught on right away, and so other companies started making them too. For the next 20 years, from the mid-1890s to the mid-1910s, these recorded recreations of a minstrel show opening were extremely popular. If you; find boxes of old records, you'll always find some of them. They're always called "minstrel first part."

He called his group the Imperial Minstrels. He only needed four people. You didn't see them, of course, so you didn't need the spectacle of all those people on stage. But four people can sound like a lot if you know how to work your audio. They became very proficient at what they were doing. Interestingly, his troupe of four people, the Imperial Minstrels, one of them was a Black man named George W. Johnson, a Black recording artist at that time. He was an ex-slave who had started recording later in his life. Johnson was valued particularly because he had a very hearty laugh. One of the things you wanted on a minstrel record was, every time a joke is told, no matter how dumb it is, there's uproarious laughter. It's hard not to laugh when somebody else is laughing.

Every record label in existence seemed to want a minstrel record in its catalog. A lot of these were made during that period. They died out around the World War I, when we had other things we were concerned about. Minstrelsy itself was receding by that time. Then they came back in the late 1920s as nostalgia. "Remember those days of Primrose and West and all those people who are dead now? They were wonderful in their day." Actually, minstrel records were made up until the 1950s. Bill Cullen and Milton Berle did full minstrel records in the early LP era. Minstrelsy recreated on record was a reality in American culture from the 1890s all the way to the 1960s or so.

Tim: After the introduction of the phonograph, which became very widespread, the next major 20th-century media was radio, which had its antecedents, but really spread in the 1920s. From the very beginning, as stations went on the air, they had minstrel shows, usually local productions. They would take their microphones out to a grange hall or something and broadcast a minstrel show.

Then there was a man named Dailey Paskman who was the general manager of a fairly prominent radio station in New York at the time, WGBS, now called WINS. Dailey Paskman wanted more humor. There's a lot of music. They wanted a little more humor. What better than the minstrel show for jokes and laughter and so forth?

Like Spencer, he put together a troupe, Dailey Paskman's Minstrels, specifically as a broadcasting troupe. They all were familiar with the special requirements of broadcasting such as working to the microphone. He put on a weekly show and it took off. This is 1925. From 1925 to 1928, Dailey Paskman's Minstrels was a major show not only in New York; it was heard all over the Northeast because of signals in those days. At that same time, the radio networks were just launching, NBC and CBS, the first two. Of course, they saw all the success he was having, so they said, "Well, maybe we ought to have a minstrel show too."

NBC got Dutch Masters cigars as a sponsor, and they started the Dutch Masters Minstrels in 1928. From 1928 to 1932 was a major hit in radio, big network production with a big orchestra, writers, and the whole network thing. As that began to wind down in the early 1930s, they looked around for a replacement and found that their Chicago station, WENR, had a local minstrel show, which was doing very well. So they sold that to the Sinclair Oil Company and that became the Sinclair Minstrels on NBC.

During the mid–1930s, that show was enormous. It was in the top five of everything on radio. It was live from Chicago, ran from 1932 to 1939, as I remember. It had a studio audience. They could accommodate 500 people. But NBC claimed it had 20,000 people on the waiting list for tickets to get in to see this thing.

In addition, there were other minstrel shows on CBS. Jack Benny did a minstrel show and Bing Crosby on his show had a minstrel show. The funniest one in the 1940s, Perry Como, who was an up-and-coming crooner at the time, had a very suave, sophisticated show called the *Chesterfield Supper Club*. And he puts on a minstrel show of all things. [Chuckles.] Perry Como is the interlocutor. Many of these shows incorporated minstrelsy and minstrel shows into their programs on radio all the way through the 1940s, both on networks and on local stations.

Craig: Next is film.

Tim: Film actually began, of course, in the 1890s, shortly after recordings as silent films. Hard to do a minstrel show on a silent film since music is the whole soul of the show, but they tried. There was something called the spook minstrels that I didn't know about in 1905. There they had a silent film of a minstrel show, and they had singers positioned behind the stage who would sing and speak in sync with the action on the silent screen. The Museum of Modern Art has one of these films. I'm going to see it shortly.

In 1913, Edison brought out a primitive sound system called the Kinetophone.

He made a series of films for it; they were about six minutes long each, which was the longest he could audio record. And one of them was the Edison Minstrels and they put on a minstrel show. It's only recently been restored by the Library of Congress—fascinating show. Buster Keaton had a minstrel show in one of his silents, a comic one.

When sound came in widespread in the late 1920s with the *Jazz Singer*, that's when minstrelsy on film really took off. Several of the early, big musical movies were built around minstrel shows. Al Jolson had a movie called *Mammy* in 1930, in which he has a huge minstrel show with all his minstrels behind him. Shirley Temple staged a minstrel show in *Dimples*.

Mickey Rooney and Judy Garland, two of the teen stars, put on a minstrel show in *Babes in Arms*. That was the first one. Rooney's in blackface, Garland is in brownface, which is a subdued blackface, which they often used for the women in that period. It was such a big hit that they did a second movie three years later called *Babes on Broadway*, where they did another minstrel show. These things were enormous. They were produced by Busby Berkeley, complete with his platoons of dancing girls and his aerial shots and all the big Hollywood production values like no minstrel show ever looked like in the 19th century.

There were minstrel shows in biographical movies. There were three different feature films made about Stephen Foster, which all included minstrel segments of course. Jolson played Christy in one of them. There were minstrel shows in Westerns, quite a few of them, and those were pretty true to life, actually. There were small troops, simple instrumentation, like what the minstrel show had been, in fact.

Nineteen forty-three was the hundredth anniversary of the Virginia Minstrels. Bing Crosby came out with a movie called *Dixie* in that year. There's a lot in the movie industry all the way through the early '50s.

Craig: Once again, supposedly minstrelsy was dead around 1890, but you've shown for the first three mediums here that it was alive and well up through 1950. Okay, so now we're entering television.

Tim: In television it spreads in the late 1940s. As television stations went on the air, they also looked to the minstrel show. I have a chart that shows how often the term minstrel show turns up in a large database of newspapers. You see a big dip during World War II, but right after the war, it comes surging back. These are listings, basically, on radio and on television of minstrel shows being shown. The networks, which had a long history with this from radio put on minstrel shows.

Fred Waring had a major show on Sunday nights following Ed Sullivan. It was an hour-long musical show. He was a real musicologist. Fred Waring really studied all aspects of American music. One of the aspects he studied was the minstrel show. He staged, on three separate occasions on CBS Television nationwide, a full-fledged blackface minstrel show. He's the interlocutor in whiteface and behind him are the Pennsylvanians, his chorus, all in blackface, which today you look at and say, "What?" But there they are. They do routines, they do some jokes, they do some songs. None of it is demeaning stuff, the songs, or the jokes.

Clearly, from the radio days, the network sensors made sure they weren't using offensive words. They were very cognizant of their audience. The only thing they would allow would be blackface if it was visual and, to some extent, dialect, although they didn't want to overemphasize that. Those things were still there.

[Fred Waring on record playing: Let's recall the early days of entertainment in America. Well, there were drawing room musicales, big-time vaudeville, and even the old medicine shows. There's one more, we haven't left it out. No, we just simply mentioned it last because, well, it's first in our minds tonight, the minstrel show. The wholesome and fascinating form of entertainment, which has been used in churches and schools and clubs all over the country for many, many years. Because minstrelsy means good, clean, fun, and wonderful music, we continue in the spirit of all good minstrel shows with the greatest of dignity and respect. Gentlemen, the opening chorus.]

Tim: It's so shocking to see today, but not in the content of what they said and not in the content of the songs that they sang—no coon songs or anything like that. He also had a minstrel routine as part of his traveling show. Fred Waring traveled around the country, putting on concerts about music of the West, music of the Irish, music of this, music of that. He brought in academic experts to make sure the shows were accurate to how they had been performed back in the previous century. They were very authentic kinds of reproductions. They're shocking today, basically because of the blackface, but not because of the content, if you listen to them.

Ed Sullivan put on a minstrel show for the 50th anniversary of the Ford Motor Company in 1953. That's the time when the protests were really beginning to ramp up.

Starting in the late '40s, for the first time, you've got concerted complaints and petitions and editorials about these being racist. That's the first time. Before, it had been low-class maybe, but nobody seemed to consider them racist even 10 years earlier. Now, this was the Truman era. It was a more liberal era. Jim Crow is coming under attack, the Jim Crow laws in the South. Civil Rights was beginning to take root, finally, and as part of that, the minstrel show was under attack.

There was a show on NBC radio in 1948 called *The National Minstrels*, which attracted a lot of negative attention. ABC announced a show called *The American Minstrels of 1949* on ABC television, which again attracted attention. Ironically, both of those shows featured African Americans in the cast. Nevertheless, the idea of a minstrel show was so toxic by that time.

In both cases, there was pushback from the Black community. There were people who would write to the Black papers and say, "No, this is our history. Why are you getting so sensitive?" pointing out there was an entrée of Blacks into show business and into American culture. There was a back and forth even within the community on that.

By the early '50s, the pressure became more and more. Also, the television networks were owned by three companies, basically. They were very dependent on their sponsors. The sponsors didn't want controversy of any kind. They certainly didn't want controversy attached to their products, their soap or whatever. There were pressure points that didn't used to exist, and the NAACP and others learned where those pressure points were and threatened boycotts of sponsors. And that was it, basically. Within a 10-year period, maybe even less than that, eight years, the minstrel show was driven out of the mass media.

Craig: If you were to look at a typical show anywhere from 1850 to 1870 and contrast it with something such as Fred Waring on television, what changed in the content?

Tim: The most fundamental change is that during that earlier period, minstrelsy always presented itself as contemporary entertainment. For terms like modern minstrels and up-to-date minstrels, they really were emphasizing that this isn't nostalgia, this is what's happening now. The songs and the jokes all played to that. It was all very contemporary. When you get to Fred Waring, the 1950s, actually, when you get past the 1920s, most of it is nostalgia for the old days. That's when Stephen Foster makes a comeback because that's the old days about what it was supposed to be like back when.

Fred Waring was doing almost an academic reconstruction of a minstrel show. If you could somehow get past the blackface, it would be a very instructive program about songs that are not offensive in any way but how they were performed. How the jokes were told back and forth, the role that each of the participants took.

Craig: This is a really tough question, but I've got to ask. If you were to give an elevator talk, 30 seconds to two minutes, how could you sum up minstrelsy, addressing both its good and its bad?

Tim: I would emphasize that it had many aspects to it beyond the obvious. It lasted a very long time for a reason. If we're to make any progress at all in justice and equality in our day, we have to understand what it really was, why it lasted so long, and what it was that finally eliminated it.

Much of this is based on written material and written material could be so distorted. I'd learn this in the Jack Johnson chapter that I wrote for *Lost Sounds*. Jack Johnson, the great Black fighter. In the press of his day, he was represented as being some kind of Muhammad Ali, over the top, speaking in uneducated gibberish.

When I actually got to hear Jack Johnson on a recording, that's not Jack Johnson at all. That's the filter that the writers are putting on him and even respectable historians don't seem to want to go beyond that filter. You have to understand groupthink. There's a large element of groupthink to this. If Abraham Lincoln goes to these shows, if they're all over everywhere, nobody's complaining, well, they must be okay. Maybe we should question a little bit more what media tells us is okay or what media tells us is not okay.

Bringing audio materials and video materials to the scholarly pursuits I think is another goal that I've fought for for many years.

I'm cognizant of the fact that I'm a white guy talking about Black culture. I'm very dedicated to what really happened. I really want to be a historian about this and not be a moral seer of some sort. I don't want to write anger, I want to write what happened. You make up your mind, but please do it based on facts.

Craig: Thank you for taking the time to put these thoughts down to allow people to make those decisions on their own.

Part III

In the Company of Music

Clifftop water tower.

23

Clifftop

Now that you're acquainted with many of my friends in the traditional music community, let me welcome you to Clifftop, officially known as the Appalachian String Band Music Festival! This annual outdoor "tribal" celebration of musicians, luthiers, historians and authors, and everyday festival players is held on a remote mountaintop in West Virginia where even locals say "you can't get there from here." The *remote* part of its location and *length of time* of the event (up to nine days of camping) is pivotal. Being sequestered in nature *is a part of the package*. Trust me, you'll get hot, cold, wet, muddy and maybe even spent … unless you pace yourself by hydrating, sleeping and eating well. But it starts as a frenzied moment to indulge in your favorite thing (traditional music) with kindred spirits (the traditional music community). What's not to like?

Okay, there are those pesky little rattlesnakes once in a while, and brown recluse spider stories from time to time, but hey. Given a good attitude, bug juice, dry or waterproof shoes, and clean underwear, odds are in your favor that a good time *will be had*.

Let's step back for a moment and consider what Clifftop really is to 21st-century humans. If past cultures had indeed been playing their own traditional music on a daily basis, it might actually look and sound a bit like Clifftop. Ancient Mayans, Egyptians, and even Romans and Greeks would be practicing what the Clifftop experience sustains, nurtures and encourages: community. *The music is shared and encouraged.*

Where the music from cultures past would carry its own signature sounds (think voices, instruments, settings), in our current, North American culture, we celebrate with instruments and history from many communities of people from all over the world. We can play an 800-year-old dance number ("Morpeth's Rant" from Scotland) on instruments from Europe (fiddles) and Africa (the banjo) for dances that also came from Africa, Europe, and here. Native Americans have contributed to our traditional music culture. In fact, this music has been around so long, it's really hard to tell who contributed what. Traditional (folk) music is what humans use to express how they feel. No one owns it, so we each can make it our own. And when we're finished, the tunes travel on down the river of time until someone else discovers them and, through them, expresses their human experience.

You can't break traditional music. But you can easily share it with others. So at

23. Clifftop

A 2015 Clifftop jam, with Brian Slattery (banjo), Charlie Shaw (bass), Roger Netherton (fiddle), and Rachel Eddy (guitar).

Since the beginning of recorded time, musical instruments appear in representations of daily life across cultures and continents. Just visit any museum. And if you want to see what the traditional music evolution looks like today, come visit Clifftop.

Clifftop and other festivals, we celebrate our collective humanity by playing these joyful tunes.

To be really technical, the Clifftop crowd plays what's called Southern Appalachian traditional music. But most of us players simply refer to it as old-time. And if you ask someone what that means, you'll probably get an amazing variety of answers. Just know the music is mostly not from here (the United States). Over the past 200 years, it's what many of our ancestors played to celebrate, console, relax and honor their experiences. The tunes are pretty repetitive, but that also makes them easier to learn. And the more folks that can play, the better the odds of using this second language to make new friends, share experiences, expand the community of participant friends and enjoy life. Clifftop can feel a bit like "church" to those of us that experienced that sense of community. In this case, the gospel, revelation or testament of old-time music would be:

- *It's good for you.* As you'll read later, it really does positively affect mental and physical health.
- *It's good for your friends and neighbors,* one's community. And, therefore…
- *It's good for the world!* Music lowers stress, promotes understanding, bonds us together as humans and, for all we know, has probably done more to keep our species alive than we will ever acknowledge.

Okay. I have some more friends I want you to meet. Here are excerpts from a few Clifftop conversations I've filmed over the years with regular attendees talking about why they make the pilgrimage. The first is Hilarie Burhans in 2015.

Hilarie Burhans—Clifftop Community Role: The *Good Samaritan.* For years, Hilarie and her husband Mark would pack up a small version of Salaam, their Athens, Ohio, restaurant and bring it to Clifftop. Then, on a scheduled basis, they would feed the masses. Long lines would lead to pleasant conversations and sometimes spontaneous jamming as friends and fellow campers enjoyed fabulous meals, free of charge (donations only). To feed such a troupe, smiling fellow campers would volunteer to help. Hilarie reported to me they were never at a loss for assistance or money. The community revels in her gifts.

"To me, Clifftop is like Brigadoon. It's a whole, beautiful community that rises from the mist, exists for nine days, and then is gone until the next year. It's the most beautiful thing!"

Last summer (2022), after two years of Covid-cancelling, Clifftop resumed with more than 2,000 attending—down from peak number of close to 4,000 a few years earlier. But it felt like a feeding frenzy! I got Hilarie to weigh in on some important topics again.

Craig: How does traditional music affect your life, let's say, physically and then mentally, emotionally?

Hilarie: It is a massive stress reliever for me. This past few years of Covid, I was teaching a lot of online lessons, and then through the whole thing, once a week, the only social thing we did was to have this jam. I put up our big festival canopy on my outdoor side patio. I gathered a small group of other old-time musicians to play music together … once a week, all the way through the pandemic. I felt like it sort of saved me. I think I would have been bonkers without that.

Craig: The music in the community was the draw?

Hilarie: Yes, and it's always been that way. If I think of my tribe. Other than my family, my tribe isn't really so much where I live, it's the community of people that I know through music, and people I learn from and I teach to, and they're my people.

One of the things about traditional music that makes it different from classical

Hilarie Burhans. Representing the best of today's Clifftop community.

music or jazz or whatever is the sheer accessibility of it. It takes a lot to get a bunch of people together to play classical music. And this event, the traditional music at Clifftop, is a way people can communicate on a really deep level with each other without years and years of study.

You can dive in early on and be sketching out chords, mostly listening, and following the jam rule which is "play either quietly or well." Most tunes have only two or three chords, and they're the same two or three chords in every key. It's a fairly narrow-ish brand of music that we play, narrow but not shallow. Very deep. You can get into this as far as you want. My husband likens it to going to the beach. You can go out and enjoy the little waves or you can wade in further and have the big waves, but everyone can enjoy it at some level.

You can, early on, have these peak moments where you and another person are communicating on this different level, other than talking or whatever. You could not know this person at all and still be involved musically in this intense if temporary relationship.

I also played in a contra dance band for years and years, and we were pretty popular. A hiring host would fly us here and there ... then with the whole hassle, and you think, "Why the heck do I do this?" Then maybe it's the second tune, maybe the third tune when all of a sudden, everything is locked together, and you're there with the other people you're playing with, and you're like, "This is why! Now I remember." It's those peak moments.

Craig: Then as you look out at the crowd, especially dancers, they're flying?

Hilarie: I love to see them all with their feet hitting the floor at exactly the same time and you become one pulsating unit. It's community with the dancers, and you can play in such a way that they dance differently. You feed off of their energy, and they feed off yours.

Just FYI—you can enjoy yourself without those really peak moments, but when they do come, it's awesome!

Hilarie used the word "tribe," a common term for our Clifftop community. Here's what another banjo-playing regular, John Herrmann, had to say about it in 2015.

John Herrmann—Clifftop Community Role: The *Revered Mystic.* John is *the* banjo player first-tier fiddlers want to play with. His in-the-field festival videos get hammered by banjo players wondering how he gets such amazing sounds and rhythms. A few years back, in his attempt to get a more desirable banjo voice, John applied plain old silver masking tape across the top of his banjo bridge. Over the course of the next two years, more and more banjo players came to Clifftop with similar tape applied. I asked one fellow why he did that. He said, "Because John Herrmann does it." "Why? What does it do?" I parried. "I dunno," was his response. Okay, so John clearly is a vetted thought-leader. But as a Zen practitioner, he's incredibly thoughtful to begin with. He naturally experiences (and warrants) such a following.

John: I go to Clifftop because that's where my tribe is. I think all my oldest friends are old-time music friends. I love to get in the situation where you've been playing for days, and you can do anything. By the third day at Clifftop, I can sit down with my banjo and *bang*! I am playing as good as I can play. There you are. Right to the core.

It doesn't happen all the time. In Zen practice, we have Sesshin, which is a week-long retreat where you sit 10–11 hours a day, with no talking, the whole week. Things happen when you practice something intensely, and you go deeper, deeper, deeper, deeper. This also happens at these festivals.

A third conversation on the timelessness of traditional music and its importance to humanity is from Phil Jamison, author, dancer, dance caller, banjo player, and former calculus instructor at Warren Wilson College. He was filmed and interviewed in 2022.

Phil Jamison—Clifftop Community Role: The *Consummate Resource for Traditional Music and Dance.* If Phil was a baseball player, one would say he "came up

John Herrmann. Master player, Clifftop legend.

through the system." He sings, plays, dances, calls dances, researches dances ... all from firsthand experience engaging in these aspects of the traditional music community. In a few chapters (Chapter 25), you'll read Dr. Josh Turknett's conversation regarding music and dance's effect on the brain. Based on the amount of time invested in those activities, I think I can safely say nobody's brain is more lit than Phil's. He lives and breathes this culture and has done his utmost to pass along his learnings and wisdom through teaching, performing, speaking and writing. I so admire this person. On top of that, he taught calculus for years at Warren Wilson College. His lit brain is a beacon of understanding, insight and inspiration for those lucky enough to know him.

Craig: If I say the term "traditional music," what are your thoughts on traditional music, and what does it mean to you?

Phil Jamison: I think of traditional music as music that is particular to a certain group of people or a community, and it is music that's passed on from generation to generation. Groups of people all over the world in different places have developed their own musical traditions, and I find it a very important part of the folk culture. It's an important thing to keep alive, it's sustainable, and it gets passed on and on. It's not like pop music that is gone with the next hottest thing.

Craig: What about it makes it sustainable? What about it inspires people to keep passing it on? Is there some magic to it?

Phil Jamison. Traditional music and dance historian.

Phil: What would make it sustainable is that it *can* be passed on from generation to generation, and it blows my mind that you can go back in a time machine 200 years, if you could find a fiddler from 200 years ago, and we would know some tunes in common. We could sit down and speak that same musical language. I think what makes it sustainable is that it's not a commercial product created by the music industry. It has a life of its own.

In my head, a lot of old-time music is traditionally about dancing. The tunes people are playing are primarily dance tunes. In the past, people didn't sit around and watch TV or videos or YouTube or anything at home; they would go out to dances.

What would it be like if you lived in an age before there was such a thing as recorded music? If all the music you'd ever heard in your whole life was made live, how much would you value those music-makers in your community?

If you wanted music, you had to go to where other people were, and that creates a community of people. The musicians had an important role in communities and were very valued, and dancing was a very common recreation in this country up until the music got commercialized and became available so you could sit at home and listen to it.

Craig: The role of traditional music is to keep us together as a community. Are there other functions or features of it, maybe the content of the tunes or the lyrics, or does anything like that play a role?

Phil: Sure. Yes, so if you're talking about vocal music, there's certain messages in the songs. In the ballads, in all of those murder ballads where Katie goes to the river with Willie and meets a tragic end…

Craig: Don't go to the river!

Phil: "Don't go to the river with Willie," that's the message. Don't get pregnant out of wedlock or this might happen to you too. It sends a message to young men: "Don't get Katie pregnant, you'll end up in the jail—and be ready to be hung if you do that kind of thing." The ballads send messages; they're not just entertainment.

Craig: This is tradition, I mean those ballads are primarily English or Irish.

Phil: Also, the religious sacred music, there's definitely a "you've got to act" message. "You have to live right if you want to get to heaven!"

And here's a fourth conversation that really sets up what happens with the Clifftop traditional music community experience and how you can internalize its values in your daily life. It's all here, from Tricia Spencer in 2022.

Tricia Spencer—Clifftop Community Role: *The Benevolent, Accomplished Teacher.* Talk about compassionate and soul-searching. Tricia grew up with music. It was her family heritage. When she ran into others playing well, she learned those styles too. But when she experienced Clifftop, she found something even more meaningful … community. How people could come together and *celebrate* this music (traditional) amazed her! That's what communities do. After some reflective time, she embraced the culture and found peace, joy and love within. It has touched her so deeply, she's dedicated her life to passing along the music—and the spirit she discovered at Clifftop that fulfills it—to others.

Tricia: My name is Tricia, I'm from Kansas. I'm at Clifftop again.

Craig: Why is that important?

Tricia: Oh, I love this place. It changed my life. Out of all the things I do, this is in the top five.

Craig: Top five?

Tricia: Yes, when you sometimes start thinking about what's most important to you in life, and what are non-negotiables—Clifftop is my non-negotiables. And I guess in some ways my everyday life mimics Clifftop. I made that change in my life. I let go of a lot of unimportant things and made this be my life.

Craig: What about Clifftop freed you to find yourself?

Tricia: Well, because I didn't live here, and I didn't know these fiddlers, I was so lucky to be adopted by the Ohio old-time fiddlers. Because I grew up in a more bluegrass tradition, I didn't know people sat around and shared this common love of tunes. I'll never forget sitting there with three, four other fiddlers who all knew the same tune, everyone else knew what they were doing, and they were in the moment.

What they were doing ... it was like breaking bread with each other, but it was with fiddle tunes. There were the stories of where the source came from, and where they might have picked it up, or who made it be playable for them. Then I realized there was this whole level of sharing music and keeping a particular genre alive that I wanted to be a part of. To me, this is heaven. I mean, what fiddler wouldn't want to do this?

Now, granted, if you want to play another genre where you might be the focus of it, you're not going to find it in old-time, because it's about group participation. It's not about your skill level and how good you are. It's more about what you know about it, and how much you love it, and who you maybe got it from, and all that kind of stuff.

Tricia Spencer. Tricia embodies the spirit of Clifftop.

Craig: Most times when people start a tribe or a community, there's a barrier to entry, but once you're inside that, you're a part of it. Is there something in this tribe you related to—or freed you? Was it the music or was there anything else?

Tricia: It's the whole thing. It's not just the tunes because, obviously, we can play tunes with people anywhere—but it's what happens here at Clifftop. When you come here and camp for seven or eight days, you're coming here with provisions to get on through the week, because it's hard to go get what you need. I love the fact that these folks come and they make these little beautiful cities here—there's the Ohio area, the New York area, the Canada area.

Craig: Texas, Philadelphia.

Tricia: And in the Texas area, Howard and I had Kansas in Texas area and California. They build these communities, they share food with each other, they share drink with each other, they share stories with each other. When I come here, I can have differences with the people who come here, but I would much rather hang with everyone here than 99.99 percent of everyone else who knows nothing about what we do here.

I knew right away that these were my people: they cared about food, they cared about community, they cared about learning and growing, they cared about nature, and they cared about tradition. They wanted something to keep going. That's how they invested, and that's how we invest here into the world. *This makes you a better person, I mean, it really does!* If you don't have the skills to come on in and play in the best jams, hardly no one here wouldn't give you "Hey, here's how you do it, here's how you get going and hold this one string down, and you can play with this," because that's what it's about. It's about sharing and building something as opposed to, like I said, promoting yourself.

I always say that, in old-time music, you're taking your skills to build tunes in the tradition, as opposed to taking your skills for your own ego. It's about the bigger picture in old-time music.

I knew this was it; not only was it here, but I wanted to do this in my own town. I wanted to build that same community where people wanted to sit for hours and play in the same key. I knew I wanted that, and I wanted to help people kind of jump on board. It's a good life. Simple, it's honest, and everybody here cares for each other.

Craig: You're really articulating it well. I want to take it up to the next level, though. We're on the mountain top, and we've all found each other, for some reason, at this place. Can we take it from here and somehow give it to the world? What is the role of traditional music with humanity?

Tricia: When you talk about this, this is part of why I do what I do. It's why I teach. It's why I perform. I think what has happened in the world is that things have become so easy for people to get instant gratification that they don't even know this exists. There's that phrase: *everybody loves old-time, they just don't know it yet.*

This music is what we did before we became really civilized. We made music with each other. That's how we connected with each other, and, yes, I think when I go home and take on students, little by little I give them this information of how cool this is. Let's do it together, and I start sharing. I do believe that makes a difference in the world, and it's the kind of world I want to live in—where tradition does mean something, and what that means is, you're paying tribute in respect to the people who carried it on before you. If I don't do my part to share this with the next generation, the young ones, then who are we going to share it with eventually?

Craig: It's giving you standards and values that are worth saving.

Tricia: Oh, yes.

Craig: If you're a part of our culture or our tribe, this is what we do and this is why we do it.

Tricia: Yes. If you're playing John Salyer's tune, and you think it's a great tune, how are you not going to know a little bit about John Salyer and why he even fiddled in his family? Whether you play it like John Salyer anymore or not, you are now connected to this music that came from somewhere else, and now you carry it on. Even if you're not very good, even if you can't remember the tune title or the name—that piece of a moment in time is being carried on.

I feel that way now. I reached my fifties, and here were all of these great fiddlers from the Midwest that I spent time with, many of them sitting knee to knee with me. This was time and energy they could have spent doing something else, but yet they gave it to me. My family music ... I didn't think it warranted me learning it.

With so much focus on Appalachian fiddling, it made me feel that my tradition was not important, and I carried a chip on my shoulder for many years, and especially while here. Then at some point, I realized Appalachian fiddling is a piece and is the essence of everything, not only the mountains, because that's what music is. You can find a lineage that goes way beyond the years we can count or recordings we have.

Finally, I was able to put the big picture together of what the music meant to me and who I was and what I was carrying on. I would be doing a great disservice if I stopped playing music today, because, honestly, in Kansas, I am the old person. Whoever wants it, I'm going to give it to them.

Craig: Is the music the touchstone which actually contains all these emotional feelings of connection and joy and family and fulfillment and security and trust? Is this the nugget you're passing along?

Tricia: Well, yes. I think so. It's not only the music, though. Like I said, to me it's the embodiment of what it's like to camp here for seven days or eight days or however long you're here. You are connected to the land. It rains on you, and it's hot, but you find a way to be connected here—and the music is our language with each other. Obviously, some people here don't play, but they are all still connected because they might be making food or they might be good listeners, and they love it.

I think you could have this anywhere. We do it at our home. Our kids jokingly talk about how we have Clifftop food and we have Clifftop nights. We basically set up our evening like we would at Clifftop. This means we turn off all the lights, and we might eat funny snack food and play tunes and pretend that we're back here again, but we're doing it in Kansas.

Finally, here's a good conversation describing community from an interview I did in 2015 with Clifftop regulars Steve Arkin, banjo player, and John Hoffman, fiddle player. If I had a **Clifftop Community Role** for these two, it would be **Good-Time, Great-Music Aficionados.** You're guaranteed to experience both whenever they play.

Craig to **Steve Arkin** and **John Hoffman:** "What's your favorite thing about old-time music?"

Steve: The joy of locking in with other musicians.

John: Community! At a festival, between tunes, I walk around and watch the joy coming out of the campground.

Steve: You get to play your heart out. You let your mind go, and your fingers will follow.

John Hoffman (left) and Steve Arkin. Lighthearted musical spirits.

Craig: As you're playing, can you make it possible for people listening to tune into that same level?

Steve: To the extent that the banjo is the flying buttress on the fiddle's cathedral, that's your job or a big part of your job: help feed the drive and the groove, which are similar and related, but not congruent.

John: But most of us want to sit down and start playing because there's a feeling to that togetherness … the place you have when the beat gets wider and wider, the time slows, and all of a sudden, what you couldn't play alone, or what you couldn't play when the groove wasn't happening, all of a sudden you can do just about anything!

What Kind of Music Is Played at Clifftop?

First, let's start with some definitions. *A traditional music community is a group of individuals actively interested in playing, supporting, and sharing traditional music.*

What is traditional music? It refers to music that has been passed down from generation to generation within a particular culture or community. This music is often associated with specific regions or countries and is considered an important part of that society's cultural heritage.

Traditional music is typically performed on instruments that are native to the culture or region, such as the bagpipes in Scotland or the sitar in India. It can also be performed on instruments specific to a genre. Southern Appalachian traditional music, commonly referred to as old-time, features fiddles, banjos, guitars, and mandolins. Other instruments like mountain dulcimers can also be included. In all cases, songs that tell stories or history or express emotions related to important events, such as religious ceremonies, weddings, dances or funerals, can be included.

In most cases, traditional music has evolved over time and has been influenced by outside cultures or musical styles. For example, traditional Irish music has been influenced by English, Scottish, and other European music as well as African American jazz and blues. Southern Appalachian music was influenced by Blacks, white immigrants from many European cultures, and indigenous Native Americans. As many interviewed for my documentaries can attest, it's difficult to separate the cultures from the music. Therefore, with Southern Appalachian traditional music, *it's not considered Black music or white music, it's both and more (i.e., Native American)*.

At some point, it happens to pretty much everyone that gets into old-time, one starts to wonder just where (in the world) does this music come from? Who played it? Should one choose to embark on that learning journey, know that it's a wonderful adventure. I started by asking "roots" questions of the old-timers I played with, mostly the aging fiddlers that were starting the tunes in my jams. I quickly learned everyone had an "inkling," either they'd heard the history "firsthand" from somebody, somewhere, or they'd also heard about somebody, somewhere who had read a story (in the past 20 years) that could place the tune, uh, with somebody, uh somewhere. Yeah, confusing. And almost assured to be anecdotal. But that's half the fun … nobody really knows. Which, in my book, opens the door to embracing the mystery and the romance of our species' shared rich, diverse history. Now, for those that really do care about the origins and entrances of traditional music to the United States, here's what I was able to find online from bona fide sources (see the bibliography).

Pre–1600s, there were musical Native Americans drumming, singing, playing instruments of their own design and dancing all across North America. I can only imagine how glorious that must have been. During the 1600–1700s, carried by early pilgrims, farmers, seekers and other adventurous types, English hymns and psalms arrived along with European ballads, sea shanties, reels, jigs, hornpipes and country dances. Also from Europe came ballroom dances, minuets and French cotillions.

During this period, one of the darkest events in human history (slavery) was silently delivering music, dance, culture and instruments to the United States. African drumming, call-and-response singing and extraordinary dances with perhaps thousands of years of history arrived in North America on slave ships, hidden in the bodies and DNA of these precious beings. But not for long. It soon emerged as a powerful energy. Homesick, enslaved Africans quickly assembled makeshift drums and stringed instruments from whatever materials were available. They learned European violin along with its accompanying repertoire and in time began introducing their musicality to the new world.

Dena Epstein's seminal book *Sinful Tunes and Spirituals* is an extraordinary collection of firsthand and secondhand testimonials from observers of their calendas and other dances along with African traditions and rituals they were performing to remind them of their home. Emotionally, it was a moving celebration for the participants as well as the observers … and they did not go unnoticed. As Tim Brooks discusses in *The Blackface Minstrel Show in Mass Media*, his 2020 book on minstrelsy, a young, emerging America was looking to define itself as different from the rest of the world. In 1890, the composer Dvorak recognized the contribution of enslaved Blacks and called it out, saying, *"Americans, look to this field. Your African American influences are your folk music."*

In the 1800s, traditional music from its original source, along with what it may have picked up along the way (i.e., at sea ports in the Caribbean), began the evolution of all traditional music: It blends with traditions from other cultures and, in the present, becomes *a new tradition.* This phenomenon is explained and demonstrated in *Folksongs of Another America: Field Recordings from the Upper Midwest, 1937–1946,* a book by Dr. James Leary, professor emeritus at the University of Wisconsin. What was composed and played a certain way on one instrument can take on a new character being played a different way on an instrument from another country. Such creations bond both players and community as its original to them, at that place in time.

As Dr. Leary observes, when traditions come together, a new one forms from the combination featuring unique characteristics of each. This is not a bad thing. This is a new thing happening since the beginning of humanity. And what works continues. As the creative musical beings we are, in a new place, with new (soon-to-be) friends, America was using music to help grow community. Music was just one of the easier applications. Foods, textiles, crops, building techniques … it was all undergoing rapid expansion thanks to the new population's desire to build, survive and, hopefully, prosper.

Appalachia was one of the first places music and dance took center stage. Blacks, whites, Native Americans and new arrivals from all over the world were cooking up new traditions. Gospel songs and spirituals, work songs, square dances, quadrilles and waltzes were the rage. And to take on some ownership of the old tradition, a new name might be created to give it a more local, even updated feel.

African ring and shout dances, juba dances and the banjo did not go unnoticed by enterprising white musicians. They were quickly adapted to become entertainment for white audiences willing to pay 15 cents (children) and 25 cents (adults) for the newly-created minstrel show. From the 1830s to the early 1900s, traveling musicians brought new music, dances, stories and more to entertainment-hungry citizens in their new country. There's more on the discussion of the phenomenon (and legacy) of minstrelsy in Chapter 22.

Later, newly-emerging genres such as old-time, blues, bluegrass, Cajun and more were introduced to audiences everywhere across the new country. Almost two hundred years later, that energy *is still there.* I know! I can find it in jams, dances, musical gatherings everywhere I go in North America. Actually, we don't just play it. Those that truly understand what it is, where it came from and how it developed (from all peoples from all places), we *celebrate* it! It's our human *legacy*!

Traditional music is often performed at festivals, concerts, and other events, and it is sometimes taught in schools.

Who Comes to Clifftop?

There's one more aspect to Clifftop that I thought worthy of discussion. Who attends? With the exception of color (way more whites than Blacks, but we're working on that), there's neurodiversity … and lots of artists—musicians, but also painters, writers, designers, weavers, photographers, sculptors, and many other categories of creators.

I'd offer that *most* of the attendees are *dedicated* artists to some degree. You have to *really* want an experience if you take nine days off and drive a thousand miles there to get inspiration from this place. They may have day jobs in the capitalistic realm, but it's probably not who these people really are. Put another way, a salary is the drug an employer pays you to forget your dreams. Based on where they invest their time, artists have different values than what you might call typical employees, the worker bees. Artists are inclined to assign greater value to their dreams. These artists are everywhere at Clifftop.

I discovered a variety of artists during my time in advertising. As worker bees, they were there to earn a living, but most were more than happy to talk about their creative passions and pastimes (painting, writing, dancing, music). I've found even more creatives through traditional music. Creativity is fascinating wherever you find it—as one never knows when or where it will appear. Often you don't see it coming, but suddenly it shows up as a solution, an inspiration, or a direction. Seems most people don't pay much attention to it. I noticed many artists during my business years. To me, they always stood out in a good and interesting way.

Creativity is pretty much everywhere at Clifftop. It could be in how someone uniquely plays a common tune, or dresses, or dresses up their campsite, or their dog or their instrument case. I take pictures of these appearances every Clifftop. And when I witness it, I love it! It's interesting and playful. Some would call it inspiring. Artists show more of themselves and their work when they feel they're in safe company. I'm pretty sure that's why more artistically-inclined people are now attending Clifftop and bringing the creative fun level even higher.

Neurodiversity

If you've worked in HR, did you ever hear "artists don't fit the norm"? As an employee, the label "artist" can work in your favor or not. If you look at the bell curve of society, the middle is filled with the more compliant, more hire-able "worker bees." Many worker bees are the people who are patted on the head right after they're told they're not artists because, as John Lennon said, "every child's an artist until they're told they're not." What a waste! If they are told that by a trusted loved one, and the young creative accepts this judgement, they'll push aside their favorite things and decide, "Okay, I'll get a job." Does this story sound familiar? I hope not for you, but it does for me (see Chapter 2: The Artist's Choice).

Giving up their first choice for a career (some form of art), they may get additional education, find work, get married, buy a house, have kids, and plan on retirement. Although they are capable of making this change, it's been my experience that artists simply aren't wired this way. Passion burns in their soul. You can only ignore it so long until, one day, the person might give themselves permission to "follow their heart." In my book, it's the best life decision *ever.*

So rather than give up on creating, they keep their inspirations handy, nearby, and they look for opportunities to bring it to the fore while maintaining an outside, stable day job. Often, though, once it emerges and becomes a focus, it can actually become their identity.

They don't just follow a different drummer; they could actually be the head percussionist. To facilitate a possible future focus on their art or project, they might turn to a second or outside job to help keep bread on the table. In my years on the road talking to people in the traditional music community, I found *these artists are everywhere.* But through the traditional music community, they found a way to make a living *through* their art. Remember Hunter S. Thompson's quote about *finding a job that suits your preferred way of living* earlier in this book? My favorite story is that of banjo builder Mike Ramsey.

Mike was always an artist, tinkering, fixing, and building things, especially motorcycles. He was also really bright. He got an education and took a job with Procter & Gamble, where he was doing well but felt bored.

As he tells the story, one night he walked into a bar on High Street and heard a group of people playing the old-time tune "Liberty"—Thomas Jefferson's favorite tune—full out! He said there was a guitar, a banjo, and a couple of fiddles, and he decided *on-the-spot,* "That's me!" He made a decision to change careers and do something that he liked more that his corporate job.

Mike chose to build banjos because he thought it was a cool instrument that would give him entrée to meeting cool people, like the folks in the High Street bar and at music festivals. He was absolutely right about that—and a legend in banjo building was born.

Mike started building banjos in the late summer, fall, and winter. In the spring he filled his car with them and started to drive across Appalachia to all the fiddle festivals, selling banjos out of his car at every stop. He wanted to be known as the Johnny Appleseed of banjos, a title he deserved and earned.

Mike built close to 4,000 banjos by the time he retired. His best friend in the

Mike Ramsey heard a bar band playing the old-time standard "Liberty." Moved by the music's excitement and energy, he decided to change his career to became a banjo builder.

banjo trade, Bart Reiter, made it to 5,000 banjos. Bart is another story. Where most banjo builders would laugh if you asked them the question "Can you make a living building banjos?" Bart was one who genuinely did.

Raised by a very structured and organized German father, Bart was a banjo-building machine. Before he started his own business, which he loved, he had learned his skills firsthand repairing all sorts of stringed instruments at his day job with Elderly Instruments. He even started building his own guitars on the side and tried to sell them at Elderly. Apparently, it wasn't the right time to offer guitars. A fellow employee said, "Why don't you try making open-back banjos? We never seem to have enough of them." And so he did!

Bart could crank out 30 banjos a month *all by himself.* And today, I'd argue his banjos are still among the best out there. One of his models, the Standard, set a standard for all other builders to live up to. They're incredible instruments.

Bart and Mike are both artists, very capable of working and succeeding in the capitalistic realm. But eventually, both said no. Both also commented to me about how much they liked being their own boss. However, something else made them feel even better about their life's work. *People in the traditional music community genuinely appreciated them. They weren't only customers, they were friends.* How rewarding.

I have to admit, I ended up loving each and every one of these builders. Bart gave me a banjo, literally gave it to me, saying, "I want to say thank you for all the banjo builders you made famous." I was humbled, almost to tears, but I didn't want to cry in front of Bart because it would have made him uncomfortable.

I do think my banjo builder films elevated the message, "Hey, if you're a creative/artist, find something you really like to do, do it well, and join a community that recognizes and appreciates what you do for them. You may not make piles of money, but you will have the respect you deserve, which in itself is income." I play Bart's banjo for kids every year at my favorite gig, the Afton Apple Orchard. To me it's as valuable as the old South Dakota fiddler's fiddle.

Getting back to neurodiversity and the traditional music community, anecdotally, I've witnessed a higher-than-average occurrence among attendees of what are considered negative labels. People openly tell me about their struggles with ADD, ADHD, dyslexia, bipolar disorder, sensory issues, anxiety, depression, and autism. Given my experience with those labels through the autism community (another side interest), *I can say with certainty it's what makes the traditional music community even richer in creativity.*

Now, here's another label worth noting.

Four Fulbright Scholars!

When I started my interviews with banjo builders, I really didn't know who or what I was going to find. It took only a few conversations for me to recognize *most of these people are artists first, business people second.* I then altered my interview approach in order to discover more of their passion for what they were doing rather

Fulbright Scholars. From left: Art Rosenbaum, Seth Swingle, Evie Ladin, James Leva.

than business results, which came later. Deeper, more meaningful conversations and fun were a direct result.

Overall, I can say these people appear happy and pleased with their life choices and style of living. Later I discovered the old-time performers and teachers were cut from the same cloth as the luthiers. Yes, all are indeed business entrepreneurs, but the majority were way more interested in discussing the design and production of their final product and lifestyles rather than business models—figuring out how they would or could make the most income.

I also discovered how deep their passions run. Without planning it, I interviewed four Fulbright scholars for my documentary series.

According to the Fulbright Scholarship website,.

> The Fulbright Program, the United States government's flagship program of international educational and cultural exchange, offers passionate and accomplished students and scholars in more than 160 countries the opportunity to study, teach, conduct research, exchange ideas, and contribute to mutual understanding. These talented Fulbrighters from all backgrounds inspire, innovate, and contribute to finding solutions to challenges facing our communities and our world.

To be awarded a Fulbright Scholarship, one not only has to be very bright but also motivated, dedicated, and passionate about positive change. Artist, musician, and teacher Art Rosenbaum, musician and historian Seth Swingle, dancer, singer and performer Evie Ladin, and performer and scholar James Leva all received Fulbright Scholarships. During their interviews, they explained how they were able to expand their learnings and generate goodwill globally, thanks to this program. Sadly, Art Rosenbaum recently passed, but Seth, Evie, and James are Clifftop regulars, deeply and socially engaged in the community and what it represents.

Yes, they are all amazing people. I can also report there are many other intelligent, compassionate, competent members of the traditional music community similarly capable of affecting positive change *in their local surroundings.* Music and community can affect people that way. A tribe establishes and reflects purpose and values. It creates opportunities and supports personal growth while fostering collaboration and friendship. Community also lowers barriers for others to join the fun. All this happens while making us happier, healthier, more secure, and less lonely.

I would argue because of all these diverse people, the Clifftop community is made stronger. Clearly, they're creative. They present new ways of thinking by thinking (and being) different. And more creativity is something this community not only appreciates but also enjoys! I'd say it is warmly and safely embraced. And once an artist feels safe, they can flourish. My camera records lots of good people flourishing at Clifftop.

It's easy to see how old-time music helps form its very own community.

The age dispersion between young and old at Clifftop is bi-modal, meaning there are groups at both ends of the age spectrum with few, if any, in the middle. On the lower end there's a cluster of young attendees, say, 12- to 34-year-olds, that first got there accompanying their old-time music–loving parents. Also on that end is a second group that joined their adventurous peers to travel to this remote mountaintop for a week of camping and hanging out with musician friends. If asked, both younger crowds would admit to finding themselves there mostly by *chance.* Two things most of them exhibit, though, is excitement and joy. They will be back!

The other end of the age spectrum, the 50- to 80-plus-year-olds, are close to the youngins in attendance. But unlike the younger crowd, they're there mostly by *choice.* To them, it's a chance to meet up with old friends and play their instruments (often a lifelong passion). Same with learning new tunes. This group seems to have an unlimited number of reasons to get out the old gear (and aspirin), saddle up for the drive, set up the equipment (often in the rain), endure little sleep, survive a week of port-a-potties, yada yada (and many more gripes). Why? Because *it's so worth it!* Remember the positives Hilarie Burhans, Tricia Spencer, John Herrmann and Phil Jameson testified to earlier? They're a pretty representative group of cheerleaders. As with the youngins, they're spokespeople for that excitement and joy.

So where are the folks in the middle, the 35- to 49-year-olds, you ask? Except for the few talented, very dedicated artists that see old-time music as their way of life (the future "flame keepers"), the rest have given up on their music passion and found day jobs. Like their peers that never discovered the music (or Clifftop), they've become the worker bees, *going to work in tall buildings* (as per John Hartford's prophetic lament). Unless there's a layoff, divorce or some other severe life change that forces one to re-evaluate their personal priorities (i.e., rediscover their true passion in life), they're too busy to make it to the mountain. Too bad. Lots of good memories made here. Not to mention life-long bonding with complete strangers. And as Tricia Spencer says, "This music makes you a better person."

Back in earlier cultures and societies, traditional music made it possible for us to bond better with each other. Researchers aren't exactly sure what the 40,000-year-old bone flutes were played for, but later cultures developed harps, lutes, and lyres for events, celebrations and individual use.

As more people joined the circles and enlarged communities, it helped us survive. Communities can develop values as well as the means to educate all to the importance of following them. In the traditional music community, some make the instruments that others play, perform on, and teach. The historians, like authors and filmmakers, save the developments for both current and future generations. Meanwhile, in real time, all of their works can gift us moments of unbridled joy. I can't make that statement without picturing a pack of kids dancing in front of me at the apple orchard. It's easy to trigger. I simply start a breakdown or a square dance on the fiddle or banjo … lighting the match. Next, the community dance comes out of nowhere. A few kids start dancing, which brings in more kids, which brings in grandparents, which brings in parents. Smiles are everywhere. Time stops. Joy starts! I'm not a Buddhist, but I clearly know these moments in time are extraordinary … and can lift my heart simply thinking about them. Every. Single. Time.

In my personal story about discovering traditional music earlier in this book, I talked about heroes and mentors in a good way. Sometimes they can present as jerks or roadblocks (hello, Dr. R.) as well as manipulative personalities. I've had my fair share of experiences with them. I'm grateful for learning how to recognize, and now avoid, such disasters. Interestingly, in the traditional music community, I feel the latter group of people described above are few and far between. Community is based on getting along and assisting. Those with rather severe issues cannot manipulate as easily and quickly move on to find easier marks. Rest easy, dear fellow artists. At Clifftop, we're all in good company.

Oh, a last comment on personalities. I don't have any statistically significant research to offer on the number of introverts versus extroverts at Clifftop. Anecdotally, I'd say most are friendly introverts. That's been my overall experience with both artists and musicians, not that an occasional extrovert can't light us all up (in delight or laughter). But where introverts normally keep to themselves, that's not so at Clifftop. Actually, it's easy to jump-start a discussion simply through topics of *relevance*. You can open up a conversation with a common subject, especially something deep, like personal feelings toward a shared interest ("I really like the sound of your banjo"). Age assists because it adds credibility. This combination can immediately open a window to trust, inviting even more conversation. At Clifftop, 48 hours after meeting someone—a complete stranger—you're talking about subjects you would barely venture on with your most trusted back-home friends. These conversations can also fill you up for a year. The gain is well worth the effort (venture).

A side note, I took my Myers–Briggs test again last year. Turns out, I'm now an INFJ* or P, depending on the day. And I have *many* deep talks at Clifftop. We even laughingly refer to them as Clifftop Conversations.

- I—Introvert, N—Intuitive, F—Feeling, J—Judging and P—Perceiving

24

Why Play Old-Time Music?

I have a favorite descriptive comment about community I heard off-camera from Clifftop camper and friend Lucy Allen. When asked what she liked most about our Clifftop tribe, she responded, "I can be myself without pretense." Many of us can't say that about our nuclear family or work peers.

The benefits that communities provide to their individual members can include:

Social support: Communities provide a sense of belonging and connectedness and can be a source of emotional and practical support for their members. You're part of the tribe.

Opportunities for personal growth and development: Being part of a community can offer opportunities for learning, skill-building, and personal development as well as the chance to take on leadership roles and contribute to the community's success. And in the case of Clifftop, encouragement is offered everywhere.

Increased sense of purpose: Being part of a community can provide a sense of purpose and direction, as members work toward common goals and contribute to something larger than themselves. As Dwight Diller once told me, "It ain't about you and how good you play, it's about the tune. You and the others should always be making the tune the best it can be."

Enhanced physical and mental health: Research has shown that social support and social connectedness are linked to better physical and mental health outcomes, including lower rates of depression, anxiety, and chronic disease. It's nice to belong to something you believe in … that believes in you.

Opportunities for collaboration and collective action: Communities can provide a platform for members to collaborate and work together toward shared goals, whether that's advocating for social change, pursuing a common interest, or addressing a community-wide issue. Some of us old Boomers still want to leave the world a better place than we found it. Traditional music can help make that happen.

And Finally, Traditional Music's Gift to Humanity

Individual Level

Very similar to the earlier listing of the benefits of music, a few more are added when you focus on this particular genre of music.

The traditional music played in Appalachia with fiddles and banjos has been known to have numerous benefits for physical, mental, emotional, and spiritual well-being.

Physically, playing the music requires physical activity and coordination, such as moving the fingers on a fretboard, strumming or plucking strings, or tapping one's feet. These activities improve dexterity, hand-eye coordination, and motor skills, which can also help to prevent or reduce the risk of developing conditions such as arthritis or carpal tunnel syndrome.

Mentally, playing traditional American music can be a form of meditation, as it requires concentration, focus, and mindfulness. And as mentioned above, playing music can help to improve cognitive function, memory, and creativity as well as reduce stress and anxiety.

Emotionally, traditional American music can evoke strong emotions and feelings of nostalgia or longing, as it often tells stories of hardship, love, and loss. It can also be a form of self-expression and emotional release, which can help to improve emotional regulation and promote emotional well-being. Traditional music is very personal. A person can make it their own by interpreting it the way it makes them feel. You can't break it, but the act of exploring through it is encouraged.

Spiritually, traditional American music has deep roots in religious and spiritual practices, such as gospel music or shape-note singing. These forms of music can also promote a sense of community, connection, and belonging, thus decreasing loneliness, and can also be a form of worship or prayer.

In past cultures, traditional American music played an important role in helping humanity survive by providing the community with a way for people to express their emotions and connect with others. It was often played during communal gatherings, such as dances or religious services, and helped to build a sense of a community's identity. It also served as a form of entertainment and distraction during difficult times, such as war or economic hardship.

Furthermore, traditional American music has been passed down from generation to generation, preserving cultural traditions and values. It has helped to create a sense of continuity and connection between past and present and has played a crucial role in shaping American culture and identity.

Now if you just walk up to a smiling musician and ask them to explain their feelings, your odds of getting *any* of the above are minimal. You've got to think about music a bit (a lot, actually) to get this far. But therein lies music's beauty. *All of these benefits are going on in the background while you're just feelin' good, smiling without effort.* And between human beings, smiles are contagious. All that good goes back into the world through those fortunate enough to be a part of a musical experience.

Even More Benefits from Traditional Music Communities

Key Findings of the Harvard Happiness Studies

The Harvard Study of Adult Development is a long-term research project that began in 1938 and has followed the lives of two groups of men for more than 80 years. The study has yielded many insights into human happiness and well-being. Here are some of the key findings:

- *Strong relationships are crucial for happiness and health.* The study found that people who had strong, supportive relationships with family, friends, *and community members* (emphasis mine) were happier and healthier than those who were isolated or lacked strong relationships.
- *Quality of relationships is more important than quantity.* It's not only the number of relationships that matters *but also the quality of those relationships.* People who had a few close, intimate relationships were happier than those who had many superficial relationships.
- *Positive emotions and attitudes have long-term benefits.* People who had a positive outlook on life, expressed gratitude, and experienced positive emotions were more likely to be happy and healthy in the long term. *Most Clifftop attendees are "happy to be here!"*
- *Personal growth and development are key to happiness.* People who had a sense of purpose, engaged in activities that challenged them, and continued to learn and grow were happier and more fulfilled than those who remained stagnant. *Learning a new instrument sure lights up your brain!*
- *Health and happiness are linked.* The study found that people who were physically and mentally healthy were more likely to be happy and satisfied with their lives. *Lots of walking at Clifftop. Feels really good after a late night jam session.*

Benefits of Delight and Awe

Additional Perks of Traditional Music

One of the fantastic benefits of engaging in a project of this scope—180-plus interviews, 12 years "in the field," more than 60,000 miles traveled, literally 1,000-plus new people met—is getting the chance to reflect on conversations and lesser "discoveries" in the "in-between times." For instance, I could be driving a car between interview recordings, editing a final part of a program, preparing a speech on my films for a high school class, writing a short article ... little things would come to mind. Most of these "epiphanies" came in sideways. For instance, in reviewing my conversations with pretty much anyone in the series, you can sense a sort of joy or happiness from within. They smile, they laugh … *a lot*. They also joke or simply relax into a pleasant discussion of the subject at hand. All of them! Hmm. I started thinking—has anyone ever been upset, snarky or perturbed at something unrelated to the filming, like, they came in upset? In all of my travels, *I never encountered anyone in a bad mood*. Now, they might feel intimidated and anxious about filming, but they're smiling and ready to do the task. Good attitudes prevailed.

Now, how can that be? Aren't we all human? Don't we all have good and bad days? How could a focus group of core traditional music people *all* be at their best at a particular moment in time? I do have some thoughts on this topic.

There are some knowns about perspectives and how they affect our attitudes. One is a rather simplistic cliché: *if you follow your passion, you will never work a day in your life*. There's more in this statement about focus and liking your subject than happiness. One could be engaged in something they love but hate the task or event at hand—maybe even to the point of avoidance. I'm sure luthiers can have a bad day by accidentally ruining a build, or a performer or teacher may encounter a non-advancing student whose parent has forced them to be there. So difficulties can arise. However, *when a person does things they enjoy, they truly can find delight*.

Those minutes can spread into hours with no acknowledgment. Time passes, yet the emotional rush stays. It's incredibly fulfilling. I heard builders talk of shaving an instrument's neck with a draw knife as being almost Zen-like. Or a performer hitting the groove on a difficult tune during a performance. Or the circle at Clifftop experiencing the elusive, life-changing "transcendent" moment with a group of strangers who then become instant lifelong friends due to the shared experience. The whole "in-the-moment" event, where you lose yourself in something really engaging and fun, comes to mind. Time stops. Joy starts. Let's drill down on "delight" for a moment.

Delight

Remember me talking in the first part of this book about the energy and joy I'd felt as a five-year-old listening to powerful classical music? That *time stops, joy starts* feeling I was experiencing is called *delight*. It can be defined as a feeling of great pleasure, happiness, or enjoyment. Interestingly, it is often associated with a sense of surprise or unexpectedness. It's an event, to some degree.

It's subjective, of course, and can vary from person to person based on their individual preferences, experiences, and expectations. Examples are easy—delight may come from trying new foods, witnessing kindness in strangers, or watching a small animal play or nuzzle into their human. Holding the hand of a loved one.

For some of us, it comes from playing music. It could be discovering a new tune, working out a difficult phrase on an instrument, relating to the storyline of the music or its history, locking into a rhythm and arrangement with other players or letting the sound and vibration of the music fill your being without analysis or judgment. Jeez, I'm feeling all that typing this.

Overall, delight is a positive emotion that is associated with an intense sense of joy or happiness. And it's good for you! But let's move on.

Awe

Another epiphany occurred to me after watching the smiling interviewees. There's a peculiar situation called awe. *Awe is a powerful emotion that arises from encountering something vast, transcendent, or sublime.* It has been associated with a range of positive physical, psychological and social outcomes, such as increased well-being, compassion, and a greater sense of meaning and purpose in life. That should make anybody smile, right? It also lowers blood pressure. I'd venture that people active in the traditional music community—especially festival-goers—are wired to find or actually create awe … in others and self. If you listen to the conversations at these festivals, attendees often describe musical experiences as "Wow! That tune was amazing! I can't believe you/I played it that well! Your/my fiddle/banjo/mandolin/spoons were awesome, too, weren't they?" Okay, nix the spoons.

Beginning in 2015, every year that I've attend Clifftop I prepare a "highlight reel" of performing musicians. They could be jamming in a tent, placed in the woods, on the lodge porch or just assembled at the side of the walking path through the campground. At night, the sound of strings is a constant, beautiful hum. Due to the advanced musicianship of many of these players and the fact that they made a long pilgrimage to this remote mountaintop, moments of delight and awe are pretty easy to find. Getting in the groove *is* the goal. What stops me in my tracks is recognizing delight on their faces: eyes wide or fixed, lips in smiles or grimaced with intense focus, body movements aligning with rhythms … especially the ubiquitous head bob. And then, often a release at the end of the tune … that could be a laugh or just silence as they all catch their collective breaths. I've had so much fun filming these moments, I've coined the "four 'f's' of filming" traditional music musicians in their circles so others know what to look for in my Clifftop highlight reels (at YouTube).

- *Faces.* Since delight is easy to see, if one of the players shows it, the others soon catch on (it's freeing and contagious). Once I spot that, my camera is already whirring.
- *Fingers.* Oh my, fingers dance on the necks of stringed instruments and it's such a beautiful thing! I can get completely mesmerized watching it through my lens. Sometimes I'll focus on just that (no faces). Often, I can frame a fiddle, guitar, banjo and sometimes bass neck all at the same time. I'm getting goose bumps again writing about it.
- *Feet.* Musical movements involve so much more than the hands. If the feet feel left out, they can subconsciously keep rhythm. I like filming feet. Sometimes when four folks are circled up knee to knee, three could be

pounding out the beat while the fourth is simply tapping a toe, barefoot. Shoes are optional here.
- *Fans.* Because most everyone at Clifftop enjoys sharing their musical experiences with others, like me, they walk around to see what's musically cookin' out there. The delight I recognize on the faces of those performing the magic in turn lights up the mirror neurons in the brains of those watching … putting them in shared delight. Like I said, it's contagious. We're all wired that way to help us connect. Think of it as "happy empathy."

If you'd like to see if music affects you this way, put this book down for a spell, head over to YouTube and search "Clifftop Craig Evans" and check out a few of my highlight reels. That should keep you delighted for a while. Then come back here for more.

Shared moments of awe facilitate community, more bonding. Awe actually expands our perspectives and challenges our preconceptions; it opens our minds. This leads us to feel more connected to others and the world around us—one last observation of the benefits of awe. If we dwell on it, we can become more aware of our own limitations and, perhaps, even mortality. And that fosters a sense of humility and gratitude. Feeling blessed yet?

We can experience awe many ways—spending time in nature or contemplating art or scientific discoveries. For us festival types, we can listen to new or different music or travel to a new place and meet new people. Unfamiliar surroundings, locations, cultures or rituals and ceremonies can also elicit feelings of awe. Moreover, social interactions with new friends involving shared experiences of wonder and amazement—such as watching a meteor shower or witnessing a breathtaking sunset or sharing a successful circle of music—foster awe.

If you have little awe in your life, *it can easily be cultivated.* Curiosity and openness to new experiences helps, as does seeking out opportunities for growth and learning. And don't forget gratitude.

As epiphanies go, awe is a good one—and it's one often found in the traditional music community. It manifests as gratitude and wonder. And it opens participants to finding greater joy, meaning, and purpose in our lives. And that's definitely worth smiling about.

Active Listening

While we're discussing ways to enhance your likelihood of experiencing delight and/or awe, here's another facilitating skill: active listening.

Today we live in the noisiest world in history. If listening wasn't difficult before, it certainly is now. And for those of us challenged with hearing issues, it's even harder.

But look around. In our ever-evolving, minute-to-minute, time-crunched world, relevant content like news changes with ever-increasing speed. To facilitate distribution, all forms of communications are being abbreviated. Historically, the USPS mailed letters quickly, but that gave way to email, which was first to have reduced words to emojis and acronyms (LOL), and then fractionalized into multiple messaging platforms. Now we have many ways to quickly receive all things indecipherable. And that's just print.

Listening among humans has never been our strong suit. Oh, parents can hear crying babies to know when to feed them. And horns make it possible not to be killed by oncoming cars or trains. And a percent of learning does take place in a school setting, either in person or electronically, but statistics show our beloved language skills are becoming even less efficient.

With the rise of technology and social media, people are becoming more distracted and less able to focus on meaningful conversations with others. This can lead to a sense of disconnection and a lack of understanding between individuals.

Research suggests that people typically remember less than half of what they hear, which means a significant portion of what is said in conversations is not fully understood or retained.

To really listen, to really understand, involves *engagement*, which means being open to another's perspective and focusing on what's being communicated. One must not only hear and process the words being spoken but also pay attention to nonverbal cues like body language and other contextual factors that help convey meaning. When was the last time you genuinely felt heard? Well, that can be changed if you yourself become an active listener. You gotta want it! Listening to respond or waiting to speak when it's your turn is not the solution. *Listening to understand is.*

Effective, engaged listening can lead to better communication, increased understanding, and improved relationships. However, it is a skill that requires practice and intentionality.

In the case of music, some already have a leg up on this social dilemma. Thanks to gifts from nature (or hard work), some of us have the ability to "learn by ear." Music and notation can assist, but they're not needed to "play along with the musical conversation." It's a real asset to those conversing in the language of music. And that spills over into real-life relationships, once again lowering the barrier to friendship and bonding.

In order to do what I do, interviewing people, *I really have to listen.* Yes, I have to juggle camera angles, make sure audio is working, try and avoid some other technical disaster while keeping the conversation moving forward and covering all the questions, but it's possible. It requires some in-the-moment acknowledgments.

First—*I'm honored to be doing what I'm doing.* I'm sitting in front of a respected, seasoned individual that's genuinely given of themselves to assist humanity—be it to make an instrument, give a lesson on how to play, sing or dance, or to write about people, times, places, and things that are meaningful. I'm thinking of what wisdom and/or history is waiting to be revealed. Nothing else going on in that moment is more important. P.S.: If you ever want to do this on your own, adjust your coffee intake and always, always start an interview with an empty bladder.

Second—*I'm also honoring them by being there.* Filming events don't just happen. I have to plan, spend money traveling, spend hours reviewing the day's work and, ultimately, present a final product that's true, accurate and well-produced. I'm preserving their history so others can benefit from their life's work. Nothing is as meaningful or powerful as the 90 minutes I get to spend at their feet listening—really hearing and understanding—their life's experience. Time stops. Joy starts! I'm smiling just thinking about it. Best job I've ever found.

Third—*Do your homework.* I do all sorts of background research before I sit with the person. Whatever I learn in advance can help facilitate the discussion by highlighting certain stories or keeping it on track, moving forward. It's so easy to get distracted with an unexpected offshoot topic and potentially lose precious recording time. It's critical to focus on the progress being made while being aware of time remaining.

Fourth—*Follow the conversation's thread in your head.* Is what they're saying making sense? I've lived and worked with lots of folks with ADD, and many have proven to be the most creative people I've ever met. They're certainly the most interesting and unpredictable. Often in conversations, topics appear along with a burst of enthusiasm for the revelation, especially in body language: the person may shift their posture (sit up straighter), make more eye contact, and speak in a louder voice. It's hard to miss, and it's easy to get caught up in the energy that the final viewer of the film also feels. But to what end? It's critical to always be thinking about "where is this going?" and "is this really relevant to the greater story?" To play it safe, I'll indulge up to two minutes to see where the thread leads. If it doesn't go anywhere, I'll be willing to give in to follow a second two-minute side story. But if that's also a dead end, to finish the conversation, I'll come back to my original planned agenda based on my research. At the end of the discussion, while the cameras are still rolling, I'll ask, "Okay, what did we miss?" I might even do that twice. It never fails to bring out more good content.

Fifth—*Unintentional bonding.* I love these people! I may have liked them before based on what I'd read or if I'd met them prior, but sitting at their feet, listening to them tell the stories of their life? It's hyper time and hyper real. I'll remember those shared moments of joy, sorrow, and adrenaline forever. Seriously. This is the highest number of genuine soul-to-soul conversations I've ever had in my life, and they're all as different as the people. But think about it—the common love is traditional music. We got together for them to relate what it means to them.

Community always comes up, but to enact it in real time with cameras rolling? To see the bonding take place? You know how I noticed the people in my films are always happy? You're watching firsthand what takes place when one human genuinely listens to another human. We're bonding in real time. We've become friends. What's not to smile about? If you've ever been stuck in an airport or some other situation where you've had a short but genuinely deep, meaningful conversation with a stranger, and then left not knowing their name, that comes close. I've always thought of those folks as angels delivering messages. In this case, I know the angel's name.

Now, imagine a late night at a music festival where you and a bunch of strangers have put all your musical contributions out there. Nothing was left on the table. That musical conversation lowered the barrier to having another discussion in words with the folks in that circle ... whether it happens right after the event or when you meet up again the next day. You can jump right to the good part, how you felt, and describe it candidly with all the smiles and positive body energy you're feeling. Don't hold back. You're now among friends.

Music Decreases Loneliness

The first week in May 2023, the U.S. Surgeon General called attention to what he termed a forthcoming "loneliness epidemic." For more than a decade, people have increasingly felt isolated, invisible and insignificant. As a society, but mostly older men, we are growing more introverted. We prefer to stay at home. Socializing—going out—was more common pre–Covid.

And the trend is not just affecting adults. From 2003 to 2019, the amount of time younger people (ages 15–24) spend with their friends fell 70 percent. Half the country reports they have three or fewer closer friends. So it's worth being reminded that socializing is *very good for our mental health*. Music and community offer positive opportunities to reconnect by providing an opportunity to explore a common interest, belong to a group and share in a range of social, physical, and mental benefits.

Music has the ability to evoke emotions, memories, and shared experiences, and it can serve as a form of self-expression and communication. Listening to music can promote relaxation, reduce stress and anxiety, and improve mood, which can help to alleviate feelings of loneliness and isolation.

Participating in musical activities, such as singing or playing an instrument, can provide opportunities for social interaction and collaboration with others, which can lead to a sense of belonging and connection. Music can also serve as common ground for people from different backgrounds and communities to come together and share in a cultural experience.

Similarly, community involvement and engagement can provide a sense of purpose, identity, and social support that can help to reduce feelings of loneliness and isolation. Being part of a community, whether it be through a shared interest, a neighborhood, or a cultural group, can provide opportunities for social interaction, emotional support, and a sense of belonging.

Studies have shown that participation in community activities can lead to improved mental health, increased social support, and reduced loneliness and isolation. This highlights the importance of creating and maintaining strong social connections and community engagement as a way to promote well-being and combat loneliness.

25

How Music Works Magic: A Conversation with Josh Turknett

Roswell, Georgia, 2023

Before we go any further, I need to introduce you to another incredible member of our music community and one of today's "brain health" thought-leaders, Dr. Josh Turknett. I interviewed Josh at his home in Roswell, Georgia, in May of 2023. At that time, "Dr. Brainjo" was already widely recognized on Banjo Hangout for a simple yet *powerfully effective learning methodology* based on his book *The Laws of Brainjo: The Art and Science of Molding a Musical Mind*.

In the book, Josh details a roadmap for people to use in harnessing the brain's learning process—neuroplasticity—to maximum effect. Dr. Turknett is not new to this understanding; he's got the background, experience and motivation to help all people of any age learn new things and maintain a healthy brain. The latter is key to bettering one's odds against dementia.

As a physician, and as a fellow human that loves playing banjo, Josh's primary motivator has been to rid the world of what he terms "mismatched disease." By that he means a condition that doesn't appear to have affected our species (like dementia) until a century or so ago. Josh has played a key role in a society of academics, historians and other concerned specialists now researching the mental and physical conditions of our species (homo sapiens) over our 250,000 years on this rock. They've already made amazing discoveries to better our health, especially our current diet (abysmal compared to what we ate for many millennia). But it's easier to let him tell the story.

"Understanding how our evolutionary history has shaped our biology is a really profound way to understand what we need right now to be healthy."

"One of the things that's become increasingly clear in the past 10, 20 years is that cognitive activity is critical for maintaining brain health and function. That doesn't just mean doing crossword puzzles. Music happens to integrate all of those things into one kind of single activity."

"The brain retains this ability to change itself in response to experience and is perfectly capable of acquiring new knowledge and skills throughout our lives until the day we die. It's always updating itself. Not only do we have the ability, doing that thing is

probably the single best thing we can do to maintain a healthy brain to prevent things like cognitive decline and dementia."

"There's no part of human cognition that's not involved with performing on a musical instrument or with dancing. I think that's probably a big reason why those two things have been part of every human culture ever discovered. They are so good for our brains, and our brains love them so much."

"Music and dance have been found in every human culture study. It's been with us for quite some time. That means that it's been a part of the brain's environment. It's something the brain has been exposed to for, at a minimum, 40,000, 50,000 years, likely much longer."

"We have to get those things that our bodies and brains need and expect because of our history as a species. We have to understand what those old ways that are still necessary are. There's a chance to get the best of both worlds, but we have to be mindful of these things."

"We should always use caution when we are removing something that was part of our life for many, many thousands of years if we don't understand exactly what it's doing for us and to us."

Old-time Community Role: The *Neurologist*. A banjo-playing brain researcher at the forefront of how we learn. He believes practicing his learning methodologies (and exercising and eating right) will help us avoid dementia while gifting us with newer, more efficient ways to learn and keep our brains healthy. As a member of the Ancestral Health Society, he is basing his work on what has been best for our species since we first appeared 250,000 years ago. So grateful Dr. Brainjo found our community.

Craig Evans: Dr. Josh Turknett of Roswell, Georgia. Thank you for sitting down with me today to talk about traditional music and more. Most of the people watching us today will know you as Dr. Brainjo, author of *The Laws of Brainjo: The Art and Science of Molding a Musical Mind*. For those that don't know you, you are a research-driven neurologist that is on the cutting edge of harnessing the brain's natural learning process.

We'll call it neuroplasticity for now, until you define it, which contributes to "learning that sticks." The good news here is that, if you have a healthy brain at any age, you can continue to learn. Even old dogs like me can pick up new tricks. And music is one of the best ways that we can light up our brain. Now, this is indeed a huge story. It's where we'll spend the bulk of our conversation today. Before we get started, I'd like to know a little bit more about you personally. Where did life start for you?

Dr. Josh Turknett: Life began here in Georgia. I was born in Columbus and then, when I was three years old, we moved to the Atlanta area. That's where I grew

25. How Music Works Magic

up and had a pretty typical, I guess, suburban Southern childhood. I was into sports, into school, particularly math and science. Always loved music too. Wanted to get into playing and performing it. Neither of my parents actively played an instrument. Probably around the age of 12 or 13, I started asking for piano lessons.

My brother and I got a keyboard around the time that synthesizers were becoming a thing. There was always some level of music in my life and experimentation—wanting to engage with it more. I didn't have any role models in that period of my life, for doing what I wanted to do with it, which was play the music that was in my head. When I'd go to teaching lessons, it wasn't what I was looking to do.

Dr. Josh Turknett—Dr. Brainjo. You can trust this doctor. He definitely knows what's good for you.

In my early experience with music, I wanted to engage with it more. I felt like there was something else out there that people were doing with it that was unavailable to me. Ultimately, I was able to reconnect with it later in high school. At that time, I was also more into science. I started getting into the brain and began thinking I might want to pursue a career in the neurosciences.

Craig: I want to back up and ask a question about your parents. What did your mom and your dad do?

Josh: They had a private psychology practice. My dad is a licensed psychologist. My mom had a degree in sociology and math, so they did family counseling for years together. Around the time I was in high school, they transitioned into doing leadership consulting with companies.

Craig: What did you guys talk about around the dinner table at night when you were young?

Josh: The Myers–Briggs.

[Laughter.]

Josh: We did get a fair amount of talk around personality, psychology, nature/nurture, who knows? It was something that was interesting to me as well. I always enjoyed trying to understand people. I appreciated that part of their work and the insights that they could give. I ended up going to college at Wesleyan University because they offered a neuroscience degree.

I made a friend there that was also interested in the brain and recommended a book by Oliver Sacks called the *Man Who Mistook His Wife for A Hat*. I didn't really, prior to that, know what a neurologist was, but I thought, "Wow, this is really cool! I could see this as a path for me." I ended up majoring in neuroscience in college and then going to medical school and specializing in neurology with a particular interest in cognition.

Craig: Let's define cognition.

Josh: Cognitive functions that we think of as being fairly unique to humans: language, thinking, memory, complex motor skills, what human brains do. Understanding that is kind of one of the last big frontiers in the world of science. I wanted to be a part of that in some way.

Craig: Okay. I want to point out the fact that you practiced here for 12 years in the Atlanta area. You're a clinical researcher. You were a medical editor of the *Journal of Evolution in Health*. You're also a bestselling author and a musician and you're a leading voice in the ancestral health movement. What is that?

Josh: I'm glad you asked. Ancestral health, broadly, just refers to understanding the roots of human health: what we need to thrive, as well as why we get sick, by looking at our ancestors and particularly our evolutionary history. Humans have been on this planet, as our current species, homo sapiens, 250,000 years, almost all of that time living in a world that looks very different than the one we find ourselves in right now in all sorts of different ways.

Largely, our biology is still adapted to that world we used to find ourselves in. That's still the world in which we will most easily thrive. If you plop us into that world, anywhere along the timeline, we're going to get what we need in terms of what we eat, what we're exposed to and the relationships we have. Understanding how our evolutionary history has shaped our biology is a really profound way to understand what we need right now to be healthy.

The Ancestral Health Society strives to understand the most common chronic diseases that are so prevalent today, which are really diseases of modern life. In the ancestral health community, we refer to them as mismatched diseases where our world today is mismatched in certain key ways that, over time, end up making us sicker. It's something that I recognized as a physician, not having the tools to help people with the conditions that they were coming to me with the most.

Craig: Tell me about the business that you're in now because clearly you left thriving enterprises here to do what you're doing.

Josh: Yes, so after medical school, I went into practice, neurology, here in Atlanta. As part of that, I was involved with a number of clinical trials investigating new treatments for various neurological conditions, including Alzheimer's. I wanted to be part of that and went into the field of neurology under the impression, as most people were at the time, that we were about to see a pretty significant change in our ability to treat those sorts of conditions. That didn't materialize.

That gets back to the whole paradigm of what we were using to try to treat these disorders and the missing pieces of ancestral health along with an understanding our evolutionary history. I'm frustrated by the lack of progress that's been made. By the same token, I now realize that there's another framework and approach that I think is going to get us a lot further than where we are.

That's part of how I've refocused those goals of helping people with cognitive disorders, helping prevent Alzheimer's. *Brainjo* is now trying to facilitate that. The purpose of the book was to outline the set of principles that go into the methodology.

Craig: While we're on it, why don't you give the web address for where people can get that information?

Josh: Sure: www.brainjo.academy.

Craig: Now that you've brought that up, I was wondering how a busy, engaged neurologist like you is using a banjo as an example of what the next step in learning or even fighting Alzheimer's might be.

Josh: Yes. First of all, a banjo is my favorite instrument. Even though I play a few instruments, I still first consider myself a banjo player. Combining banjo and brain with Brainjo, it's just too good to resist. [Laughs.] One of the things that's become increasingly clear in the past 10, 20 years is that cognitive activity is critical for maintaining brain health and function. That doesn't just mean doing crossword puzzles. Music happens to integrate all of those things into one kind of single activity. If we don't add that piece of something cognitively stimulating into our later lives, anything that we try to throw at the brain to stave off decline is not going to help, just in the same way physical activity aids the body.

Craig: Is it safe to say "if we don't use it, we lose it"?

Josh: That's the perfect way to encapsulate it. Whether we're talking about the body physically or we're talking about the brain, our health and our physiology is fundamentally driven by what we ask of it.

Craig: I noticed that in some of your materials, you made the comment, "The health of the brain is inversely correlated to the proportion of time we spend on autopilot." Can you define autopilot?

Josh: The double-edged sword of our brain is that once we learn a particular domain or skill, we can perform that thing while our conscious attention is elsewhere. We all have a collection of skills that we have accumulated over the course of our lives. During childhood, we spend all of our time building those skills, building those skills that we need to become a functioning, independent adult.

Once they're there, it's great if you want things to be easy and comfortable (autopilot), but it's not so great from the standpoint of our brain. We know that the health of our brain, our brain tissue, is directly correlated to how much we ask of it. The amount we stimulate the brain can be measured in the amount of plasticity that is occurring. Anytime we're trying to acquire some new piece of knowledge, some new skill, the brain has to change in response to that.

Craig: Let's define neuroplasticity at this point.

Josh: Yes. It's the brain's ability to change its own structure and function in response to experience in order to acquire new knowledge and skills. For years, a large part of the 20th century, there was a belief, even in the scientific community, that the potential for the brain to change tapered off and ended by our early 20s. Some very important work done in the late 20th century showed that that was absolutely not true.

The brain retains this ability to change itself in response to experience and is perfectly capable of acquiring new knowledge and skills throughout our lives until the day we die. It's always updating itself. Not only do we have the ability, doing that sort of thing is probably the single best thing we can do to maintain a healthy brain to prevent things like cognitive decline and dementia. In the case where a particular habit has become automated, it's hard not to do it. You play a song a certain way and you want to update it, you want to change it. Once that habit is there, it's harder to not do it than it is to do it. New learning has to make the new routine suppress the old one.

Craig: I want to segue over now to music. You and I have had a previous conversation about if you want to exercise your brain, one of the things that lights up your brain the most is music.

Josh: Every time you are overcoming some obstacle like that, there's nothing better for your brain. Every time you're stimulating that type of plasticity that would effectively rewire things and create a new pathway, there's nothing better that you could be doing. By the same token, this is another reason why I encourage people who've never had any musical experience whatsoever, no matter what their age, to try it out.

The worse you are at something, the less skilled you are, the more change must happen in order for you to acquire that new piece, new skill, or new knowledge. There's nothing better for your brain than being a beginner, than being totally inept. From one frame, it might look like, "Oh, I'm terrible at this. What's the point?" If you're looking from the standpoint of health and function of brain tissue, there could be nothing better.

25. How Music Works Magic

Craig: Some of the people that will be watching this conversation are familiar with Dr. Brainjo, but others are not. Could you define the Dr. Brainjo technique just as an example of how this method of learning works?

Josh: There are multiple things that are involved here, one of which is just recognizing that the purpose of your practice is to provide the brain the data that it needs to try to make a new neural network, to try to restructure itself to support the skill you're trying to learn. It's not to get better right there, then, because all of that remodeling and neuroplasticity isn't happening when you're actually practicing. It's happening later on and almost exclusively during sleep. The main function when you're practicing is simply to give the brain good inputs. Short, focused practice sessions are far better than long, less focused.

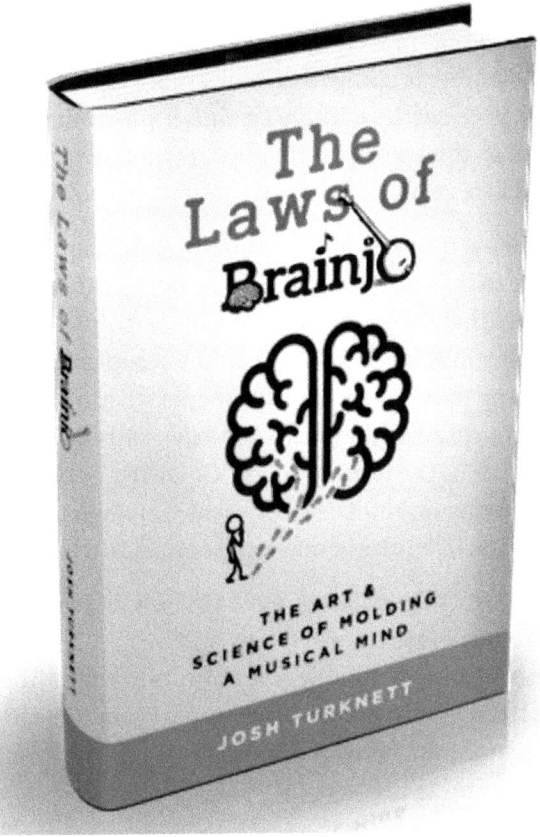

The Laws of Brainjo: The Art & Science of Molding a Musical Mind by Dr. Josh Turknett, M.D.

Craig: Is there a time of day?

Josh: There is likely a time of day. Some of that's individual. There's such a thing as a chronotype, which is what time of day is best for you. Different people have different times of day where their focus and attention is best. That's, typically, for most people, going to be between the hours of 10:00 a.m. and 2:00 p.m. The reason that matters is because the main signal to our brain to change is what we pay attention to. That's also another reason why short learning sessions are better … we have a hard time sustaining our focused attention for long periods of time. Twenty minutes, when you're feeling fresh, is the ideal.

Craig: To put it in a common person's language, if I'm really alert at nine o'clock in the morning and I really want to learn a new traditional music tune—one with an A part and a B part, 32 bars each—if I sit down and start in on the A part of this tune and spend 20 minutes learning it, should I stop at that point?

Josh: If your goal is to maximize the neuroplastic change that's happening in response to that practice, to get the most from your brain remodeling, it's unlikely that doing more is going to give you more results. It's possible that doing more could, actually, give you less. There's another phenomenon called interference, whereas if you were to then work on the B part right away, the B part can interfere with the A part and vice versa.

Craig: Okay. If I worked on just the A part, slept that night, how many days in a row do I have to do something like this before I can see a result?

Josh: That's a great question. That's going to be very individual, depending on what level you're at. Depending on the complexity of the thing you're learning, you're likely going to see some improvements within a couple of days. You're also going to be reaping continued benefits for weeks and months to come, because the changes that happen in the brain that are supporting the acquisition of a new skill like that are happening on multiple, different timetables. Even what you set in motion from that one practice session may not come to full fruition for weeks to months.

Craig: Okay. I'm exercising my brain now. If I'm working on one part of my brain, is the rest of my brain improving as well?

Josh: Probably to a degree. I do think it is important that we are mindful of doing activities that exercise our whole brain. One of the things about modern life is that we tend to spend a lot of time exercising abstract domains of thought, less with complex motor skills.

Craig: Let's give examples of abstract.

Josh: Having a conversation, reading a book, doing a math problem, working on a computer, the things of modern life where you're mostly in your head. Whereas a huge part of our brain, including our brain's cognitive apparatus, is devoted to movement, it's devoted to learning complex movements, probably initially because we were hunters. That was a huge part of our evolution as a species—our ability to make tools, our ability to use them.

Craig: And run for cover!

Josh: Yes, exactly. Also crucial. We have all of this cognitive machinery that's devoted to movement, and there's a tendency to overlook that when we think about cognitive activities. With movement, you're getting that. With dance, you're getting that. This is why it's such a great and prototypical whole-brain activity. There's no part of human cognition that's not involved with performing on a musical instrument or with dancing. I think that's probably a big reason why those two things have been part of every human culture ever discovered. They are so good for our brains, and our brains love them so much.

Craig: Okay. In your tenured experience, is there anything better for the human brain right now than learning to play a musical instrument?

Josh: I wouldn't say there's anything better. There may be things that are as good, but if we want to get a whole-brain workout, all of the parts of the brain that are involved with cognitive activity, you can't get something better than music. Even just listening to music, if you put someone under a functional MRI scanner where you can look at brain activity, all sorts of areas of the brain are being lit up just during the act of listening to music.

Craig: To be healthy for my brain, is it better to be a music grazer? In addition to my favorite traditional music, do I put on classical music? Do I put on rap music? Do I put on something different than what I was trying to learn this morning?

Josh: I think there's room for both, and I think we should think about having both. The greatest benefits likely come during our initial exposure to something with which we are completely unfamiliar. If you're completely unfamiliar with classical music, it's going to be a great stimulus for your brain because it's having to figure out patterns that it hasn't previously encountered. As you become more acquainted with it, it's that phenomenon of automaticity. When your brain starts to figure it out, it starts to extract those patterns automatically, that's where your enjoyment of it starts to kick in.

At some point, it's worthwhile to also be including new areas, new ventures. This is one of the things that adults start *not* doing. We do all this time as kids; we're always exploring new avenues. We tend to do less and less of it over time. That seems to be one of the driving factors for why brains decline over time as we lose those novel stimuli.

Craig: We've talked a fair amount about music. In fact, you made one comment, "Humans are a musical species. It is reasonable to speculate that music is an essential nutrient and that it played an essential role in our cognitive evolution."

Josh: I mentioned before, music and dance have been found in every human culture study. It's been with us for quite some time. That means that it's been a part of the brain's environment. It's something the brain has been exposed to for, at a minimum, 40,000, 50,000 years, likely much longer.

Craig: Is that based on the bone flute?

Josh: Yes, right. When we found the earliest musical instruments, themselves somewhat advanced, they indicate a fairly advanced understanding of music. Just that fact alone tells us that it's been in our brain's environment for quite some time. I spoke about ancestral health before. We should always use caution when we are removing something that was part of our life for many, many thousands of years if we don't understand exactly what it's doing for us and to us.

It's very plausible that it is shaping human brain development in some fundamental ways.

Then there's the fact that we crave it so much, that it's so rewarding and that we seek it out. Why is that? Why is it so pleasurable? With our brain, its core feature is extracting patterns of the information that it processes. Music is just patterns upon patterns of all different kinds. Our brain finds doing that extraordinarily rewarding. We should be interpreting that as "This is really good for me." If you couple that with the fact of how long it's been around, you can make a pretty good case that it is an essential nutrient for the brain because of what it's doing for our brain, one of the main reasons why we find it so rewarding.

Craig: How do you quantify the benefits of music?

Josh: When we are engaging with music, when we are listening to music, when we are giving that stimulation to our brain, it's having to adapt. It's stimulating neuroplastic remodeling and so forth. It's having to recruit all the nutrients. It's trying to up-regulate vascular supply, the blood flow. In the same way that lifting weights improves our physical health, it's having to recruit all of the necessary factors needed to support muscle and tissue growth.

Music appears to be doing that exact same thing for our brains. In that way, it is globally keeping brain health at its peak function. It is of great value for emotional and mental health.

We can't help but think of music as a human endeavor, something that connects us to other people. When we look at how music has been part of human cultures, it's almost always done collectively, and it's oftentimes done as a form of connection, as a form of ritual. When we engage with music, it's almost impossible to disentangle ... just hearing it as an isolated thing rather than it bringing all that with it. That feeling of connectedness, that feeling of belonging is also part of the experience and part of what makes it so meaningful.

Craig: As I started to get involved with Southern Appalachian traditional music (also known as old-time), I began to spend nights around a campfire listening to people, playing with people. It lowered barriers to entry, it provided for more bonding. No longer strangers, we would see each other the next day and say hi. What has astonished me about this music, traditional music, is if you go to any museum anywhere in the world and walk back through the cultures ... when you look at the Mayans and the Incans and the Greeks and the Romans and the Egyptians, often you can find in there a traditional instrument of some sort.

Now, we don't necessarily know what they were playing, but sometimes it's around a king or a queen, or it's a funeral or some event like that. This music just seems to have always been an undercurrent throughout humanity. I'm just astonished that more people haven't paid attention to it for how it maintains our health, our community, and that's why I'm so excited about the work that you're doing on the humble banjo.

Josh: I think the banjo is also a part of that. It's been part of those ritualistic ceremonies and it feels like an accessible instrument in that way. Getting back to this idea of mismatch, when you talk about all of the different cultures and how integrated music was, having participatory collective expressions of music and dance has been so ubiquitous, it's reasonable to consider that a mismatch in modern life.

That there are consequences because, as you've experienced, when you're involved in those things, playing music with others, playing for a dance, it is an extraordinarily rewarding thing. Once people do it, they want to keep doing it. We should listen to that.

Craig: We started this conversation with you talking about how life today has increased its pace. Although you didn't use the word technology, it's clear the brain is trying to keep up with it as best it can. And in the process of us trying to keep up, we seem to have jettisoned some of the things that got us where we are over the past 250,000 years. Community, for example. Ritualistic things involved with music. You are on the cutting edge here, finding out that "yes, that seems to be the way the brain is wired. We should be doing more of that." Your research is, hopefully, going to show us that "wow, it has been great for us all along. We need to do more of it."

Josh: Yes, absolutely. I think that's a great point. It's easy with technological advancements to, like you said, forget what got us here. To forget how essential the things that we were doing are for us. It doesn't mean rejecting the new; it means making sure we're still embracing the old and the fundamentals. The fundamentals will always be the fundamentals no matter how technologically advanced.

We have to get those things that our bodies and brains need and expect because of our history as a species. We have the opportunity, because of technology, to thrive in ways we never have before. But we have to integrate both of those things if we want to do it. We have to understand what those old ways that are still necessary are. There's a chance to get the best of both worlds, but we have to be mindful of these things.

Craig: You've already put forward a methodology to do this in *Brainjo*. What is next? What other areas are you looking to introduce something that the Brainjo concept will be utilized?

Josh: What is next is trying to continue to advance the idea of the importance of whole-brain activities, music and dance in particular. Brainjo began as an endeavor to apply the best practices for learning to help people learn things that are complex at any age. Now the second phase here is in helping to spread the word about just how important doing that is for the health and function of our brain. If we want to make a dent in any of the conditions that I began my career trying to help, part of why I've pivoted into this is because I fundamentally believe that music, dance, and whole-brain activities offer more potential than all of the drugs that I was researching.

I think that will always be true, getting better and better about understanding how we fully utilize that to help humans thrive throughout their lives, is where, fundamentally, I've directed my efforts. That includes expanding the courses, the opportunities for musical learning, different instruments, incorporating some instruction around dance, and then, largely, doing whatever I can to spread these ideas and to help people understand just how crucial and important they are.

Craig: I hope you have a long, long career.
  Josh: [Laughs.] Thank you.

Craig: Have fun introducing all this stuff. Because it's such a gift to humanity.
  Josh: It is a lot of fun. What's great for us and what's fun are perfectly aligned. [Laughs.]

Craig: Wow. Doesn't get much better than that.
  Josh: No. [Chuckles.]

More on Ancestral Health ... and the Importance of Recognizing the (Possibly Hidden) Value of Traditions

When Josh talked about how important music and dance are to our brains, and that, based on how rewarded it makes us feel, and how it brings us together as a community, maybe there *is* something to be said for being extra cautious about throwing out too much of tradition, justifying the removal as it being past its time (that is, irrelevant). So I poked around a bit on the web to learn what the Ancestral Health Society thinks about the dilemma of living in a time-starved society and what to give up.

The ancestral health movement is based on the premise that human beings evolved over millions of years to thrive on a diet and lifestyle that was very different from what most people follow today. This ancestral lifestyle is characterized by a diet of whole, unprocessed foods, regular physical activity, ample sleep and sunlight exposure, *and a strong social support network.*

While technology is not necessarily seen as inherently negative by the ancestral health movement, proponents of the movement argue that it is important to use technology in a way *that is consistent with our evolutionary heritage* and *does not undermine our physical and mental health.*

The excessive use of technology, particularly digital devices such as smartphones and computers, has been linked to a number of mental health problems, including anxiety and depression, and sleep disturbances. This is thought to be due to a variety of factors including the constant stimulation of social media and other digital platforms, and *the impact of technology on social interaction and relationships.*

I kept coming up with more questions. In this case, did our species actually invent music and dance? Thought that was a good question for ChatGPT. Here's that answer:

> There is growing evidence to suggest that music and dance have been a part of human culture for tens of thousands of years, and that they played an important role in human social and cultural development. Studies of archaeological artifacts and early human remains suggest that musical instruments have been used by humans for at least 40,000 years. Similarly,

evidence of dance has been found in cave paintings and other ancient artworks dating back tens of thousands of years.

While it's possible that other species, such as Neanderthals, may have also used music and dance, the evidence for this is still relatively limited. However, given that music and dance have been a part of human culture for so long, it seems likely that they played an important role in the development of human societies and culture.

There's something to be said for the physical, mental, emotional and spiritual positives of carrying on the tradition of our traditional music and dance. For those of us that have been celebrating it with others for decades, welcome to the club. Come on in and join the fun!

May our time together expand not only the joy in the moments we're sharing but also the additional moments of smiling it is adding on the back end of our lives. I sincerely hope by now, dear reader, you understand why I'm so in love the music and community. If I were to define "heaven on earth," I think I can say I found it.

Oh, and I found a book I'm going to put on my Christmas list later this year, *The Singing Neanderthals: The Origins of Music, Language, Mind and Body* which explores the evolution of music and its relationship to language and social behavior. Maybe I'll interview Steven Mithen, the author, next.

Now It's Up to You...

Okay, dear reader. Do you see what I've done here? I figure some of you have been reading between the lines. Yes, most everything in this book is my life's learning. Where the noisy media focuses on popularity, style and money as success, it's not real life. Unfortunately, it took a 20-plus-year crash and burn following that false capitalistic model to finally wake me up. There are way more important aspects of life to engage, often right in front of you. The music, community, kindness and concern I'd witnessed as a kid in Early, Iowa? That was real truth. Same with those smiling luthiers and performers I listened to, telling me their stories of happiness and belonging, serving roles in the North American traditional music community. Being one's self, delivering handmade products and soul-sharing music (and instruction) with peers at home or at Clifftop, engaging, laughing, enjoying ... that's also the real deal.

What I've put down here, in this book is for all the artists and creatives, oddballs, individualists, lost souls and others who would really like to find themselves ... meaning ... *satisfaction in life and, more important, truth and love.*

I found myself, my joy, my role and my place on this rock through traditional music and the community that celebrates it. I wrote this book from that pivotal experience. It may or may not be yours. If you're musically inclined, my route may work for you. If not

- look for a community of *people like you* that celebrate *your* interest. Even if you have to form your own community, start by really listening to people ... *hear* them with your heart as well as your head.

- engage these connections and begin looking for your own unique role to contribute to the community. It may be through strengths and gifts you've never considered of value. But others in the community can prosper through them.
- Be selfless. As a part of the community, invite and welcome others. Listen, understand and celebrate. Encourage their finding a role using their unique gifts.

Even of you have to form your own community, follow the above and *love on them*! If you understand and accept them for who they are, odds are high they will return that trust. Take it and pass it along. To me, that's why we're all here. It's not wasted. Keep moving forward.

Dwight Diller's testimonial to the power of love, community and music are now my themes in life. Music changes people; so does community. Yes, it's a mystery, and no, you don't need to know why. Accept the gifts that come with it. Let it feed you and you it. And water that garden so others can grow along with you … even after you're gone.

Is putting yourself out there worth it? Absolutely! In fact, I'd appreciate hearing your stories. If I'm still around. Look me up and tell me of your experience. In the meantime, know you're loved as you are. And find a place and people to share that love. You're deserving.

Epilogue:
An Invitation to Join the Fun

So! Have you read enough now to feel you should start playing an instrument? If the emotional, mental, and physical benefits of both music and community have convinced you it's time to add fun to your life, this epilogue will help you find your tribe.

You can start by visiting a local ukulele club, as there are many in most cities across the United States. Often many folks there would be happy to help you find your way and might even accompany you. Or you can head over to a music store, strum a few ukes, and ask the people there what's happening around town.

Here are some more suggestions for getting in touch with people in the know who can help you out:

- *Check out online forums and local classifieds:* Look for online communities or classifieds where local musicians might post ads or announcements seeking other musicians to play with. Craigslist and Meetup are two popular sites where you can find local musicians looking for other players.
- *Attend music events and open mics:* Attending open mics, music festivals, or other local events is a great way to meet other musicians in your area. Bring your instrument, if you already have one, and be prepared to network and talk to other players.
- *Join a music group or club:* Many cities have local music groups or clubs that welcome new members. You can check with your local music store or community center to see if there are any groups in your area.
- *Take lessons:* If you're just starting out, taking lessons from a music teacher is a great way to improve your skills and meet other musicians. Often, music teachers can introduce you to other students who are also looking for someone to play with.
- *Utilize social media:* You can also use social media to connect with other musicians. Try posting in local music groups on Facebook, Twitter, or Instagram to find other players in your area.

Remember, finding someone to play music with takes time and effort, so be persistent and don't get discouraged if it takes a while to find the right people. Keep practicing and networking, and you'll eventually find other musicians who share your passion.

Now, I've been talking about starting your musical adventure on a ukulele, but you actually have many choices. For those who didn't grow up with music, the uke is a great and universal entry point.

Here's a list of some other considerations:

- Ukulele: The ukulele is a small, four-stringed instrument that is easy to learn and can be played by people of all ages. It has a mellow, happy sound and is commonly used in folk and pop music.
- Keyboard/Piano: The keyboard or piano is a versatile instrument that can be played in a variety of genres, from classical to jazz to pop. It's also relatively easy to learn, as the notes are laid out in a logical, linear fashion.
- Guitar: The guitar is another popular choice for beginners, as it's portable and can be played in a variety of styles, from folk to rock to blues. The basic chords are easy to learn, and countless online resources are available to help you get started.
- Harmonica: The harmonica is a small, portable instrument that can be played in a variety of styles, from blues to folk to country. It's also relatively easy to learn, as the basic technique involves blowing and drawing air through the holes.

Know that as you're "putting yourself out there" with this action of deciding to play a musical instrument, you're in good company. Indications are that certain hobbies, such as playing musical instruments, are on the rise. For example, a 2019 survey by the National Association of Music Merchants found that sales of musical instruments in the United States had increased by 3.6 percent from 2018 to 2019, with particular growth in sales of ukuleles and electronic drums. There's one more consideration you should know about that might give you encouragement that *this is the right time to step out and play.*

Don't wait any longer to head out and join the fun! Good adventures and better health await you. I sincerely hope you experience moments where time stops and joy starts. Perhaps you too will agree it's as good as life can get.

See you at the jam! I'll be one of many smiling.

Bibliography

Adler, Sarah Elizabeth. "Music Can Be a Great Mood Booster." AARP, June 30, 2020 (updated January 31, 2024). https://www.aarp.org/health/brain-health/info-2020/music-mental-health.html.

Allen, William Francis, Charles Pickard Ware, and Lucky McKim Garrison, editors. *Slave Songs of the United States*. Chapel Hill: University of North Carolina Press, 2014.

Block, Peter. *Community: The Structure of Belonging*. Oakland: Berrett-Koehler, 2018.

Brawley, Benjamin. *The Social History of the American Negro*. New York: Macmillan, 1921.

Brooks, Tim. *The Blackface Minstrel Show in Mass Media*. Jefferson: McFarland, 2020.

Brown, Laura Lewis. "The Benefits of Music Education." PBS Kids for Parents, May 7, 2012. https://www.pbs.org/parents/thrive/the-benefits-of-music-education.

Christeson, R.P. *The Old-Time Fiddler's Repertory: 245 Traditional Tunes*. Columbia: University of Missouri, 1973.

Dissanayake, Ellen. *Art and Intimacy: How the Arts Began*. Seattle: University of Washington Press, 2012.

Dubois, Laurent. *The Banjo: America's African Instrument*. Cambridge: Belknap Press of Harvard University Press, 2016.

Duggan, Anne S. *Folk Dances of the United States and Mexico*. New York: Ronald Press, 1948.

Eisler, Melissa. "5 Healing Benefits of Listening to Music. Music Connects Spiritually." Chopra, April 28, 2017. https://chopra.com/articles/5-healing-benefits-of-listening-to-music.

Frost, Alexandra. "How Music Can Improve Your Mental Health." The Jed Foundation, n.d. https://jedfoundation.org/resource/how-music-can-improve-your-mental-health/.

Gray, Andrea. "Music Can Influence Your Mood." PPL PRS United for Music, January 6, 2022. https://pplprs.co.uk/health-wellbeing/music-reduce-stress/.

Greenway, John. *American Folk Songs of Protest*. Philadelphia: University of Pennsylvania Press, 1953.

Harvard Study of Adult Development. https://www.adultdevelopmentstudy.org/.

"How Music Affects the Mood." Pandora, n.d. https://cloudcovermusic.com/music-psychology/mood.

Jamison, Phil. *Hoedowns, Reels, and Frolics: Roots and Branches of Southern Appalachian Dance*. Urbana: University of Illinois Press, 2015.

Karapetsas, Argyris V., and Irini Rodopi M. Laskarki. "Coping with Loneliness Through Music." *Encephalos Journal* 52 (2015). http://www.encephalos.gr/pdf/52-1-03e.pdf.

"Keep Your Brain Young with Music." Johns Hopkins Medicine, n.d. https://www.hopkinsmedicine.org/health/wellness-and-prevention/keep-your-brain-young-with-music.

Keller, Kate Van Winkle. *If the Company Can Do It: Technique in Eighteenth-Century American Social Dance*. Annapolis: The Colonial Music Institute, 2007.

Leary, James. *Folksongs of Another America*. Madison: University of Wisconsin Press, 2015.

MacRitchie, Jennifer, Matthew Breaden, Andrew J. Milne, and Sarah MacIntyre. "Cognitive, Motor and Social Factors of Music Instrument Training Programs for Older Adults' Improved Wellbeing." *Frontiers in Psychology* 10 (2019). https://www.ncbi.nlm.nih.gov/pmc/articles/PMC6968490/.

Malone, Bill. *Country Music, USA*. Austin: University of Texas Press, 2018.

Murthy, Vivek H. *Together: The Healing Power of Human Connection in a Sometimes Lonely World*. New York: HarperCollins, 2020.

"Music and Health: What You Need to Know." National Center for Complementary and Integrative Health, U.S. Department of Health and Human Services, National Institutes of Health, n.d. https://www.nccih.nih.gov/health/music-and-health-what-you-need-to-know.

"Music and Spirituality." Smithsonian Institution, n.d. https://www.si.edu/spotlight/music-and-spirituality.

Myers–Briggs Foundation. https://www.myersbriggs.org/.

Rousseau, Mary F. *Community: The Tie That Binds*. Lanham, MD: University Press of America, 1991.

Southern, Eileen. *The Music of Black Americans*. New York: W.W. Norton, 1997.

Struble, John Warthen. *The History of American Classical Music*. New York: Checkmark Books, 1996.

Taruskin, Richard. *The Oxford History of Western Music*. Oxford: Oxford University Press, 2019.

"20 Benefits of Studying Music." Community Music School, Lehigh Valley, Berks, June 1, 2020. https://cmslv.org/20-benefits-of-studying-music/.

Vogl, Charles H. *The Art of Community: Seven Principles for Belonging*. Oakland: Berrett-Koehler, 2016.

Wade, Stephen. *The Beautiful Music All Around Us: Field Recordings and the American Experience*. Urbana: University of Illinois Press, 2017.

Walter, Yoshija, and Andreas Altorfer. "The Psychological Role of Music and Attentional Control for Religious Experiences in Worship." *Quarterly Journal of Experimental Psychology* 75, no. 12 (Dec. 2022): 2272–2286. https://www.ncbi.nlm.nih.gov/pmc/articles/PMC9619243/.

Index

Across the Blue Ridge CD 170
active listening 255
Acuff, Roy 119, 190
Adams, Jerry 155–160
Adams, Sheila Kay 154–162
ADD/ADHD and creativity 37
African American Legacy series by Smithsonian Folkways 207
Allen, Lucy 250
American Folklore Society 55, 175
The American Songster 199, 206
Ancestral Health Society 260, 262, 270
Andreessen, Mark 40
Aquinas, Thomas 174
Arkin, Steve 238
Ashley, Tom 148
Autobiography of an Ex-Colored Man (James Weldon Johnson) 204
awe benefits health 23, 25, 252, 254–255

Backwoods Band 152
Bamboozled (Spike Lee) 204
The Banjo (Laurent Dubois) 275
Bard 25, 157–158
Battle of Blair Mountain 179
Benford, Mac 147–153
Bergey, Barry 161
Bernstein, Ira 114
Black Banjo Gathering 198, 203, 205–206, 208
blackface 23, 136–137, 204, 212–213, 218–219, 223–225, 241, 275
The Blackface Minstrel Show in Mass Media (Tim Brooks) 241, 275
A Blue Ridge Mountain Holiday program 170
Boggs, Doc 149
Bones and Tambo 137, 218–221
Boosinger, Laura 122
Bowlin, John 59
Bradford, Perry 203
Breaking Up Christmas—Bill Clifton: America's Bluegrass Ambassador to the World (Dr. Bill Malone) 196
Brooks, Tim 209–226, 241
Brown, Paul 114, 163–171

Brown, the Reverend Pearly 133
Buddhist proverbs 49, 51
Buffalo soldiers 134, 207
Burhans, Hilarie 230–232, 247
Burr Burton Academy 107
Busby Berkeley 211, 223
Busted Toe Mud Thumpers Band 150

Callahan Brothers Band 190
Camp Creek Boys Band 169
Cannon, Gus 204
capitalism 39, 41, 54
Cardozo, Dr. Richard 34–36
Carlin, Bob 203
Carolina Chocolate Drops Band 198–199, 206
Carter Family Band 149, 190, 195
Chandler, Inez 156
"Christmas in the Trenches" 178–179
Christy, Edwin 217
Christy Minstrels 24, 217–219, 221
Chuck Wagon gang 190
Civil Rights Movement 133–134, 177, 179
Civil War 53, 120, 133–134, 138, 213, 218–220, 229
Clifftop 3, 51, 64, 66, 110, 112, 116, 172–173, 228–254, 271, 277; age dispersion 247
Clifton, Bill 196
Clifton, Verlen 169
Cockerham, Fred 168–169
Cohen, John 114, 174
Collins, Judy 200
Columbia Record Club 23–24
communities are constructs 20
community benefits mental and physical health 250–251
community decreases loneliness 252, 258
Confucius 5
Conway, Cece 203
Cornell University, Ithaca, NY 151
COVID-19 230, 258
creatives and artists 36–37, 107, 242, 271
Creed, Kyle 148–149, 168
Crockett, Davy 209, 213
Crosby, Bing 137, 222–223

David Holt's State of Music program 127
Deadwood, South Dakota 26
delight 253–254
Diabate, Cheick Hamala 203
Dickens, Hazel 195, 197
Diller, Dwight 9–11, 43–47, 53, 155, 160, 181–187, 250, 272
Dr. Brainjo 259–270
Dr. Humbead's New Tranquility String Band and Medicine Show 150
Don't Get Above Your Raisin': Country Music and the Southern Working Class (Dr. Bill Malone) 195
Dornfeld, Ruthie 115
Douglass, Frederick 215–216, 219
Dvorak, Antonin 209, 216, 241
Dylan, Bob 106, 177, 200, 202

Early, Judge D. Carr 14
Early, Iowa 15–16, 20, 28, 47, 271
Ed and Lonnie Young Band 201
Eelpout Stringers Band 52–53
egalitarianism 84
Enoch, Kevin 55, 57, 70
Epstein, Dena 88, 240
Evans Construction Company 18

Farmer Al Falfa cartoons 147–148
Fat City String Band 150
Fielding, Will 61, 69
Fink, Mike 209, 213
Fire on the Mountain 126
Fisherman's Wharf 147, 150
500-channel universe 38
Flemons, Dom 198–208
Folksongs of Another America: Field Recordings from the Upper Midwest, 1937–1946 (Dr. James P. Leary) 241, 275
Foster, Stephen 214, 217, 223, 225
Freight Hoppers String Band 115
Fulbright scholars 245–246

Galbreath, Greg 60
Gellert, Dan 111, 113, 118
Gellert, Rayna 110–118
"Gentlemen be seated" 211, 217, 221
Georgia Minstrels Band 219

277

Index

Giddens, Rhiannon 203, 205–206
Golden Gate Park 147, 149
Gordon, Lo 47, 59
Grand Ole Opry 123, 190, 199
Grange Hall 80, 222

Hammonds, Burl 182–184
Hammonds, Emmy 184
Hammonds, Lee 183
Hammonds, Maggie 184
Hammonds, Ruie 184
Hammonds, Sherman 184
Harlan County Brookside strike 176
Hartford, John 126, 247
Harvard Happiness Study 49, 52, 252, 275
Haverly, Colonel Jack 220
Hee Haw (television) 43, 119–120, 122, 125
Hendrix, Jimmy 120
Hentoff, Nat 192
Herrmann, John 114, 232–233
Highwoods String Band 2, 5, 147, 150–152
Hinton, Algia Mae 203
History of Nashville Publishing 189
The History of Rock 'n' Roll (PBS series) 200, 202
The History of the Civil War (Susan B. Katz) 133
Hoedowns, Reels, and Frolics: Roots and Branches of Southern Appalachian Dance (Phil Jamison) 275
Hoffman, John 238–239
Holcomb, Roscoe 174–175
Holt, David 43, 119–128
Holt, George 161
Hoyt, Zachary 90–97
Huff, (Patrick) Doc 77–83

International Storytelling Festival 129
intuitive information processing 35, 40

Jackson, Jim 204
Jamison, Phil 112–113, 232–235
Jarrell, Tommy 126, 152, 168, 175
John C. Campbell Folk School 117
Johnson, James Weldon 204
Jolson, Al 223
Jones, Rhys 113
Joplin, Janis 200
Jump Jim Crow 209, 213
Just Banjo '99 CD 9, 44–45

Kahn, Si 176
Kate Wolf Festival 173
Keaton, Buster 223
Kennedy Center 129
Kingston Trio Band 148
Koken, Walt 3–4, 109, 140, 145, 152

Lao Tzu 52, 54
The Laws of Brainjo: The Art and Science of Molding a Musical Mind (Dr. Josh Turknett) 259–260, 265
Lead Belly 198, 205–206
Leary, Dr. James 241, 275
Lee, Chuck 70
Lee, Spike 204
Lennon, John 27, 29, 243
Lost Sounds: Blacks and the Birth of the Recording Industry, 1890–1919 (Tim Brooks) 210–211, 216, 220
Louis, Jerry Lee 183, 201
Lunsford, Bascom Lamar 201

Ma, Yo-Yo 162
Malone, Dr. Bill 188–197
Malone, Dr. John 38
March on Washington 177–178
Marketing Channels: Infomercials and the Future of Televised Marketing (Craig R. Evans) 37
Masten, Brooks 57, 66–67
McCutcheon, John 125, 172–179
McGhee, Brownie 165, 201
Memphis Jug Band 204
mentors 31
Menzies, Jeff 55–56
Milliner, Clare 1–4, 109, 140–146
Mingus, Charles 106, 206
Minnesota Bluegrass and Old-time Music Association (MBOTMA) 49
minstrel show/minstrelsy 137, 204, 209–224
Mississippi John Hurt 201
Mississippi Sheiks Band 205–206
Mr. Interlocutor 137, 221–224
Monroe, Bill 190
Moreland, Peg 190
Morton, Jelly Roll 205
Mosheim, William Seeders 103–108
Mountain Stage 129
Murrow, Edward R. 169
music benefits 48; decreases loneliness 258, 275; mental and physical health 48
Music from the True Vine: Mike Seeger—Life and Musical Journey (Dr. Bill Malone; Mike Seeger) 195
Musicalia 172–173
Myer's Briggs Personality Inventory 37, 40, 249, 262, 275

Nashville Network 126
National Cowboy Poetry Gathering 207
National Endowment for the Arts 154–155, 161–162
National Federation of Community Broadcasters, Silver Reel 170
National Heritage Fellow 154–155

neurodiversity at Clifftop 242–243, 245
neurology 260
neuroplasticity 48, 259–260, 264–265
New Christy Minstrels Band 24, 28, 30
New Lost City Ramblers Band 149
Newport Folk Festival (documentary by Murray Lerner) 201
Nietzsche, Friedrich 5
Norton, Dellie Chandler 155–156
NPR 130, 154, 163–164, 170

Oberlin College 167
Ochs, Phil 200
old-time music 140, 251
Orpheus Foundation 146

Papa Charlie 204
Parker, Charlie 192
Parks, DeAnne L. 54
Passing (Nella Larsen) 204
Pastor, Tony 220
Patton, Charlie 206
Peer, Ralph 203
Perkins, Carl 201
Peter, Paul and Mary Band 24–25, 28, 177
Platin, Mark 58, 70, 75
Plato 5
Poole, Charlie 151
Potts, Bob 150–152
pragmatic information processing 35, 40
A Prairie Home Companion (radio show) 14, 94, 170
presentism and historicism 211
Presley, Elvis 201, 211
Pudd'nhead Wilson (Mark Twain) 204

Ramblin' Jack Elliott 200
Rawlings, David 117
Ray, Byard 123, 160
Reeves, Bass 207
Reiter, Bart 70–76, 106
Rickard, Bill 98–102
Rinzler, Ralph 151
Robinson, Justin 206
Rooftop Singers Band 148
Roots of the Blues (album; Alan Lomax) 203, 205
Ross, Pete 84–89
Rucker, James Sparky 129–139

San Francisco State Campus 147, 150
Sankofa Strings Band 205–206
Scruggs, Earl 149, 165
Seeger, Mike 114, 151, 168, 175, 195, 203
Seeger, Pete 149, 152, 176, 178
Serendipity Singers Band 28
Shelton Brothers Band 190
Sinful Tunes and Spirituals (Dena Epstein) 240

Index

Sing Me Back Home: Southern Roots and Country Music (Dr. Bill Malone) 197
Singleton Street Band 190
Smith, Bechard 179
Smith, Mamie 203
The Smithsonian Collection of Classical Country Music (Dr. Bill Malone) 196
Smithsonian Folklife Festival 129, 150–151, 154
Smithsonian Folkways 6, 61, 196, 207–208
Sodom, NC 155–156, 159
Sore Fingers Week 117
Sorensen-Boeh, Debbie 50–51
Southern Appalachian traditional music 9, 66, 240, 268
Southern Music, American Music (Dr. Bill Malone) 194
Spencer, Tricia 235–238, 248
Sprague, Carl 121
Stamps Quartet Band 190
Stanley, Ralph 121, 149
Stovall, Babe 133

Sullivan, Ed 223–224
Summerhill (A.S. Neill) 149
Sykes, Robert 169

Target Program at Burr Burton Academy 107
Temple, Shirley 223
Terry, Sonny 165, 201
Thompson, Hunter S. 65, 243
Thompson, Joe 198, 203, 205–206
Ting Tea Room 132
"Tramp on the Street" 133
Turknett, Dr. Josh 259–270

Uncle Dave Macon 126, 149
Uncle Earl Band 113, 115–116
Unger, Doug 59

Vappie, Don 203
Virginia Minstrels Band 213, 216, 223, 232

Waldorf Astoria 38
Ward, Wade 148–149
Waring, Fred 23–24, 223–225

Warren Wilson College 112, 119, 122, 232–233
Washington, Booker T. 203
Watson, Doc 119, 125–127, 201
Weaver, William Sherman 17
Weavers Band 148
Weiner, Alan 39
Weirs Cove Baptist Church 175
Welch, Gillian 117
Williams, Bert 212
Willie 157, 192, 235
Wilson, Sule Greg 202
Woody Guthrie Folk Songs (Woody Guthrie) 178
Workman, Nimrod 179
WPAQ radio (Mount Airy, NC) 169–170

XERF radio station (Ciudad Acurna, Mexico) 190

Zen 232, 253
"Zip Coon" 138, 214–215

www.ingramcontent.com/pod-product-compliance
Ingram Content Group UK Ltd.
Pitfield, Milton Keynes, MK11 3LW, UK
UKHW050539150426
5217IPUK00026B/2004